NIRVANASARA

NIRVANASARA

Radical Transcendentalism
and the Introduction of
Advaitayana Buddhism

by Da Free John

THE DAWN HORSE PRESS
CLEARLAKE, CALIFORNIA

© 1982 The Johannine Daist Communion. All rights reserved.
No part of this book may be used or reproduced in any manner without written permission, except in the case of brief quotations embodied in critical articles and reviews.

First edition, April 1982
Printed in the United States of America
International Standard Book Number paper: 0-913922-65-X

Produced by The Johannine Daist Communion
in cooperation with The Dawn Horse Press

CONTENTS

	Introduction by Georg Feuerstein	7
I	The Purification of Doubt and Differences via the Introduction of Advaitayana Buddhism	57
II	Buddhas and Buddhism	74
III	The Spiritual Advaitism of Jesus of Nazareth	74
IV	God as the Creator, the Good, and the Real	77
V	Pain, Independence, and the Discovery of Consciousness	87
VI	Ancient and Traditional Buddhism and Upanishadic Advaitism Seen in Relation to the Radical Way of Advaitayana Buddhism	98
VII	The Three Views of Consciousness and Light	117
VIII	The Great Principle	138
IX	The Three Ways of Buddhism	139
X	Nirvana and Samsara Are Not the Same	140
XI	Gautama's Problem	163
XII	Three Fires	172
XIII	Worldliness, Selfishness, and Transcendence	194
XIV	Realization and Belief	196
XV	The Practices of Insight and Devotional Idealism in the Way of Divine Ignorance	208
XVI	Insight, Intuition, and the Heresy of Progressive Enlightenment	215
XVII	The Way of Radical Understanding and the Traditional Formulae of Enlightenment	220
XVIII	Atman, Brahman, Shunyata, and Nirvana	229
XIX	Transcending the Hierarchy of Errors	230
XX	Transcendentalism	234
XXI	Advaita Vedanta, Classical Buddhism, and the Way of Radical Understanding	235
XXII	The Three Teachings of the One Way	236
XXIII	Nirvanasara	241
	About Da Free John	245
	About The Johannine Daist Communion	252
	An Invitation	254
	Index	255

Introduction

by Georg Feuerstein

1. From Scholarship to Understanding

How does one introduce a great adept (*mahā-siddha*), a living Buddha, and his compassionate, prophetic teaching? In the following essay I have given my own answer to this question. I have tried to keep myself open to, and to faithfully represent, the teaching of Master Da Free John, while at the same time endeavoring to remain sensitive to the naturally skeptical posture which, I suspect, most readers will maintain while perusing this volume.

I have written as one who has committed himself to a particular way of life, namely the spiritual path hewn out by Master Da. Simultaneously, I have brought to bear on my presentation whatever scholarly skills I have acquired in my professional career as an indologist. I must state at the outset that in making this communication I have had only one purpose in mind: to aid the understanding of those who, like myself, approach life rationally but who, nevertheless, are capable of acts of intuitive recognition and spiritual appreciation.

This book will only make sense if the reader is willing to at least seriously consider two possibilities (which I myself have come to accept as facts):

1. There is a transcendental Reality.
2. This transcendental Reality is the Condition of body, mind and world.

These are bold propositions for the agnostic and pragmatist, but this book does not defer to the professional skeptic or materialist at all. It is mainly directed at all those who sit on the fence: those who are too wise to fool themselves with materialistic values and concerns, but also too indecisive to take the plunge into spiritual life; those who wish their life would be different but do not know how to change it; those who are tired of the thraldom to arid scholasticism and quietly hunger for a more meaningful way to use their cerebral dexterity; those who are prepared to change their life but have been waiting for the right stimulus and context.

It is my heartfelt hope that this book can tip the balance for them—to the side of a full spiritual life.

For those who can see eye to eye with the above two propositions, it will only be a small step to the acceptance of the idea that in some individuals the transcendental Essence is "out front," that they have, paradoxically, died as separate entities while continuing to be alive, and that this has nothing whatsoever to do with schizophrenia. Once this has been understood, it will not be too difficult to further realize that such rare beings could indeed have a special function to fulfill in spiritual life. Where a real leap of understanding (rather than of faith) has to be made is in the recognition that the adept, or the enlightened being, could be instrumental in one's personal spiritual endeavor.

Although this volume contains essays by Master Da Free John which do not match the scholarly stereotype of the adept as a "naive bumpkin," as Master Da put it recently, nevertheless they are all authored from the adept's point of view. Master Da concedes that there may have been adepts who would fit the "naive bumpkin" myth, invented by scholars mainly to buffer their profession against interference by adepts. However, the higher adepts, especially of the sixth and seventh stages of spiritual life, typically communicate a very sophisticated teaching (see pp. 22ff.). Such adepts, having transcended the discursive mind, operate from within a different frame of consciousness. Thus, Master Da Free John creates his essays spontaneously, and they are not merely the product of his ruminations on what he has studied. In point of fact, Master Da reads very little, and the ideas which he expresses are simply grounded on his "psychic relationship" to the traditions and to literature.

His communications are an expression of his "free attention," and they freely and directly reflect, as he puts it, an

Introduction

ultimate transcendental consciousness. Hence the "adept's point of view" is, quite simply, to serve the enlightenment of others. So, even whilst Master Da is responding on a level of consideration that scholars will presumably find stimulating, he does not write as a scholar or theoretician nor in order to indulge the scholastic mind. His technical essays on Buddhism and Advaitism are simply a new way of expressing his teaching, and as such they complement his many other oral and written communications.

Several of my friends and colleagues have expressed their surprise at the fact that a self-transcending adept should write at all. In doing so they have—in the politest or perhaps the most disingenuous fashion—given vent to their basic disbelief. But the question springs from a fundamental misunderstanding of the nature of a realized adept. If one is willing to concede that an enlightened being can eat (much or little), walk (barely or long distances), talk (ecstatically or didactically), be humorous or serious, and sleep (hardly ever or like everyone else), then why should he not write as well if it serves the purpose of his teaching work?

The *siddha-puruṣa* cannot be gauged or measured by his apparent behavior. The "awakened one" *is* the transcendental Reality. The processes which occur in, and the conduct of, his body-mind are devoid of an ego. They happen spontaneously, just as the body-mind of the ordinary person "happens" spontaneously, though he superimposes a false identity on it and becomes enamored of and possessed by it. And because there is no ego obstacle in the realizer, his body-mind is fine-tuned to the Invisible and acts as a powerful transmitting agent for those who are spiritually attuned.

I consider myself most fortunate to have entered the ambience of one of the truly great spiritual Lights of today's world. Master Da Free John's compassionate presence has already greatly transformed my life. His Teaching has definitely lured me down from the fence on which I had been sitting uneasily for a good many years. Many others have experienced a similarly profound change and the benefits accruing from this. But, of course, spiritual life does not unfold mechanically. It requires passionate commitment and constant application to the art of self-transcendence. However, the adept's efficacious presence and, in this case, the most rounded spiritual teaching help one to pass through the necessary transformation more surely.

I am aware that the stance I have taken in my introduction to this auspicious volume is incompatible with the current "objective" fashion of science. But this has ceased to trouble me. What concerns me, though, is whether the reader—regardless of whether he is a scientist or a "layman"—will be sufficiently sensitive to his own intellectual predilections and emotional predisposition so as not to allow them to muffle the clear message in the essays by Master Da Free John. I sincerely hope that at least one or the other reader can actually "hear" the adept's central argument. It is always the same argument, irrespective of the subject of his consideration or the style in which it is conducted. It is always an insistent call to actual spiritual awakening and practice, the essence of which is perpetual and unsparing self-transcendence.

There is another aspect to Master Da Free John's essays which is likely to perplex and possibly even incense one or the other staunch adherent of Buddhism. This is the declaration of his radical teaching as the Fourth Vehicle of Buddhism. Again, I can do no more than point out that this is an adept's enunciation and as such warrants a most careful, open-minded consideration. I am confident that, if the reader is a seriously practicing Buddhist who truly experiences "the heresy of the assertion of an ego" (*Visuddhi-Magga* XVII), he will have no difficulty whatsoever with this declaration of Advaitayana Buddhism or its essential teaching.

I am grateful to have been given the opportunity to do *guru-seva* in the shape of this introduction, and I respectfully bow to Master Da Free John.

2. Frog Perspective vs. Bird's Eye View

When, in 1336, Francesco Petrarca climbed Mont Ventoux in the South of France, he effectively freed himself from the tunnel vision of the reigning structure of consciousness of his time. His vision of the valleys far below jolted him out of the dream-like self-containedness that characterizes the "mythical consciousness"[1] of medieval Gothic art, piety, and feudalism. He awakened to a new mode of perceiving the world; he began to see things in conscious perspective. And Petrarca (1304–74) was aware that his "discovery" of perspectival space would be of far-reaching importance to others.

Petrarca stood at the threshold of the Renaissance which, in a certain sense, can be said to have reached its climax in the genius of Leonardo da Vinci (1452–1519) who was the first to solve the theoretical problems of perspectivity. His achievement was paralleled and augmented by the heliocentric "revolution" of Nikolaus Copernicus, Christopher Columbus (who opened up earth's space), Galileo Galilei (who used the telescope to disclose the vastness of outer space), Johannes Kepler (who replaced the ancient idealistic circular model of planetary motion by calculated ellipses), Andreas Vesalius, Europe's first great anatomist (who explored the body's inner space), and so on.

Petrarca's Mont Ventoux experience has nothing in common with the sense of achievement, of egoic pride and self-confirmation, that the veteran mountaineer feels when he has successfully scaled and "conquered" a particularly difficult peak. Nor must it be compared with the feeling of mere aesthetic pleasure of the occasional wanderer who, picnicking on a modest peak, admires the panoramic scenery of the valley beneath him. For Petrarca the experience was a sudden widening of his cognitive horizon, a strengthening of his capacity for world-understanding and self-insight. His was an experiential encounter

---

1. I have borrowed this concept from J. Gebser, *Ursprung und Gegenwart*, 3d ed., 3 vols. (Munich, 1973).

with a new "paradigm." Although it occurred on the personal level, it was yet thematizing a new general awareness which was shared by other sensitive thinkers of his period and which, before long, became a part of the sensibility of the Western European civilization and its epigones.

I have begun this introductory essay with Petrarca's auspicious discovery for two reasons. Firstly, because the full awakening to spatial consciousness which typifies the Renaissance is the psycho-historical foundation for the hypertrophy of reason, in the form of materialistic rationalism, witnessed today in all areas of human life. Secondly, because Petrarca's Mont Ventoux experience affords a fitting metaphor both for the vantage point of Master Da Free John's teaching in relation to religious or scientistic doctrines, and the implicit demand his communications make on the reader. Like Petrarca, the reader is expected to burst through his familiar cognitive universe into the wide-open horizon which informs Master Da's teaching. In other words, he is encouraged to share Master Da Free John's panoramic vision of existence as seen from the very summit of human life.

In the *Yoga-Bhāṣya* (I. 47), the oldest extant commentary on Patañjali's *Yoga-Sūtra,* an ancient stanza is cited which speaks of the *yogin* who has realized the *summum bonum* as follows:

> Having ascended to the tranquillity of gnosis (*prajñā*), the man-of-gnosis beholds all grief-stricken creatures as one standing on [the top of] a mountain [beholds] the valley-dwellers.[2]

The same idea is epitomized in the well-known Sanskrit concept of *kūṭastha* which literally means "summit-abiding" or "standing on the peak." The expression is for the first time met with in the *Bhagavad-Gītā,* which dates back to the fourth or fifth century B.C. There it is applied to the adept who is fully "yoked":

---

2. This is a recurrent metaphor in the Sanskrit literature of Hinduism and Buddhism.

> The *yogin* whose self is content in gnosis (*jñāna*) and world-knowledge (*vijñāna*), standing on the peak with his senses subdued: he is called "yoked" (*yukta*), and to him clods-of-earth, stones and gold are the same. (VI. 8)

In two other stanzas (viz., XII. 3 and XV. 16), the term *kūṭastha* is employed to refer to the transcendental Reality *per se*. This second usage is in keeping with the fundamental notion that the wholly realized adept is coessential with the Ultimate.

Interestingly, R. C. Zaehner[3] drew attention to a striking parallel in the writings of two little-known but important Christian mystics, Hugh of St. Victor and Richard of St. Victor. In his *De Vanitate Mundi*, which is a commentary on Ecclesiastes, Hugh speaks of the "flight" of the soul whose "keen perception"—from the bird's eye view—"naturally reaches further when directed from above on things that lie below, when it sees all things, so to speak, together."[4]

Even more remarkable in its similarity with the Hindu metaphor are the following two passages in Richard's *Benjamin Minor*:

> The high peak of knowledge is perfect self-knowledge. The full understanding of a rational spirit is as it were a high and great mountain. . . . O man, learn to think, learn to reflect upon yourself and you will have risen to the deep heart! (75)

> Let a man rise up to the heart's high place, climb up the mountain if he desire to attain and know what is above the human mind. Let him rise up by himself above himself, and from self-knowledge to the knowledge of God. (83)[5]

---

3. See R. C. Zaehner, "'Standing on the Peak': A Concept Common to the Victorines," *Studies in Mysticism and Religion Presented to Gershom G. Scholem on His Seventieth Birthday* (Jerusalem, 1967), pp. 381–7.

4. Ibid., p. 384.

5. Ibid., p. 386.

The above considerations describe, I trust, most aptly the particular context in which the present essays and all the other oral and written communications by Master Da Free John must be placed if one is to do full justice to them. Master Da always and necessarily speaks as a realized adept or transcender. He has no secular ambitions and, in particular, no scholarly axe to grind. His "motive" is compassion (*karuṇā*), which is the natural complement of his transcendental realization (*prajñā*). If, in this volume, he addresses some perhaps more technical and intricate matters, it is because he has recently been moved to respond on this level of sophistication.

This volume of essays is, then, an invitation and a challenge to the reader to examine and understand the inherent presuppositions of his own world-view and, having identified its intrinsic limitations, to ultimately and actually remove his cathexis in regard to it. In fact, only when such a *metanoia* has occurred in the reader can he hope to "hear" the essential argument of these essays. Prior to that he will be handicapped by the restraining influence of his personal "world hypotheses" which, for the most part, are only rarely the product of deliberate philosophical effort rather than subconscious "information" stemming from one's socio-cultural environment and individual biography.

Thus, the reader is expected to make an advance comparable to Petrarca's. He has to climb the mountain, that is, he has to countervail his own cognitive tendencies and habits of thought. But once he has reached the peak, that is, when he has successfully checked his resistance to change his mental outlook, all effort must cease. He must simply remain open, as Petrarca succeeded in doing for at least part of his experience, to take in the new vista and let it act upon his whole being. For some this may prove easier than for others, but in every case an epochistic[6] bracketing of presuppositions is required: a mental holding of the

---

6. This refers to the phenomenological act of *epoché* as formulated by E. Husserl. See M. Farber, *The Foundation of Phenomenology*, 3d ed. (Albany, N.Y., 1968), pp. 526f.

breath as it were, when all doubt and superficial criticism is at least temporarily suspended, and when one has ears to hear and eyes to see.

This free, open, unneurotic attitude is essential in reading this book. For, what Master Da Free John seeks to convey in his essays is both subtle and profound. It will only be offensive to those who have cut-and-dried answers to the big questions of life and who entertain hard-shelled preconceptions and prejudices about religion, spirituality, and in particular the Indian traditions. They will find that Master Da does not cater to any conventional expectations. He writes and speaks as a realized adept, not as a philosopher, scientist, politician, or novelist. He does not presume any of the usual limitations. In other words, he does not play the game. This is always vexing for those who fail to understand that their reaction to such enlightened "spoil-sports" is an expression of their neurotic relationship to life as a whole.

Scientists are, perhaps, especially prone to "cast the first stone" at any maverick who, as they would have it, encroaches on their pet discipline but does not play according to their rules. There is a high degree of conformism among scientists (as a subculture), which may partly be due to the world-wide streamlining of government-financed research since the 1940s. But in part it is undoubtedly also bound up with the scientists' self-perception as a group of specialists overtly or covertly cherishing the quasi-religious presumption of possessing the "true knowledge," the key to understanding existence. In the course of the gradual debunking of the post-Enlightenment ideal of scientific objectivity, doubt has also been cast on the integrity of the scientist as a manipulator of data. And rightly so. The scientist is first and foremost a human being, and this means that his scientific activity, like any other activity he may engage in, is embedded in his total psychology. That is to say, he is subject to misunderstanding, ignorance, prejudice, misrepresentation, and even deliberate distortion of reality ("tailoring of facts"). In sum, he does not enjoy the adept's "view from the peak."

Even where, as Isaac Newton has done, the scientist helps to institute a new "paradigm," a new framework for formulating and interpreting scientific data, his vision remains partial and angular. This has to do on the one hand with the psychological and cognitive limitations of the scientist as a member of the species *homo sapiens,* but on the other hand also with the inherent boundaries of science itself. For, as Master Da Free John has explained in his illuminating talk "The Asana of Science," science is a particular way of seeing the world. In his own words:

> Science is an invention of Man that represents the development of one specific convention of interpreting reality exclusive of other possible conventions. . . . To do science, you must take on a pose. That pose is not the disposition, however, of Man as a whole contemplating Infinity.[7]

Science, as we know it today, is thus a product of the particular consciousness-frequency which, at least for Europe, emerged in the Renaissance and was developed *ad absurdum* in the nineteenth and twentieth centuries.

Science is more than the organized and institutionalized study of phenomena with the view of predicting events in the material cosmos; it is more than the sum of accumulated knowledge acquired by applying the scientific methodological canons; and it is more than the cooperative effort of a group of specialists. It is also, and primarily, a specific cognitive mode. Master Da describes the scientific method as a <u>mood of doubt</u>. And he further indicates that in its globalization as scientism or scientific materialism it is, as Master Da styles it, a veritable <u>culture of doubt</u>. Scientism is not only a calling into question of everything, while being unhappily wedded to the psychological need for absolute certainty (even when it is cautiously expressed in probabilistic terms); it is also a concealed form of cynicism or nihilism insofar as its program excludes *a priori* certain "bother-

---

7. Unpublished talk (October 25, 1980).

some" questions, subject-matters, and methods which are disparagingly branded "metaphysical."

Although the methodological *credo* of scientism is to excise the observer from the process of knowledge in order to arrive at the "objective" truth, science as scientism has yet the most profound personal and social repercussions chiefly through the medium of technology. Indeed, it implicates the "observer" to the point of usurping and traumatizing him. The scientistic method of certainty-through-doubt has, in fact, become a way of life, a "metaphysics," for millions of people. As Master Da Free John noted:

> We are so used to the presence of science and technology in our culture that we believe science is a natural activity, a sort of professionalization or technical elaboration of something that everybody is already doing. But this may not be the case. The activity of science may not be natural at all.[8]

Today, scientism or scientific materialism is firmly entrenched in the cerebral pathways of the vast majority of "consumers" of the high-technology nations of the world; and, as a surreptitious component of the technological export package, it is beginning to take its toll also in the so-called Third World.

In his first essay in the present collection, Master Da Free John contrasts the scientistic culture of doubt with the culture of certainty which is rooted in what he styles the "Great Tradition," that is, the religio-spiritual traditions of the world. The *punctum dolens* which separates science and scientism from the Great Tradition is the existential status of the "invisible" or immaterial dimension of the universe. The scientist flatly denies the existence of what is valued most in the Great Tradition or, if he is inclined to make any concession at all, argues that if "higher" cosmic dimensions did exist, science could never know anything

---

8. Ibid.

about them since their very invisibility or immateriality precluded scientific experimentation. The left-brained scientist demands "concrete" evidence which can be translated into instrumental measurements. His favorite sense is sight—not the *visio Dei* but the perspectival image conjured up by the neurons of the brain and the rods and cones of the material eyes. Naturally, the Invisible is beyond the pale of physical vision and therefore also does not figure in the scientific interpretation of the universe. The fundamental scientistic doctrine, amounting to a metaphysical axiom, is that "seeing is believing." But "seeing" is always given a very restricted meaning, and "inner vision" is dubbed hallucination.

It is important to understand that in making the contrast between scientism and the Great Tradition, Master Da Free John does not merely restate in so many words the age-old scission between rational scientific knowledge and irrational, religious faith. For he tacitly affirms that the method of science and the *methodos* ("way") of the religio-spiritual traditions of mankind are, on a comparable level, both generative of knowledge. Implicit in his argument is the predication that the Great Tradition is not primarily a culture of (blind) faith—as against the scientistic culture of (pure) knowledge and (absolute) certainty—but a culture of experiential knowledge. The "scientific method" of the Great Tradition is an inversion of the orthodox scientific procedure inasmuch as it is founded on the implication of the subject in the noetic process. In fact, the "theory" of the Great Tradition rejects the observer model of science as introducing an artificial disjunction between subject and object. This leaves it free, on the "experimental level," to resort to epistemic means generally outlawed by orthodox science, viz., introspection and suprasensuous cognition which, in India, is known as "yogic perception" (*yogi-pratyakṣa*).[9] And the "instrumentarium" for the practi-

---

9. All spiritual traditions of India are agreed on the possibilty of suprasensuous knowledge. A distinction is made between paranormal cognition and the immediate apprehension (*sākṣātkāra*) in mystical experiencing.

tioner of the Great Tradition is his own body-mind.

However, as Master Da Free John explains in subsequent essays, the respective forms of knowledge yielded by scientific materialism and the Great Tradition are, ultimately, both to be transcended. For, from the realized adept's "summit" point of view, both are still mere representations of reality, and not Reality *per se*. But, whereas scientific materialism, confining itself to segments of the visible realm of cosmic existence only, is a dogmatic commitment to the frog perspective of unillumined intelligence, the Great Tradition has the intrinsic potential of generating the bird's-eye view of the self- and world-transcending adept. Possibly, the phrase "bird's-eye view" is still misleadingly suggestive of perspectival and hence one-sided knowledge. In actuality, the adept's authentic *locus* is in what Master Da styles "Divine Ignorance"[10] or "seventh-stage wisdom." The adept, to be sure, is not a knower but a transcender of knowledge, knower, and known. His transcognitive stance, or mood of certainty-through-Realization, truly enables him to serve and not merely ideologically exploit the world. The *kūṭastha* has, it is implied in the *Bhagavad-Gītā*, "become the Absolute" (*brahma-bhūta*), and the Absolute is not hampered by the perceptual-cognitive apparatus of the body-mind; rather, it is traditionally styled "omniscient" (*sarva-jña*), though this omniscience is not knowledge of particularized objects.

Scientific materialism and the cultural attitude which it informs are implicitly atheistic, and where they are tenuously associated with theism, the latter is typically of a highly secularized, demythologized cast of religiosity. In his essay "God as the Creator, the Good and the Real," Master Da Free John comments that "atheism proposes a myth and a method for ego-fulfillment." This, *mutatis mutandis,* is also true of conventional religion and, to a degree, even of the modes of higher esotericism. Atheism is

---

10. The phrase "Divine Ignorance" simply refers to the highest or "seventh-stage" Realization of the One Being beyond all experience and knowledge. From a practical point of view it is bodily surrender into the indeterminate Reality and abidance as the Transcendental Consciousness which is devoid of all content.

camouflaged religiosity. As Vincent P. Miceli observed, "Atheism's vigor arises from its heroic will to create mythical gods in place of the true God."[11] Atheism is, therefore, as much an opiate for the masses as Karl Marx thought religion was. Moreover, as Master Da points out, in their political dimension both atheism and religion resort to materialistic modes of control. Both are manifestations of the ego and as such are partial approaches to Reality, angular visions of the Truth. Both may be regarded as instances of what one might call "the fallacy of misplaced finality": the confusion of experiential knowledge of reality with Reality itself, that is, the absolutization or deification of fragments of reality.

> It is only when the egoic root of our functional, worldly, and religious spiritual life is inspected, understood, and transcended that self, and world, and God are seen in Truth. (See below, p. 84.)

The "mountain peak" of spirituality ascends so steeply that the ego cannot find a foothold on it. One could also say that the ego belongs to the climber's gear which must be abandoned in the course of his ascent. The peak will only sustain the most sublime. Indeed, if I may stretch this metaphor still further, the mountain's pinnacle looms into the truly rarefied atmosphere of the Invisible and therefore cannot sustain anything but that which is, or has become, invisible itself.

Whilst one may characterize atheism as the religion (or irreligion) of the visible, the *raison d'être* of religion is the Invisible. Scientific materialism, which is *per definitionem* atheistic, is the glorification of the visible aspect of the universe. And by "visible" is here meant the entire spectrum of phenomena amenable to "verification" and translatable into ocular proof or its analogues. It is a left-brained monopolization of truth, seeking to grasp reality by way of "rationalization," that is, literally, the

---

11. V. P. Miceli, *The Gods of Atheism* (New Rochelle, N.Y., 1971), p. xiv.

"reckoning" by parting, dividing, fragmenting, atomizing, or quantizing. Now, the Invisible can never be rendered visible. It is inconvertible. But the visible can be rendered transparent to evince its invisible, hidden foundation. That is the domain of religiosity and spirituality.

Master Da Free John's teaching is securely founded on his personal realization of the ultimate Condition. And it is from the realizer's or adept's point of view, and not merely from the limited perspective of the theoretician, that he engages in metaphysical considerations. It is this fact which must be duly appreciated, for it lends uniqueness and authority to the following essays. This is, to all intents and purposes, the very first time that a *mahā-siddha* communicates the realizer's apical view in the medium of the contemporary mind. By virtue of this, Master Da's communication is intelligently critical of the conceptual and ideological structures that are today's forms of ego affirmation or denial, rather than transcendence. And, for the same reason, his message is not only searching and profound but also encompassing. In his own words:

> My Way is a radical Teaching that enters into consideration of all the stages of life and the entire Great Tradition of the ancients and their modern representatives. (See below, p. 71.)

And:

> Just as Buddhism and Advaitism stand in critical relation to the traditions and stages of life that precede them, and just as each advancing stage of Buddhism and Advaitism stands in critical relation to its precedents, my own Work also develops a form of Argument based on criticism (positive and creative rather than merely sectarian and destructive) of the entire Great Tradition that is our Treasured Inheritance and all of the developing stages of life that are our school of transcendence. (See below, p. 108.)

3. The Seven Stages of Life

The main conceptual tool by which Master Da Free John appraises, and allows others to similarly understand, the spiritual status of the many idiosyncratic expressions of human life and thought is the schema of the seven stages of life. The seven-stage model, which is among Master Da's original contributions to the theory and practice of spiritual life, is a map of man's total potential for psycho-spiritual development. As Master Da explains:

> In the traditions of spiritual culture, the development of a human being has commonly been described in terms of seven stages, each spanning a period of seven years. There is a rational basis in Awakened Wisdom for this scheme. That basis is the very structure of the total bodily being (or body-mind) of every human individual. We are a composite made of elements and of functional relations, a coherent life-form expressed via the nervous system and brain, and levels of mind that may consciously reflect not only the gross or "material" realm but the realms of Life-Energy and all the cosmic realms or media of light. At the root of this system is the heart, the primal organ not only of life but of consciousness in man. It is here that the presumption and conception of egoic independence, or the separate "I," arises in every moment. It is on the basis of this presumption that the human individual is predetermined to a reactive life of fear, vulnerability, flight from mortality, and a universal constitutional state of contraction. That contraction encloses consciousness in the limits of skin and thought, and it separates the whole bodily being of Man from the Divine Radiance and Perfect Consciousness that is otherwise native to it and eternally available to it in every part. . . .
>
> The culture of the Way of Divine Ignorance may also be related to the traditional scheme of seven stages of growth.

But it is founded on the Awakening of the heart, from self-possession to free feeling-attention, via all functions, in all relations, under all conditions. Indeed, the whole Way is the Way of the heart.[12]

Now, the human body springs from a single cell. Researchers on human development conceptualize this original cell as being "totipotent," that is, as possessing the capacity to become the fundamental structures which compose the fully developed body. This primary cell carries a kind of blueprint of the mature organism into which it can develop. However, in order to manifest these differentiated structures, the cell must forego its "totipotency" in favor of specialization and individuation.

One can usefully apply this biological insight to the sphere of man's overall psycho-spiritual evolution. As neonate the individual has only a dim awareness which allows him to relate to his environment just sufficiently for his survival within a protective, caring human society. World and ego are as yet a kind of primordial soup. Most of man's neonatal behavior is purely reflexive or instinctive, and his "life-style" is one of utter helplessness and complete dependence.

The first stage of life relates to the individual's physical adaptation to the world into which he was born. Here he learns "simple" skills like focusing with the eyes, grasping and manipulating objects, walking, talking, controlling bladder and bowels, thinking conceptually, and relating to his fellow-beings. At the end of this phase, the growing individual is a fully mobile ego who, providing that no serious maladaptation has occurred, is a strongly self-centered but educable person.

The second stage of life, which extends approximately from the eighth to the fourteenth year of life, concerns primarily the maturing individual's emotional and sexual development. With

---

12. Bubba [Da] Free John, *The Enlightenment of the Whole Body* (Middletown, Calif., 1978), pp. 189–90.

the growing awareness of himself as a social being in a shared life-world, the young personality is confronted with increasing outside demands that conflict with the egoic tendency towards self-assertion and autonomy. In particular the awakening of sexuality is a possible source of great tension and inner conflict and must be integrated into the total emotional development of the individual. Sexual maturity depends on the ability to enter into a mature emotional relationship with others. Master Da Free John observes:

> Because of the generalized antisexual taboo to which so-called civilized societies oblige their members to adapt, people today tend not to grow and adapt to full relational sexuality. Instead, the individual tends to remain more or less bound to the primitive and infantile sexuality of his or her own bodily self.
>
> The pleasurable and sexual nature of one's own bodily being becomes clear in the earliest years of life. But the ecstatic or self-released fulfillment of bodily life is possible only in intimate and feeling submission in relationship. However, the antisexual influences that pervade our experience even in childhood suppress our relational adaptation and leave us self-conscious in our natural relations. . . .
>
> [When spiritually sex-positive] influences are not present to oblige people to sane, human, and higher use of their sexuality, the body of the individual tends to remain as the field of sexual practice. Thus, even when a sexual partner is available, the uninitiated and irresponsible individual tends to remain essentially hidden and self-possessed in his or her practice. Love and desire tend to be more or less crippled in such people. Indeed, love and desire even seem to be in conflict. But love-desire, the single force of sexual ecstasy, is the necessary foundation of sexual relationships and sexual embrace.[13]

13. Bubba [Da] Free John, *Love of the Two-Armed Form* (Middletown, Calif., 1978), p. 64.

In the third stage of life, stretching approximately from the fifteenth to the twenty-first year, the person, ideally, comes to full intellectual maturity. The underlying theme of this phase is mental-intentional adaptation to life and the integration of the skills acquired, and the lessons learned, in the first stages. When this process is complete, the individual will have a clear self-image and be capable of relating functionally to the world. As Master Da Free John explains:

> The third stage of life is mature when the individual enjoys integrated responsibility for the whole of the living being (physical, emotional-sexual, and mental). Thus, he is in that case able to be present as a clear will and as love under all the otherwise frustrating or pleasurable conditions of lower experience. Those who seek to begin spiritual life must be mature in this sense in order to move on to higher maturity.[14]

That not a few people fail to arrive at this point is borne out by the leviathan of social problems, like alcoholism, drug addiction, violence, racism, chronic depression, suicide, and so forth.

Fewer still take the next step—into the fourth stage of psychic adaptation. Those who succeed in doing so have actively entered spiritual life. The first three stages happen to overlap with the individual's psycho-physical epigenesis from neonate to adult. In their spiritual aspect, however, they call for a conscious application to his personal integration by which he can move beyond the mere functional adaptation expected of a mature member of human society. With the fourth stage of life, the commitment to ego-transcendence, tacitly present already at the culmination of the third stage, has become a sustained, if still limited, obligation. Master Da notes that this stage "is characterized by submission and adaptation of all functions of the lower body-mind to the sacrificial and moral disposition of the feeling

---

14. Bubba [Da] Free John, *The Enlightenment of the Whole Body*, p. 196.

or psychic being."[15] Now the individual cultivates the practice of faith, love, trust, and surrender in relation to the transcendental Being. This coincides with the opening of the "heart," leading to an acute awareness of the tendency towards self-encapsulation, the recoil from Ecstasy or the Bliss of the transcendental Being.

This awareness or sensitivity is heightened in the fifth stage of life. Here the individual's awareness shifts from the perception of the physical dimension to the experience of the "subtle physiology" of the body (and mind). This extends the radius of his cognitive field, and offers him new opportunities for self-transcendence. This is the demesne and area of obligation of the conventional mystic and *yogin*. It is the field of all forms of esotericism involving the activation of the subtle or higher psycho-physical structures of the body-mind. As Master Da elucidates, attention and the "Life-Current" become established in the brain core. On the level of conscious experiencing this manifests in the form of supraconscious states (*samādhi*). He comments:

> In the fifth stage of life, yogic mysticism raises attention into the extremities of subtle experience—or the heavens of ascended knowledge. But Liberation in God is not Realized at that stage or by such means. In order for the Life-Current to cross the Divide between the "third eye" and the "sahasrar," or between the body-mind and Infinity, the gesture of attention and the illusion of an independent conscious self must be utterly Dissolved in the true Self.
>
> The highest extreme of the ascent of attention is called "nirvikalpa samadhi," or total Absorption of self-consciousness in Radiant Transcendental Consciousness. But, in fact, the seed of differentiated self remains in such ascended Absorption of attention. Attention is yet extended outside the heart, or the root of self-consciousness, as a gesture

---

15. Ibid., p. 206.

toward an independent Object, and, therefore, such "samadhi" is not only temporary, but it remains a form of subject-object Contemplation.[16]

Through further spiritual growth, by means of the transcendence of the ego that has been disclosed in the experiences of the first five stages, the spiritual practitioner arrives at what is traditionally known as Self-realization (*ātma-bodha*). At this point the individual awakens to his transcendental Identity or *ātman* or *puruṣa*. More precisely, he awakens as the Self. He now knows himself to be different from the ego, or the limited body-mind, which he once believed to be his true identity. The sixth-stage adept, in the language of Hindu non-dualism, has become the transcendental "witness" (*sākṣin*) of all phenomenal processes. The sixth stage coincides with the uprooting of the "gesture of attention," which is the transcendence of all object consciousness.

This is the condition of conventional liberation, variously styled *apavarga, mukti, mokṣa,* or *kaivalya*. In the non-idealist language of (original) Buddhism, which does not revolve around the conceptualization of a transcendental Self-essence, this superlative condition or attainment is regarded as the "extinction" (*nirvāṇa*) of the desires which bind the individual to the world of objects and suffering. *Nirvāṇa* is thus the realization of the "object" of the Buddha's silence. The idealist schools of later Buddhism gave voice to that silence about metaphysical matters by formulating a philosophical position approximating that of the Hindu schools of non-dualism (Advaita Vedānta). Yet, in terms of the practical consequences on the level of the sixth stage of life, it makes no difference whether the self is seen, in the language of Buddhist realism, as "non-self" (*anātman*) or merely as the abstract name for a "bundle of factors," or whether, in the language of Hindu idealism, it is seen as "non-Self" (*anātman*) or

---

16. Ibid., pp. 422–23.

the antithesis of the transcendental Self. Both approaches share the sixth-stage characteristic of the transcendence of the self and of attention.

However, and this is the pivotal point of Master Da Free John's teaching, a further moment of growth is possible which perfects the whole protracted endeavor towards ego-transcendence: In the seventh stage of life, the liberated "individual" recognizes the incompleteness of his self-sacrifice and, in doing so, enters *sahaja-samādhi*, the enstasy "with open eyes" as Master Da names it. This is equivalent to God-realization, for now the transcendental Self is no longer pitted against the phenomenal world. But, through a last act of self-sacrifice (which is from then on repeated *ad infinitum*), the world is recognized as continuously arising in the Ultimate Being which is coessential with Self. This is how Master Da explains this ultimate Realization:

> Thus, in the seventh stage of life, or the Way of Radical Intuition, the soul Exists in Ecstasy, <u>as</u> the Heart[17] (rather than in the heart, or the inner being). And in this Perfect stage of life the Bodily Life-Current is Released or Liberated from the body-mind and all association with the internal mechanisms of the brain core. When the devotee abides as the Heart, re-cognizing all phenomena as only unnecessary modification of Itself, while It neither embraces nor resists any experiential condition—then the Bodily Life-Current becomes not only naturally polarized toward the brain, and thereby Released from concentration in the lower functional body, but it is actually Released even from concentration in the brain. This is due to the fact that the mind, or the independent gesture of attention, is itself Dissolved through re-cognition in the Heart.[18]

---

17. The "Heart" is another name for the Divine Self, the Intuition or Realization of the Radiant Transcendental Being or God.

18. Bubba [Da] Free John, *The Enlightenment of the Whole Body*, p. 424.

4. Religion as Seen from the Adept's Vantage-Point

The scientific study of religion (*Religionswissenschaft*) was sparked off by early encounters between one religion and another which gave rise to curiosity and a degree of speculation among mythologers, poets, artists, historians, and philosophers of antiquity. However, the methodological exploration of religion is a phenomenon of more modern times made possible mainly by the severance of the bond between theology and philosophy and by the whole trend towards secularization and specialization. One of the specialized branches of *Religionswissenschaft* is the study of the history of religions which is primarily concerned with questions of origin, development, dependence, and influence.

In his presentation and critique of the traditional religio-spiritual responses to the Invisible, Master Da Free John adopts a historical-typological framework. He speaks of "the magical or shamanistic cultures" as the origins of religio-spiritual thought, and regards "animism" as the essential feature of these archaic cultures and their religio-spiritual legacy.

The term "animism" was coined by the senior of British anthropology, Edward B. Tylor.[19] He considered the archaic belief in a soul (*anima/animus*)—typically based on the experience of sleep, dream, ecstasy, illness, and death— as the historical origin of religion. By means of projection[20] the primitive mind, as he saw it, would then attribute a soul to all other beings and things

---

19. See E. B. Tylor, *Religion in Primitive Culture* (1871; reprint ed., New York, 1958).

20. However, as P. A. Angeles astutely observed in a recent paper: "To the animistic mind there is no projection but a 'finding,' or direct confrontation with life-and-self-qualities in things." P. A. Angeles, "God-Entities and Scientific-Entities," *International Yearbook for the Sociology of Religion* (1967), 3:168.

("animatism"). This gave rise to what he styled "manism" (ancestor worship) and "fetishism" (iconolatry). Subsequent evolutionary stages of religious thought and experience were, according to him, "polytheism" and then "monotheism." Other scholars have proposed somewhat different sequential models. Particularly the anthropological fieldwork of the last few decades has toppled some of the ivory-towered speculations of earlier scholarship. Though, again, there are those who are reluctant to extrapolate from the anthropological data on contemporary "primitive" tribal peoples to the consciousness and religion of *homo sapiens'* earliest progenitors. Perhaps rightly so, for on the basis of the evidence amassed by anthropologists one would have to almost invert the Tylorean schema and treat monotheism as the very earliest form of religion.[21]

Historians of religion have, by silent consensus, ceased to concern themselves with the question of the origins of religion, and in academic circles today the topic is firmly taboo. However, this reticence is not shared by psycho-historians who approach history from the point of view of evolving structures of consciousness. And it is in the light of this new and increasingly vigorous discipline that one may with fewer misgivings (and with impunity) renewedly address this whole question and even subscribe to some form of the now so anathematized evolutionism.

Master Da Free John evidently uses the term "animism" in a wider sense than is customary, and his specification of this concept appears to overlap with that of "dynamism" as formulated by J. King who sought to refute Tylor's "soul" model.[22] "Dynamism" is denotative of the primitive belief in an impersonal dynamic life-force, such as the *mana* of the Melanesians and Polynesians, the *megbe* of the Congo Pygmies, the *waken* or

---

21. This has in fact been seriously suggested by W. Schmidt, *Ursprung der Gottesidee*, 12 vols. (Münster, 1926–55).

22. See J. King, *The Supernatural: Its Origin, Nature and Evolution* (London, 1892).

wakonda of the Sioux, and so forth.

However, Master Da avoids the pitfall of turning this into a mere abstract belief, but implies that this is always a theory-practice continuum centering on the "presumption" (and experience) of the invisible "energy" or "energies" that animate the world. In this extended sense, animism is really a generic term for conventional religiosity and spirituality. Master Da, moreover, posits an earlier phase of "pluralistic animism," setting it into typological relation to "polytheistic" developments, and a later phase for which one may coin the term "singularistic animism" which is the logical antecedent of "monotheism." He, furthermore, calls the bifurcated pretheistic stage "magical animism." Pluralistic animism is the experiential projection of multiple, discrete "energies" or invisible agencies onto nature. With increased hypostatization this led to the postulation of a plurality of deities (personalized, multifunctional agents), often organized into a pantheon. By "singularistic animism," again, is meant the tendency to "see" a more impersonal, singular "energy" active behind the visible world. The extreme hypostatization of this "energy" results in the concept of the "one god." Master Da Free John makes the point that the idea of the Creator God, as the most typical expression of the monotheistic model, is fashioned on the egoic perceptual-conceptual apparatus (see below, p. 77).

Master Da further distinguishes, on the horizontal level, between an esoteric and an exoteric aspect of polytheism and monotheism, and he makes the same distinction on the vertical (diachronic) level whereby the earlier magical animistic developments become "esoteric" and the later theistic developments "exoteric." Thus one arrives at the following stemma:

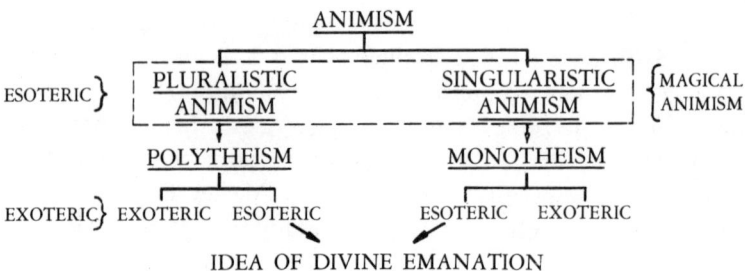

IDEA OF DIVINE EMANATION

As is obvious from the above diagram, the esoteric branches of polytheism and monotheism have formulated a single dominant idea, namely, as Master Da puts it, that of "divine emanation." This is the notion, based on the "energic" world-view of animism, that "conceives of all of Nature (including every part, thing, or individual being) to be set upon, pervaded by, or at best emanated from an ultimate (and thus Divine and Transcendental) and invisible (and thus spiritual) Source." (See below, p. 67.) Thus, according to this theorem, the visible world is in some sense dependent on the Invisible. The universe may be understood either in terms of its being a *de facto* emanation of the Divine or as being coessential with or, thirdly, eclipsed by the ultimate Reality.

In contrast to the emanationist view of reality, materialistic schools of thought—from scientific materialism to Hīnayāna Buddhism—rest on an explicit or implicit denial of the ideal of emanation. In the case of scientific materialism this denial is part of the larger disaffirmation of the transcendental Reality itself. The situation is different with Buddhism. Gautama, the founder of Buddhism, was an enlightened adept favoring a pragmatic and individual-oriented approach. He was conversant with the diverse philosophical schools of his day but considered them all as mere "opinions" or "dogmatisms" (*dṛṣṭi-vāda*) and refuted them as such. In his "middle path" (*madhyamā pratipad*) he carefully avoided the extremes of both the "nihilistic doctrine" (*uccheda-*

vāda) and the "essentialist doctrine" (*ātma-vāda*).

His own metaphysical "solution" to the problem was to maintain an agnostic attitude of silence. He refused to join in the metaphysical speculations of his contemporaries. The Buddhist tradition recognizes fourteen metaphysical "inexpressibles" (*avyākṛta-vastu*) which may be summarized in the following set of four propositional questions:[23]

1. Is the world eternal, or transient, or both, or neither?
2. Is the world finite, or infinite, or both, or neither?
3. Does the Buddha exist after death, or does he not, or both, or neither?
4. Is the soul identical with the body or different from it?[24]

For the Buddha these conundrums do not profit the spiritual practitioner and therefore they should be ignored (see *Majjhima-Nikāya* I. 63). He likens the speculative metaphysician to a gravely ill person who has been wounded by a poison arrow but who refuses to be treated until the caste status of the physician is ascertained (ibid.).

On at least one point, though, the Buddha was most definite: the world process, and even *nirvāṇa,* the *summum bonum* of his noble eightfold path, lacks an abiding "essence" or "self" (*ātman*). Now, the Pāli texts are adamant in emphasizing that the Buddha did not espouse any form of dogmatism (or ideology). We read, for instance, in the *Majjhima-Nikāya* (I. 72) that the Buddha is "free from all theories." However, with the hindsight of over two millennia of philosophical history, we know this claim to be problematical. All knowledge is "procrustean," that is to say, it is embedded in theory even though it may be precritical and unexamined. Perhaps what this canonical statement means is

---

23. See T. R. V. Murti, *The Central Philosophy of Buddhism: A Study of the Madhyamika System,* 2d ed. (London, 1960), p. 38.

24. As T. R. V. Murti, op. cit., points out, this last question could of course also be formulated according to the quaternary model of the other three.

this: The Buddha is not concerned with grey theory, but his teaching is rooted in the adept's "free" understanding of existence. The same holds true of the founding genius of Advaitayana Buddhism, Master Da Free John, though unlike the Buddha he is willing to avail himself of emanationist as well as radical transcendentalist language.

Because of the preeminence of monotheism—in the form of Judaism, Christianity, and Islam claiming a total of some one and a half billion (at least nominal) adherents—Master Da enters into a more detailed consideration of the creator idea. He shows how the idea of God as Creator or Author of the world is the first member of a logical chain that characterizes theological thinking. The other links of this chain are the idea of God as the Good, the notion of the existence of evil (often personified in the figure of the Devil) as being the very antithesis of God, the idea of God's saving interest in the world (i.e., his love for the devotee and his wrath for the transgressor), the assumption that God's creatures have free will, and lastly the idea that by religious means man can realign his will to the Will of God and thus escape the machinations of the Devil.

From the adept's vantage-point, however, the <u>concept</u> of God as Creator is supplanted by the <u>realization</u> of God as "the Real, or the tacitly obvious Condition of all existence" (see below, p. 86). And with the obviation of this key notion of theism, the other links of the theo-logical chain also collapse. Master Da Free John points out that good and evil are simply tendencies within the dynamism of nature which, in combination, serve to perpetuate the "play" of nature. In his own words, "Nature is a transformer, not merely a creator or a destroyer" (see below, p. 85).

This being the case, the religious struggle against nature ("the flesh"), or the spiritual aspiration to take flight from nature, becomes a quixotic undertaking. However, when it is recognized that life is a non-binding modality of the all-encompassing Reality, then the ego—which is the motor of all antagonistic struggle against, or flight from, life—is transcended. And the transcendence of the ego is the quintessence of authentic spirituality. All forms of religiosity and spirituality are, in the last analysis, expressions of the ego. They are all grounded on a more or less circumscribed understanding of existence. As Master Da Free John makes clear, only the adept who enjoys the fullness of realization is wholly aware of the inherent limitations of the "language" used by the *religieux* to map out the interface between the visible and the Invisible. Having transcended the ego, the adept alone is in the unique position of rendering the ego transparent in the processes of life and thought.

It is the God-as-Father image against which also some iconoclastic theologians have recently arrayed their skills and ingenuity. Paul Tillich, one of the most able and best known spokesmen of this group, has stated his case as follows:

> The being of God cannot be understood as the existence of a being alongside others or above others. If God is *a* being, he is subject to the categories of finitude, especially to space and substance. . . . Many confusions in the doctrine of God and many apologetic weaknesses could be avoided if God were understood first of all as being-itself or as the ground of being.[25]

Thus, the theological death of God is his metaphysical resurrection as *ipsum esse* which is beyond finitude and infinity, beyond any of the brain-born categories of theology or philosophy. Paul Tillich, like his colleagues, has reached this formulation by the expedients of intuition and logic—hence theology, the verbal-conceptual understanding (*logos*) about God (*theos*). By contrast, the adept's speech about God-as-Being is not of the abstract-argumentative type but it is a testimony of his realization of that very Being, his *theosis* rather than theology.

In his memorable essay entitled "Nirvana and Samsara Are

---

25. P. Tillich, *Systematic Theology*, 2d ed., 3 vols. in 1 (Chicago, 1967), 3:235.

Not the Same" (p. 155), Master Da Free John launches into a specific critique of "popular" religion and spirituality as they are rampant today. By extension, his critique is also leveled against the other manifestations of the modern mass culture such as "pop politics" or "pop science." These, he observes, are typically reductionistic and belligerent in their fundamental attitude of what one might call "ideocentrism," a kind of ideological cultism which makes no demands on the person. Above all, in their basic orientation to pamper the "usual man," these "pop"-cultural manifestations tend towards disastrous falsification. They furnish a person with a false sense of reality and sanity and bolster up his illusion and hubris that all is well with him and his ways.

For Master Da one of the most serious consequences of such popularization and vulgarization is the fact "that the great ideas are promoted as mere ideas (capable of being believed and asserted as Truth by the ordinary or un-Enlightened mind) rather than as ideational expressions of higher mind or a mind-transcending Enlightenment." (See below, p. 151.) This is really the crux of his criticism of mass culture. The beliefs which motivate the "usual man," or by which he explains or seeks to justify his life-style, are not integrated into his life as a whole. They float, if I may use this strong simile, like frothy scum on a polluted river. At best these beliefs, as Master Da comments, are conducive to material productivity or social benignity. But even in this optimal form they are geared towards pleasuring the ego. They do not favor and, in the last analysis, are actually inimical to the ideal of ego-transcendence.

5. Indian Orthodoxy and the Heterodox Traditions in the Light of Advaitayana Buddhism

As did Gautama the Buddha with his own teaching in the sixth century B.C., Master Da Free John is introducing

Advaitayana Buddhism—the Fourth Vehicle—on the basis of a rigorous critique of antecedent and contemporaneous religio-philosophical formulations. In order to be able to adequately understand Master Da's unique contribution to human spirituality, it is necessary to furnish an outline of the historical-cultural background of the two principal targets of his critical consideration—Hinduism and Buddhism.

The Indian religious and philosophical genius has created a rich tapestry of spiritual-soteriological traditions. From the perspective of mainstream Indian thought, viz. Hinduism, two broad categories can be distinguished: the "orthodox" (*āstika*) and the "heterodox" (*nāstika*) schools of thought.[26] The former group, representing Hinduism proper, comprises the six philosophical systems and the schools associated with them as well as their common historical-cultural foundation, which is the sacred Vedic tradition. The Vedic revelation is embodied in the four hymnodies or "collections" (*saṃhitā*), viz., the *Ṛgveda, Yajurveda,* and *Sāmaveda,* and, as a somewhat later incorporation, the *Atharvaveda*. To this voluminous scriptural codex one must also count the corpus of ritualistic texts elaborating on the doctrinal and liturgical matters in the ancient hymnodies— the *Brāhmaṇas* and *Āraṇyakas*—and also the esoteric instructional literature, that is, the *Upaniṣads*.

The six classical systems or "views" (*darśana*) of Hinduism are Mīmāṃsā, Vedānta, Nyāya, Vaiśeṣika, Sāṃkhya, and Yoga. They represent pointed formulations of ideas current already since ancient times in a diffuse and undeveloped way. The Mīmāṃsā (lit. "inquiry") school is a philosophy of ritualism which does not subscribe to a belief in God-as-Creator. It shares this "atheism" with the Sāṃkhya and the Yoga schools in their classical formulation. The Vedānta (lit. "Veda end"), also known as the "Later" (*uttara*) Mīmāṃsā, is a continuation of the philosophical speculations and the wisdom of the Vedic seers and

---

26. The term *āstika* and *nāstika* refer to the acceptance ("it is," *asti*) or the rejection ("it is not," *na asti*) of the Vedic revelation.

sages. The Nyāya school is primarily a system of logic and epistemology, though in the service of the ideal of liberation. This ultimate soteriological orientation is also true of the Vaiśeṣika school of thought which examines the categories of existence and is thus an early form of ontology. Ontological investigation is also the forte of the Sāṃkhya system which teaches a strict dualism between the noumenal ground of the world, called *prakṛti*, and the noumenal ground of the subjective consciousness, known as *puruṣa*. The Sāṃkhya dualist metaphysics is also shared by the philosophy of Classical Yoga as founded in the *Yoga-Sūtra* of Patañjali, though it has its own unique elements of interpretation.

Of these six classical schools, the Nyāya,Vaiseṣika, Sāṃkhya, and Yoga are the least integrated into the "orthodox" fold of Hinduism. Notably the two last-mentioned pay only lip service to the vedic revelation but are really quite self-reliant philosophical efforts. In their metaphysics they stand at the perimeter of Hindu orthodoxy, while still presenting a considerable cultural force within it.

The single most important tradition of the six schools, which now overshadows all the others, is Vedānta. It is often equated with Hinduism *per se.* This is the philosophy as embodied in the teachings of the *Upaniṣad*s and the *Bhagavad-Gītā* which is esteemed as an "honorary" *Upaniṣad*. These texts give voice to many teachings, but all of them declare Reality to be non-dual (*advaita*). Master Da Free John speaks of these schools collectively as "Upanishadic Advaitism," but extends the use of this term also to the later Vedānta schools which favor a non-dualist or monistic interpretation, notably the Kevala-Advaita of Śaṅkarācārya (trad. 780–820 A.D., but possibly earlier).

The principal "heterodox" traditions of India, which Master Da Free John considers as part of the "underground," are Jainism and Buddhism. Both sprung up on the fertile soil of the ascetical (*śramaṇa*) sub-culture which did not recognize the Vedic revelation and its sacerdotal guardians, the hereditary priesthood of Brahmanism. The origins of this sub-culture are veiled, though some of its strongest roots must have been sunk into the pre-

Aryan culture indigenous to India, perhaps even into the cultural world of the epigones of the once great Indus civilization. It was these ascetic freethinkers who contributed greatly to the progress of the natural sciences, medicine, and mathematics but also to the typically Indian psycho-technology.

By the time of the Buddha they had split up into a large number of schools or sects. The Pāli Buddhist *Brahmajāla-Sutta* refers to 62 "wrong views," and the Jaina *Sūtrakṛtāṅga* makes mention of 363 such "heretical" doctrines. Besides the Buddhist order, the chief organized schools of that epoch were the Ājīvikas (or peripatetic teachers of fatalism), the Lokāyata school of naturalists of a materialistic type who were also known as the "Do-as-you-please" philosophers (*yadṛcchāvādin*), the Ajñāna tradition which espoused a strict agnosticism, and the Jaina tradition which appears to be the oldest of them all.

Like Buddhism, Jainism is more than a mere philosophical system. It is a whole way of life or culture with its own distinct ethical and religious practices and a vast literature, written mostly in the Prākṛta language. Its philosophical stance is a type of realist pluralism: There are many objects which are all real. What marks this philosophy, though, is its unparalleled tolerance to other views which it exercises on the basis of the *syād-vāda* or doctrine of the relativity of judgments about reality. According to this doctrine every statement is to be qualified by the phrase "somehow" (*syāt*) in order to forestall absolutist claims. This is an aspect of the ethical norm of universal non-violence or *ahiṃsā* honored in Jainism more than in any other religion. In describing Jainism as a "religion," it must be remembered that its founder Mahāvīra, who was an earlier contemporary of the Buddha, did not embrace theism. According to the Jaina canon there is no divine Creator, but there are countless liberated adepts (*siddha*) who are omnipresent, omnipotent, and omniscient.

The realist-pluralist orientation in Jainism is still more pronounced in Buddhism. Gautama the Buddha had a pragmatic bent of mind and was disinclined to speculate about metaphysical realities. He was primarily interested in the reality of suffering (*duḥkha*) and the means by which a person could conquer it. In his very first sermon, delivered in the Deer Park of Sarnath near Benares in 528 B.C., the Buddha announced to a group of only five disciples the doctrine of the "Four Noble Truths":

1. Existence is suffering;
2. Suffering has a cause, since everything is conditional on something else;
3. It is possible to annul suffering, because the removal of the cause eliminates its effect;
4. The way to prevent suffering is through the "Noble Eightfold Path."

This schema summarizes the Buddhist "problem" consciousness and the consequent "strategic" approach which, as Master Da explains, is the inherent limitation of conventional Buddhism.

Central to the Buddha's soteriology is the whole argument about "dependent origination" (*pratītya-samutpāda*), or the nexus of arising conditions. This represents a non-substantialist theorem which, fundamentally, depicts "objects" as occupying the space between reality and nothingness. It characterizes the Buddha's "middle path" between the extremes of eternalism and nihilism.

The Pāli scriptures contain several versions of this nexus, but the classic form has twelve "links," viz.: (1) Ignorance gives rise to (2) action-intentions, which are the precondition for (3) rudimentary awareness, which gives rise to (4) the psycho-physical organism, which is responsible for the appearance of (5) the sixfold sphere of sense-contact, which gives rise to (6) sensory contact, on which depends (7) sensory experience, which gives rise to (8) "thirst" or the craving for further enjoyment, which is the precondition for (9) "clinging," on which rests (10) the will-to-be, which gives rise to (11) (re)birth, which, in turn, is responsible for (12) old age and death. A corollary of this teaching is the "doctrine of momentariness," according to which all arising conditions are necessarily only fleeting phenomena.

Even the so greatly treasured human personality is, in this view, merely a collocation of impermanent conditions. There is no permanent, continuous self. Everything is simply a beginningless succession of momentary phenomena (*dharma*), rather like the Heraclitean river into which one cannot step twice. The Buddha did not deny the reality of the ego, but he did not elevate it to a metaphysical principle. The personality is a bundle of five transient factors, viz., the material organism, sensation, perception, action-intentions, and awareness. This epitomizes what Master Da, in his essay "The Three Views," puts forward as the first view or model of consciousness.

The means by which one can terminate the incessant flux of phenomenal conditions is the eightfold path, viz., (1) right view, (2) right resolve, (3) right speech, (4) right conduct, (5) right livelihood, (6) right effort, (7) right awareness, (8) right concentration. The practitioner who follows this path to its end conquers all suffering through the event of his enlightenment and liberation. His enlightenment is in no way different from that of the Buddha. However, owing to the fact that he has been instructed, whereas the Buddha realized *nirvāṇa* on his own initiative, he bears the title of "worthy one" (*arahant*) rather than "awakened one" (*buddha*).

Although there is no way scholarship can ascertain which, if any, of the recorded sermons in the Pāli canon are the *ipsissima verba* of Gautama Siddhārtha, the above outline of his teaching can be taken to be roughly representative of the principal tenets of his "dharma." However, as is the case with all schools of thought that continue beyond the lifetime of its founder, over time changes were introduced which gave rise to splinter groups and schismatic movements. In later periods there were as many as thirty chief schools of Buddhism. In view of the fact that Master Da Free John, in this book, explicitly aligns his teaching with the tradition of Buddhism, it seems warranted to briefly outline the highlights of Buddhist history.

Approximately two hundred years after the Buddha's death, the Buddhist order split into two camps, the Theravāda

("Teaching of the Elders") or Sthaviravāda as it is called in Sanskrit, and the Mahāsaṅgha ("Great Assembly"). The former gave rise to three important sub-schools, viz., the Pudgalavāda, which postulated, after all, a permanent entity or person (*pudgala*); the Sarvāstivāda, which developed the teachings of the Theravāda; and the Sautrāntika school, which assumed a consciousness substratum and thus was the historical predecessor of the later idealist schools of Buddhism, referred to in the following essays.

The Mahāsaṅgha was responsible for the innovation of the *bodhisattva* ideal and the doctrine of voidness (*śūnyata*). Thus, it was most immediately connected with the origin of Mahāyāna Buddhism in Southern India around the first century A.D. The Mahāyāna ("Great Vehicle") is also typified as Bodhisattvāyana because of the prominence which it gives to the figure of the *bodhisattva* and his particular way, which is different from the ancient eightfold path. The *bodhisattva* has to fulfill six perfections before he can become a *buddha*, viz., open-handedness, discipline, patience, will-power, contemplation, and wisdom. In the course of his struggle for enlightenment (*bodhi*), he must also enlighten all other beings. This is his vow: to postpone his entry into *nirvāṇa* until even the last being is saved. His entire spiritual discipline is conducted as an exercise of universal compassion (*karuṇā*). The Mahāyana masters are fond of contrasting this teaching with the ideal of the *arahant* in the older Buddhist schools, which they dub somewhat pejoratively the Hīnayāna ("Lesser Vehicle"). Their criticism is especially directed against the *pratyeka-buddha* or the "solitary awakened one" who is not stirred to teach others the way to enlightenment.

The Mahāyāna, *inter alia*, also introduced a new emphasis in the interpretation of reality, tending towards a more idealist explanation. This became palpably obvious in the second century A.D. with the establishment of the Mādhyamika school, founded by Nāgārjuna, and even more so in the Yogācāra or Vijñānavāda school of the brothers Asaṅga and Vasubandhu who lived in the fourth century A.D. They broke with the Buddha's policy of silence on the metaphysical matters and spoke eloquently about the ultimate Reality in such terms as "Voidness" (*śūnyatā*), "Thusness" (*tathatā*), and "Storehouse-Consciousness" (*ālaya-vijñāna*). They thus approached the Upaniṣadic doctrine of the Absolute (*brahman*), the kind of eternalism that the founder of Buddhism had sought to avoid.

This trend towards idealist formulations was continued in the Tantrayāna, the "Third Vehicle" of Buddhism whose beginnings may be dated back to the sixth century A.D. As the name indicates, this is the Buddhist teaching as given out in the *Tantra*s. This form of Buddhism comprises four major traditions, viz., Mantrayāna, Vajrayāna (in Tibet), Sahajayāna, and Kālacakrayāna (the latest school to arise). The Tantrayāna is, broadly speaking, the vehicle of complex esoteric rituals, involving difficult visualization and meditation practices. This Buddhist Tantrism, like its Hindu counterpart, understood itself as a new revelation of the Buddha's teaching. Its innovations were meant to better accommodate the needs and diminished capabilities of humanity in the "dark age" (*kali-yuga*). Particularly the Sahajayāna with its de-emphasis on ritualism presented itself as an "easy" or "natural" way for the "modern" man.

The strength of the Buddhist tradition in India was broken with the Moslem invasions during the tenth to twelfth century A.D. By that time Buddhism had become more of an elitist movement than a popular religion which could stir the great masses outside the cloistered world of the monastic intelligentsia. The destruction of the Buddhist seats of learning and the slaughter of thousands of monks, therefore, proved fatal. But the conquest of Buddhism did not mean the triumph of Islam but the victory of the resilient, all-absorbing tradition of native Hinduism, more particularly of Advaita Vedānta. However, Buddhism did not disappear from its land of origin without having first cross-fertilized its age-old antagonist, Hinduism. The single most important figure in this osmosis was, as far as the available documents permit one to assert, Śaṅkara's teacher's teacher, Gauḍapāda, the author of the famous *Māṇḍūkya-Kārikā*.

Gauḍapāda's unconcealed sympathy for Buddhism was not shared by Śaṅkara, even though the latter's work is unthinkable without the former's.

The colorful and remarkable history of Hinduism and Buddhism can be seen as an untiring quest to find new and better ways of expressing the Inexpressible, of improving upon either the silence of the Buddha or the naive animism and polytheism of the ancient Vedic scriptures. In all these countless attempts, language evinces itself to be astonishingly pliable—but not pliable enough to fit snugly onto Reality. In the end, language must be abandoned to let Reality speak for itself. As a tool for drawing man's attention away from the mechanicalness of his routine existence, language is of incomparable usefulness.

Master Da Free John's selection of (early) Buddhism and Advaitism for particular consideration makes implicit sense. For they represent typological extremes in the "language game" about Reality. Their difference may be summed up in the well-known distinction between "realism" and "idealism." Master Da brings a new dimension of understanding to this theme when he characterizes the Advaitist idealism as an "emanationist" teaching, regarding it as a logical development of the ancient Vedic animism and contrasting it with the Buddha's "non-emanationist" realism.

However, his discussion of these linguistic-conceptual differences is not from an abstract point of view. He pursues a very practical goal insofar as he shows that the diverse ways of speaking about ultimate matters (and even silence is a "language" in this sense), fall into a limited number of categories, and that the two cardinal formulations are realism/non-emanationism vs. idealism/emanationism. Whereas the first "language" focuses on an analysis of the phenomenal conditions or realities, the second begins from the other end, with the postulation of a noumenal Reality which is set off against conditioned existence.

Master Da's next step is to demonstrate the inherent limitations in both "languages" and to institute a *tertium*: the non-problem-based radical "language" of Advaitayana Buddhism.

But he does so without sacrificing the advantages of the realist and idealist modes of approach. Thus his teaching transcends the earlier three vehicles of Buddhism without one-sidedly opposing them.

At the same time, Advaitayana Buddhism transcends the Advaitism of the *Upaniṣads* and the later more systematized schools, including Śaṅkara's influential philosophical elaboration of the non-dualist tradition. Inasmuch as Master Da Free John's teaching is grounded on the non-dual Realization of the One Being, it can rightly be considered a continuation also of the highest modes of Hindu esotericism. However, Advaitayana Buddhism goes beyond the traditional forms of the *advaita-vāda* for exactly the same reason that it transcends the three vehicles of Buddhism: By abandoning the traditional problem-and-strategy approach, Master Da's Radical Transcendentalism gives the most direct expression to the highest possible spiritual Realization which is otherwise obscured by the inadequacies of "realist" or "idealist" conceptualizations. This linguistic-conceptual radicalness has, of course, far-reaching practical consequences, and these are spelled out in several of Master Da's other writings, notably *The Enlightenment of the Whole Body*.[27]

6. Radical Transcendentalism or Advaitayana Buddhism: Light in a Dark Age

In his tract *De pace seu concordantia fidei* (1453), Nicolaus of Cues made the revolutionary suggestion that spokesmen of the various faiths should, through a free exchange of ideas, endeavor to establish one religion which would most pristinely reflect the unity of the Divine. A hundred years later, in India, the Moslem emperor Akbar (1556–1605) instituted a "synagogue" in

---

27. Bubba [Da] Free John, *The Enlightenment of the Whole Body*.

which representatives of many different religions gathered regularly to consider theological matters. He even went so far as to found a "religion of God" (*dīn-i'ilāhi*).

Akbar's spirit of ecumenism was revived by Rām Mohan Roy, the founder of the Brāhma Samaj (1815). He too sought to accomplish a higher, unitarian synthesis among all religions, notably Hinduism and Christianity. In 1881, the immensely popular Keshab Chandra Sen, a former member of the Brāhma Samaj, founded his Nava Vidhāna ("New Order"). His life's vision was the "universal church" that would unite all of humanity, but after his death the movement which he had called into life rapidly lost influence. Other similar ventures are the Baha'i religion, an Islam-based unitarian faith, and the Sufi Society founded by Hazrat Inayat Khan.

On a different and non-syncretistic level, the ecumenical idea is kept alive in organizations which derive their impetus from the famous World Parliament of Religions which convened in 1893. Among these efforts are the International Association for Liberal Christianity and Religious Freedom, the Universal Religious Alliance, the World Congress of Faiths, the World Fellowship of Religions, and so on.

In contrast to the religious societies mentioned earlier, these organizations do not seek to bring about a unified form of doctrine or worship. Rather, they mean to promote, on the basis of a tacit understanding of the transcendental unity of all religions, the cooperation between religions in order to further the moral and social welfare of mankind. Thus, while they genuinely acknowledge that the multiple religious and spiritual expressions are merely man-made variations on the single theme of the transcendental Truth or Being, they do not recognize that this variety is incidental to the ego and that, moreover, the shadow which the ego necessarily casts on Truth is removable. Therefore all these undoubtedly well-meaning and, to some degree, helpful and constructive endeavors are ultimately negligible.

That the world is in dire need of unification—both secular

and religious—is, I think, beyond dispute. That this desideratum cannot be met by syncretistic church building or ecumenic cooperation should also become apparent to anyone reading Master Da Free John's essays with an open mind. The only passable avenue to achieve a true world community is through the hard school of individual ego-transcendence. This has always been understood by the real practitioners of the esoteric aspects of the faiths, just as it has always been misunderstood by the nominal followers of religious exotericism, that is, by the believers in the "letter" but not the fiery spirit that animates it.

Master Da's communication is an adept's (com)passionate gesture towards those in the valley of quotidian existence. It is a prophetic vision of the possible world, the *civitas Dei*, that humanity might inhabit if it could shake off the trammels of routine existence and the mediocre habits of the first three stages of life.

Master Da Free John styles his teaching "the ultimate development of the tradition of Transcendental Realization" (see below, p. 107). He explains:

> I view the traditions of Buddhism and Advaitism to be the ultimate, most advanced, or sixth to seventh stage dimension of the Great Tradition. But my Work is also to reconsider and purify what we have inherited from the Great Tradition as a whole, and, therefore, my Work stands in critical relation even to the Buddhist and Advaitic traditions themselves. (ibid.)

His teaching, then, is the keystone of the arch of the Great Tradition that has been erected in the course of mankind's religious history. It is the final or ultimate touch to past and present spiritual traditions. The reason and justification for this claim is connected with the second connotation that one may discern in the term "ultimate": His teaching is the most immediate and the most radical pointer to the Ultimate. As Master Da Free John puts it in his brief essay entitled "Transcendentalism" (see below, p. 235):

> From the point of view of Radical Transcendentalism, or the Way that I Teach, there is, simply and only, Radiant Transcendental Being—and self, mind, body, world, and God are not other than This, but all are inherently transparent when recognized as This Only.

For Master Da, Truth is one. But it can be expressed in many ways. This is the adept's testimony and confirmation of the "transcendental unity of religions" which is debated by philosophers of religion. He thus reaffirms the ancient Vedic revelation "The wise speak of the One Real in many ways" (*ekaṃ sad viprā bahudhā vadanti, Ṛgveda* I. 164. 46). But—and he does not hide the realizer's Light under a bushel—there are more or less adequate ways of expressing the same Truth, more or less insightful, reality-based and complete visions or perspectives of the *ens realissimum*. In the communication of that One Truth, Master Da employs a multi-language approach, but his most characteristic way of symbolizing the Truth is by means of the radical language of pure Transcendentalism.

As is obvious from the first quote above, he considers his teaching as an instrument of catharsis of the conceptual, linguistic, and practical dimensions of the religiosity or spirituality of the Great Tradition. This austere declaration is reminiscent of the prophecies about another great teacher who lived nearly two thousand years ago:

> The winnowing fan is in His hand and He will thoroughly clean His threshing floor. His wheat He will store in the granary, but the chaff He will burn with fire that cannot be put out.[28]

Presumably, most readers of this book will have been brought up in the Christian tradition, which is the cultural basis

---

28. *Matthew* 4:12. Cited from *The New Testament of Our Lord and Saviour Jesus Christ* (n.p., 1979).

Introduction

of our contemporary Western society. They may not even be nominal Christians, but they will have been at least exposed to typically Christian values. Therefore, they may also be familiar with Jesus of Nazareth's self-understanding as *Messias praedestinatus*, who felt called upon to fulfill the "Will of God," and who had foreknowledge of his death as a necessary and crucial step towards the establishment of the "Kingdom of God."[29] However, nearly two thousand years of exoteric ecclesiastical interpretation have done much to obscure the universal spiritual significance of this heroic adept of Judaism. And today, the undoubtedly historical fact of his death is taken as a symbol for the "Son of God's" atonement for all sin: Jesus' crucifixion was the ransom paid to the Devil for the delivery of man. This *theologia crucis* has occasioned a laissez-faire attitude which neither does justice to the original teaching of Jesus nor proves at all helpful to the religious practitioner—quite simply because it takes much of the "heat" out of his practice.

Master Da Free John is very outspoken about this "popular" Christianity:

> The popular Myth of Jesus is an Idol of mass religion. It was created by the exoteric Christian Church, when it moved to legitimize itself in the eyes of the secular State of Rome. That Idol is worshipped by popular belief, and many have been and continue to be deluded and oppressed by the Cult of that Idol. . . .
>
> The popular Myth of Jesus is founded on archaic cosmological archetypes. Jesus is believed to have come down from Heaven (or the sky of stars above the Earth) and become a blood sacrifice (in the ancient style of cults that ritually killed animals and men), and then he is supposed to have risen up into the sky again—back to Heaven. The man Jesus is popularly believed to be God, the Creator of the Universe, and his death is glorified as a necessary Cosmic

---

29. See *Mark* 9:9.

Event that somehow makes it unnecessary for any believer to suffer permanent mortal death.

All of this, and more, may have made some kind of imaginative, street-level sense in the days of the Roman Empire, but it is nothing more than benighted silliness in the last quarter of the twentieth century. And, in any case, none of this Idolatry was the teaching or the intention of Jesus or any of the other great spiritual Adepts of the world.[30]

Thus, the true meaning and consummate value of the Christ's "sacrifice" is not to be found in any idolatrous attitude of mind, but in one's actual *imitatio Christi*. And, once the egoic *idée fixe* of Jesus' absolute uniqueness is abandoned, then one will also come to see that the sacrifice to which he willingly submitted himself is the same sacrifice that is the true disposition of all ego-transcending adepts or God-realizers. Then it will be understood that the spiritual path, when stripped of its traditional or doctrinal elaborations, is essentially an *imitatio Dei*, an emulation of the very nature of the Divine, a dropping of the dross of what the conventional mind prizes highest: the whole web of "I," "me," and "mine."

Master Da Free John clearly and unequivocally speaks as a realized adept, and he makes the uncompromising spiritual demands of a World Teacher. This in itself is sufficient to make his message unpopular. There is a wide-spread natural disinclination to believe that the Invisible (if it is assumed to exist at all) could break through into the visible realm. Theophanies do not form part of the grammar of secular thought. And even those few who are spiritually "musical" will be inclined to hedge and remain sitting on the fence. Most probably, they will rationalize their hesitancy by pointing to the superabundance of "false prophets" that clamor and compete for attention today. But, to be sure, the real reason for their reluctance is the fear of having to make a real

---

30. Da Free John, *Scientific Proof of the Existence of God Will Soon Be Announced by the White House!* (Middletown, Calif., 1980), p. 211.

change in their life, the fear of the fire of authentic spiritual life. Little do they realize that, in the Buddha's words, existence itself is fire. Only when one has come to understand and feel that life, on whatever level it is lived, is indeed suffering and unhappiness, does one reach the position where one can truly appreciate the advantage of the fire or "heat" (*tapas*) of self-transcending practice. In this way alone can one ever hope to awaken to the "Transcendental Fire" of which Master Da speaks in his essay "Three Fires" (see below, p.191ff.). Elsewhere he states this fact aphoristically thus:

> To survive, we must change, and grow, and evolve.
> To change, and grow, and evolve, we must transcend ourselves.
> To transcend ourselves, we must become a love-sacrifice into the Radiant Life-Principle.[31]

Adepts like Gautama the Buddha, Jesus of Nazareth, Ramana Maharshi of Tiruvannamalai, Sai Baba of Shirdi, Anandamayi Ma of Dacca (now Varanasi), and Master Da Free John not only evince the reality of the Invisible but are the actual gateways to it. Having perfectly transcended the illusion of the ego, they have rendered the human body (in its totality as a multi-level structure) transparent to the Invisible. And by virtue of this transparency, they are agents of psycho-physical transformation in those who approach them in the spirit of sacrifice, of surrender to the Divine. However, by no means do all God-realized adepts have the potential function of a World Teacher. Indeed, rightly regarded, such a function is fully realizable only today. For it is only since the globe has been overlaid with a rapid communication network of increasing density that the diverse cultures and cultural enclaves of humanity are swiftly growing into a "world culture." But even then, an adept may fulfill his transcendental destiny as a World Teacher only if he meets with the right

---

31. Ibid., p. 153.

response. Master Da Free John has spelled this out for us:

> Whether my birth and my association with people can represent the force of some great age, a great transformation of the world, is to be seen. My work can be relatively modest and local, as Shirdi Sai Baba's work was in his lifetime, or my work can be associated with a global transformation. It will depend on recognition, surrender, and acceptance of a lawful order of existence by many, many, many people.[32]

There can be no doubt that the time has come for a global renaissance if mankind intends to survive and grow spiritually.

> There is simply no light abroad in the world today. There is nothing but corruption, nothing but the failure to accept the Way of God. There is absolutely no sign of the Way of Truth, except in rare instances of individuals and small groups of people. The Truth is essentially hidden and secondary. . . . There are no signs of an imminent Golden Age in the disposition or condition of humanity at large. Rather, the signs are of the necessity for a great purification, a great reestablishment of order, a righteous readjustment of the whole world.[33]

Yet, despite the sheer absurdity of his task in the face of such universal opposition to the Truth, the God-realized adept will persist in his struggle to awaken others.

Now, what is most remarkable: Notwithstanding its fatuous intransigence, the conventional mind—where it has not been completely stupefied by the anaesthetic of the materialist opiate—has a deep presentiment about the necessity for the world-wide catharsis that lies at the heart of the adept. This surfaces in the folk traditions, both of the religious and the secular

---

32. Da Free John, *The Bodily Location of Happiness* (Clearlake, Calif., 1982), p. 88.

33. Da Free John, *Scientific Proof of the Existence of God Will Soon Be Announced by the White House!*, p. 383.

variety. Yesterday it was the belief in the recurrent return of divine incarnations (*avatāra*) at the darkest hours of human history. Today it is the belief in the "intervention" by intelligent beings from outer space, or the saving grace of tomorrow's supertechnology. What both types of belief have in common is the fatal projection of the saving agent into the future. This hypermetropia is the reason why mankind as a whole has never been "saved." It is always only a few individuals who "have ears to listen" (*Matthew* 11:15) because they are able and willing to assume responsibility for their life here and now.

Having broached the subject of "divine incarnations," I should like to dilate somewhat on this topic. The popular conception is not entirely wrong. But, perhaps, the world is always in a "dark age," though possibly adepts make their presence felt more at particularly critical junctures of time. This, however, is not essential to the argument.

The Sanskrit word *avatāra* means literally "descent," being derived from the prefix *ava* ("down") and the verbal root *tṝ* ("to cross"). An *avatāra* is thus the Divine which has, so to speak, crossed the abyss between the Unmanifest or Invisible and the manifest or visible. Hindu theologians have waxed eloquent about the nature and number of such "incarnations" of God, and in the *Bhāgavata-Purāṇa* (X), which was probably compiled in the ninth and tenth centuries A.D., a list of twenty-two *avataras* (of Viṣṇu) is given, including the names of the Buddha and the future messiah Kalkin.

The idea is not alien to Buddhism either. All the Buddhist traditions recognize that Gautama the Buddha was only one among many "awakened ones" (*buddha*). But it is also acknowledged that among all enlightened beings, these successive Buddhas hold a superior position, perhaps precisely because they were understood as World Teachers. Buddhism also has its counterpart to the Hindu Kalkin—Maitreya (in Pāli: Metteya), meaning 'the Compassionate." His coming was, according to the Pāli canon, prophesied by the Buddha himself,[34] but as with

---

34. See *Dīgha-Nikāya* III. 76.

Kalkin the mythological embellishments are so fantastic that no practical conclusions can be drawn from these prophecies. However, although the Pāli texts may not have preserved the words of the Buddha with absolute fidelity, the tradition regarding his prophecy about the future Buddha Maitreya could still be substantially authentic, in which case it would be pertinent to investigate its relevance to the auspicious event of the renewed "turning of the wheel of the Law" by Master Da Free John.

In this connection it may also serve to recall the prophecy of the great Tibetan adept Padmasambhava (eighth century A.D.) who is reported to have said:

> When the iron bird flies, and horses run on wheels,
> The Tibetan people will be scattered like ants across the World,
> And the Dharma will come to the land of the Red Man.[35]

There is another well-known Tibetan prophecy which is given in Bu-ston's *Chos-ḥbyung* or "History of Buddhism" (written in 1322). In this text the Buddha is depicted as announcing to the goddess Vimala the following:

> Twenty-five hundred years after I have passed away into Nirvana, the Highest Doctrine will become spread in the country of the red-faced people.

More recent and perhaps more significant is the prophecy made by the great Hindu adept Sri Upasani Baba to the Śaṅkarācārya of Jyoti Math in February 1939, when he declared that an "incarnation" would soon manifest in a "European" country. (The term "European" is commonly used in India to refer to Americans as well as the white-skinned races of Europe, and is therefore a racial rather than a geographical qualification.) That incarnation, he is reported to have said, would bear down

---

35. Quoted from *The Annals of the Nyingma Lineage in America*, 1:4.

everything before him and would firmly reestablish the Vedic Dharma in India.³⁶ Master Da Free John, who according to his own testimony (see below, p. 72) is the prophesied "Dharma Bearer," was conceived in the month of Sri Upasani Baba's prophecies and was born on November 3 of that year.

But regardless of such prophecies, we have a *mahā-siddha* in our midst who means to fulfill his destiny as a World Teacher. Have we become enlightened enough to relate to him maturely? Or will we again merely idolize him or perhaps even seek to crucify him?

I should like to conclude this essay with the following quote from one of Master Da's works:

> A Transcendental Adept or true Spiritual Master is a Transparent Reminder of the Living One, a Guide to Ecstatic Remembrance of the One in Whom all conditions arise and change and pass away. Such an Adept is not to be made into the Idol of a Cult, as if God were exclusively contained in the objective person and subjective beliefs of a particular sect. Rather, right relationship to an Adept Spiritual Master takes the form of free ecstatic surrender to the Living Divine based on recognition of the Living One in the Revelation of Freedom, Happiness, Love, Wisdom, Help, and Radiant Power that Shines in the Company of the Adept. Right relationship to a true Spiritual Master is the most fundamental basis of the universal process that is true religion, and there is no basis for "religious differences" at the level of actual practice and Realization.³⁷

---

36. See B. V. Narasimha Swami and S. Subbarao, *Sage of Sakuri,* 4th ed. (Sakuri, 1966), p. 204.

37. Da Free John, *Scientific Proof of the Existence of God Will Soon Be Announced by the White House!,* p. 314.

I
The Purification of Doubt and Differences via the Introduction of Advaitayana Buddhism

1.

In this age of scientific materialism, doubt is the only certainty and the only substance of mind. Therefore, people in this age are profoundly crippled in their ability to grasp matters of higher certainty or to relate to subtler mental and physical processes. Likewise, they have been wounded in the root wherein we are naturally moved toward Truth (rather than what is merely and temporarily factual or true). Therefore, this is an age in which people demonstrate little ability to understand and practice real religion or spirituality. Transcendental Awakening or Divine Realization has been reduced in the popular mind to the status of mere literary mythology. Because of all of this, my Teaching Work suffers a vague reception, and what I have made plain is commonly regarded to be unreal.

The Great Tradition* suffers in this same situation. The modern interpreters of the traditions generally do not approach their subject as practitioners and wise advocates. Rather, they approach their subject with this "scientific mind," empty of everything but doubt and doubt's opinion. The usual interpreters of religion and spirituality are not themselves really religious or spiritually motivated. At most they may represent some conventional and profoundly secularized "religious" mind (such as tends to characterize contemporary Christianity), but there is a great range of presumptions common to the traditional structures of religious and spiritual consciousness that such individuals

---

* This term refers to the totality of mankind's religio-spiritual traditions, past and present.

simply cannot uphold. Such presumptions include the certainty of the continuation of existence after death, experiential presumptions about the "invisible" or non-elemental (or at least higher elemental) dimensions of the cosmos of Nature, presumptions about the reality of spirits, ghosts, subtle entities and powers, magic, miracles, mystical ascent and experience, the laws of karma (or the cause and effect laws that necessarily produce the future from the actions or motions of all present processes), and the supremely valuable resource or instrument of Help represented by individuals who are either highly evolved or perfectly Awakened. It is the blind or weakness represented by the inability to make such presumptions that causes scholars to misinterpret, secularize, and generally underestimate the traditional sources. And it is this same disability that makes popular interest, understanding, practice, and ultimate conversion to the Way of Truth so unlikely in this age.

The tendencies I have just described represent an obstacle to the consideration of the Way that I Teach as well as the Great Tradition. The common tendency is to reduce the expressions and offerings of profound religious and spiritual consciousness to structures of mind that are basically non-religious and even anti-spiritual, characterized by doubt and minimal levels of presumption relative to what is beyond elemental or materialistic conception. The popular and scholarly commentaries of our day tend to communicate and justify a materialistic, secularized or this-worldly, humanistic or conventionally socialized point of view. Everything else is regarded to be at best doubtful if not unreal, fanciful, and the product of undeveloped or neurotic human tendencies.

Before the Great Tradition and the Way that I Teach can be rightly evaluated and fully embraced, there must be a restoration of human balance and a renewal of the total mind of Man. Some individuals may be free enough to respond even now, but most of humanity must soon go through a difficult trial of purification, rebalancing, and regeneration of higher and subtler knowledge about the structures of manifest existence before the real religious or spiritual response can move them to the Real again.

The Purification of Doubt and Differences via the
Introduction of Advaitayana Buddhism

2.

The ancient traditional origins of religious and spiritual philosophy are in the magical or shamanistic cultures. Thus, conventional religious or spiritual consciousness is basically founded on the presumptions of "animism." There are many different belief systems that are animistic (and thus religious or spiritual), but what characterizes them all is the basic presumption that energy, invisible life, or spirit-force is "behind" all and every part of Nature. It is this invisible part that is embraced via every form of magical, religious, worshipful, mystical, yogic, or spiritual belief and practice. And it is the failure to presume (really and profoundly) the existence and the availability of such energy (or Power) that characterizes the non-religious, anti-spiritual, or merely materialistic consciousness.

Just so, the differences in presumption relative to the status of invisible energies (or Energy) are what differentiate (and ultimately result in conflicts between) religious or spiritual traditions.

The traditions of elemental magic, or the earliest and most primitive cultures of religion, conceive of the invisible in terms of the obvious pluralities of gross awareness. Therefore, every thing and every one is presumed to be animated and otherwise manipulated by individual spirits. And the practice of religion is therefore directed toward the attainment of positive and useful relations with spirit-entities of all kinds.

In contrast to such pluralistic animism (and the polytheistic religions that are built on that basis), the later developments of animism (ultimately represented by the monotheistic cultures) tend to produce religious and spiritual practice on the basis of the presumption that there is only one invisible force (or Divine Spirit) behind (and ultimately transcending) all of Nature.

The religious orthodoxy of any particular time and place is always critical of other systems. Therefore, the animistic cultures that developed monotheistic religion rigidly denied value (and even the right to exist) to the cults and practices of pluralistic animism. The early Hebrews, for example, engaged in systematic and even aggressive criticism of the magical practices, "idol" worship, and polytheistic cultism that were extant in the territories they wanted to acquire. Their principle of opposition was not truly a complaint against the cultic use of holy objects to serve access to or even represent the invisible spirit-influence. The Hebrews themselves used various kinds of such cultic machinery (from the ark of the covenant to the temple and all of its trappings). Rather, the principle of opposition was the difference between the mind of pluralistic or polytheistic animism and the mind of monotheistic animism.

The monotheistic religions developed forms of religious practice that were intended to cultivate positive and useful relations, in the present life and beyond, with the One Spirit-Entity (both directly and in the form of all human relations). And the monotheistic cults (dominantly represented by the militant and politically oriented cults of the ancient Middle East—Judaism, Christianity, and Islam) systematically suppressed and eliminated the tendency toward pluralistic animism. (A more recent example of a monotheistic culture's suppressing a culture of pluralistic animism during a drive to acquire and politicize a territory can be seen in the suppression of the American Indians during the settlement that became the United States of America.)

The knowledge and the psyche represented by magical animism is gradually lost as the monotheistic cults gain a dominant political and cultural position. In place of the magical culture (in which very real association with the individualized spirits, powers, and personalities that compose the manifest world has anciently been maintained) a characteristically monotheistic spiritual or mystical culture emerges. The exoteric or outer culture of monotheism has always been associated with the cult of ethical and prayerful relations with the Spirit-God. But the esoteric or inner culture of monotheism has always been directed toward mystical knowledge of God via the shamanism of "sky magic," or mystical and yogic ascent to the Heavenly Abode of God (above and beyond the pluralities of the gross and even the subtle worlds).

It was in the traditions of mystical or esoteric polytheism and monotheism that the principal traditional religious and spiritual idea was developed. That idea encompasses the entire range of experience developed in the phase of magical pluralism (and its outer or exoteric form, which is conventional polytheism) and the phase of both outer and inner monotheism. It is the idea of Divine Emanation.

The common thread of all conventional and traditional religion and spirituality (represented by the cultures of the first five stages of life) is the idea of Divine Emanation. Basically, this idea is the ultimate conception of animism. It conceives of all of Nature (including every part, thing, or individual being) to be set upon, pervaded by, or at least emanated from an ultimate (and thus Divine and Transcendental) and invisible (and thus Spiritual) Source. This is the principal conception of all conventional religion and spirituality, and it is the underlying basis of all dogmas, doctrines, belief systems, cultic practices, systems of authority, and methods of association, reception, and return relative to the Source of all emanations.

Whenever there is a breakdown in the ability of people to base their existence on this fundamental presumption, religion and spirituality tend to be degraded into materialistic secularization and to disappear in the culture of materialistic pluralism. Such is the case in the present age, and it will remain the case until science grows beyond the prejudices of materialism and acknowledges that the psychology represented by the scientific method is a specialization of mind and thus neither the Way to Truth nor the only legitimate means (or specialization of mind) for acquiring knowledge about self and world.

The exclusive dominance of materialistic scientism has resulted in the common disavowal of the basic idea of Divine or Transcendental Emanation. The exclusive dominance of monotheism resulted in the common disavowal of magic and psychism. It tended, therefore, even to eliminate from the common culture the necessarily psychic processes of monotheistic mystical ascent, and so a sharp division between the esoteric (or secret and mystical religion or spirituality) and the exoteric (or public, social, and conventionally ethical religion) developed. Indeed, the outer stance of the monotheistic cults tends to be associated with strong taboos against mystical experience as well as magic and psychism of all kinds. (The "Garden of Eden" story in the *Old Testament* book of *Genesis* is a prime example of the taboo against esotericism that is often promoted in the exoteric domain of cultic monotheism.) This practice reinforced the separation between the exoteric and the esoteric divisions of the cult. The mystical saints were supposed to remain hidden. Neither their powers nor their state of mind was to be revealed to the masses in any manner that would upset the order of common society. And if the ecstatic saints became too public in their esoteric teaching, the cult itself would try to suppress them. Eventually, as the monotheistic cults gained broad political and social power, the esoteric dimension of the cults was eliminated by the pressures of the exoteric cult and its mind.

Modern secular society is simply an extreme development of the exclusive exotericism of the monotheistic cults that were in power previous to the age of scientific materialism. Just as the monotheistic cults suppressed and eliminated the magical cultus of pluralistic and polytheistic animism, the modern cult of non-religious and anti-spiritual or non-animistic materialism has also suppressed and generally eliminated the mystical and the religious cultus of monotheistic animism and the entire world-view based on Divine or Spiritual Emanation.

My own consideration with you involves two principal reflections on this entire history. First of all, we must review and critically examine the entire process, so that we can regain a renewed capacity for association with the invisible dimensions of Nature. Only on that basis can we again be what we are—which is a naturally or inherently living, animated, or spiritually Radiant and religiously Awakened being. And the second aspect of my consideration goes beyond the conventions of all that may be gained by such a renewal. It is a matter of understanding and transcending the individualistic or self-based limitations of the first five stages of life (represented by both pluralistic and singularistic animism) and the sixth stage of life (represented by systematic exclusion or negation of Nature and the manifest self).

3.

Materialism is an ancient philosophical tendency. It is the product of mechanical mind, an analytical (or left-brained) and sense-bound (or merely perceptual) consciousness that is fixed upon elemental processes. It is a view that presumes no invisible or spiritual forces behind and independent of matter (or reality conceived via the bodily senses). It presumes no ultimate Invisible Spirit-Power or Creative Energy that is prior to and independent of matter. And, therefore, it does not presume the world and the self to be arising dependent upon the Process of Divine or Spiritual Emanation and ultimately or inherently existing in the Condition of utter Identification with the Divine or Transcendental Being, Consciousness, Freedom, Power, or Bliss.

When this materialistic or sense-based egoity becomes the principle of general cultural, social, and political organization, we see the development of totalitarian, utopian, and merely humanistic regimes. In our day, such attempts at organizing human beings on the basis of materialistic idealism and realism are profoundly evident in the world-wide growth of technologically based political materialism. The movements motivated by such a view of life obviously include socialistic, communistic, revolutionary, radical, and dictatorial political efforts of all kinds. But this same idealism, since it is the conventional basis of scientific culture, is transforming even democratic and traditionally free societies.

Wherever political materialism (which controls bodily existence and action) and scientific materialism (or the control of mind, psyche, and knowledge on the basis of materialistic views) are dominant, there inevitably is cultural suppression of non-materialistic, spiritually based, religious culture. In the worst of such regimes, aggressive military or police tactics are used. But in all cases, at least highly organized propaganda techniques are everywhere in evidence. Thus, in Russia, aggressive political efforts are made to prevent (or at least profoundly control) exoteric or conventional religious cults from interfering with the orientation of the masses toward the purposes of social idealism. But in America there is the tendency, even at the level of the State, to use religion as a means for maintaining the secular or merely social ideal. Even though religious freedom is proclaimed, the social order is infected by a bias toward exoteric Christian monotheism and the social idealism of white Protestantism. Racial and religious bigotry are as characteristic of American society as they are of any other society in the modern world. And the roots of all of this are in the materialistic persuasion of the egoic mind.

Historically, there have also been attempts to create religion on the basis of certain basic features of the materialistic view. The ancient world developed a number of traditions on this basis, the primary one still in existence being that of Buddhism. Buddhism, particularly in its original form (represented now by the Theravada or Hinayana school) developed on the basis of an even more ancient "underground" tradition of asceticism. It arose in India, where most of the many schools of religion and spirituality were commonly based on the ancient Vedic tradition. The Vedic tradition was the ancient Indian version of the culture of animism. It was associated with pluralistic animism (or the tradition of elemental magic and shamanism) and polytheism. And even though India began to develop monotheistic trends only relatively late in its development, the ancient polytheistic and animistic mystical tradition was already firmly based in the fundamental religious or spiritual idea, which is that of Divine or Spiritual Emanation.

As I have indicated, there was also in the Vedic period an underground, secondary, or non-Vedic (and thus non-Emanationist) cultural process. The schools of Samkhya, Jainism, and

Buddhism were built on that cultural base (although Samkhya and Jainism, like the traditional Emanationist schools, were founded on the point of view of subjective "idealism"—or the idea that consciousness, or the self-essence, is the Ultimate Principle—whereas Buddhism, at least in its earliest form, was founded on the strict conceptions of "realism," which are concerned with the methodical transcendence of conditional existence rather than the method of meditative identification with the self-essence). Even the more modern school of Advaita (or non-dualistic) Vedanta was to some degree built on that base, because of its strictly Transcendentalist orientation, but it also continues the basic line of the Vedic tradition, and it is firmly established on the base of the Vedic Upanishads and the idea of the world as Divine or Spiritual Emanation. Indeed, the Samkhya tradition was also assimilated into the mainstream of Vedic conceptions (as can be seen in the *Bhagavad Gita*). But the Jain and the Buddhist traditions were more resistive to this tendency to conform to the animistic or non-materialistic conception of the phenomenal world. To the degree those traditions remain intact in the Indian cultural process, they have been adapted in one or another manner to the scheme of Divine or Spiritual Emanation (so that Jain and Buddhist saints are seen in terms of Emanation cosmology and the sacred history of Divine intervention in the human world). But neither the Jain nor the Buddhist tradition has continued as a major cultural force in India. Basically, Jainism disappeared into the mass of relatively insignificant sub-sects, and Buddhism left India to develop in other parts of the Orient where the popular traditions were more congenial to its basic conceptions.

In any case, Buddhism is not a materialistic cultural influence in the same or negative sense that applies to the gross exoteric or worldly influences of scientific and political materialism. It is essentially a Way of Transcendental Realization that is based on materialistic "realism" rather than spiritual or subjective "idealism." Ultimately, the Way of Buddhism Realizes the same Transcendental Reality or Truth that is finally Realized via the

Ways built upon the concepts and presumptions of the basic ancient tradition of Divine or Spiritual Emanation.

The materialistic conceptions of classical Buddhism point to a problem (that of material or conditional existence itself) to be overcome or transcended. The Buddhist Way is to overcome or transcend that problem, and successful overcoming or transcendence of material or conditional existence is the essence of the Buddhist conception of Realization or Enlightenment. Therefore, it is not materialism itself that is valued in the Buddhist view, but That which is Realized in its overcoming. And the Buddhist Way is not oriented toward outer-directed, merely social or worldly and self-indulgent purposes. Rather, even though it often employs positive social and personal means, it is oriented toward transcendence and freedom from all kinds of craving, strife, and limitation.

Just so, the spiritual idealism of the traditional ancient view, founded on animism and the idea of Divine or Spiritual Emanation, viewed conditional existence as a structure of planes of manifestation emanating from the Divine or Transcendental Source. Thus, the Way of the Hindus, even though it also generally employed positive social and personal disciplines, was ultimately directed toward the transcendence of all conditions (or planes of manifest possibility), and all forms of birth, suffering, and death, in the Divine and Transcendental Source-Reality, prior to all conditional emanations.

Therefore, both materialistic realism and spiritual idealism have anciently provided the basis for the same ultimate Realization of the Transcendental Reality or Condition. The spiritual or animistic view has produced pluralistic or magical animism, polytheism, and both exoteric and esoteric monotheism. It has also provided the conceptual basis for all conventional religious and spiritual language, as well as the experiential basis for the traditional cultures of the first five stages of life. Even the sixth and seventh stages of life can be described in terms of the basic spiritual concepts of Divine or Spiritual Emanation. (And such has been done, particularly in the schools of Advaita Vedanta.)

My own Teaching makes use of such language in the service of those who are culturally adapted to the religious ideas of spiritual idealism. But I have from the beginning also considered and described the Way in more radical terms, and the Buddhist tradition as a whole is, therefore, also a precedent for my own Teaching Work, since it placed the sixth and seventh stages (and even the earlier stages) on a basis that did not necessarily require the presumptions of spiritual idealism, animism, and Divine or Spiritual Emanation (or the presumption that Nature and the manifest self are necessary, and are thus to be embraced rather than transcended).

It is true that, to one degree or another, the later schools of Buddhism (in the Mahayana and Vajrayana or Tantrayana traditions) reorganized the Buddhist philosophy and practice on a basis that less and less reflected the early materialistic realism of Gautama. The later schools grew more and more along the lines of spiritual and metaphysical idealism, and they eventually created their own version of the idea of the world as Divine or Spiritual Emanation. As such, the later Buddhist schools closely resemble the later Hindu schools of Advaita Vedanta, tantrism, yoga, social idealism, and exoteric religious and devotional worship. But the original Buddhist tradition represents an alternative conceptual basis for considering and practicing the Way of Transcendental Realization.

In the original language of Gautama, or in the language of materialistic realism, the conditions of manifest existence (or of self and not-self) do not arise by emanation from a Divine Creative Cause or Source. According to that view, all limited conditions are caused by previous limited conditions. The world (and thus every self) is not emanated (and thus made necessary) by a Divine Cause. Rather, the world, or every moment of conditional existence, arises as an effect of a beginningless and endless chain of causation. Therefore, the original Buddhist Way is not to meditate on God, or the Divine Being within or behind the conditional self, but to examine and awaken insight into the conditional states of self and its objects, until there is an

Awakening that inherently transcends conditional existence.

The "Nirvana" of original Buddhism is not annihilation but perfect transcendence. The Way is described in negative terms (a problem is to be transcended), but the Transcendental Realization is valued above all. That Realization is not described in Itself (since all language is the bearer of conditional limitations or "false views"), but It is clearly pointed to in the Teaching of Gautama, and his own Realization is clearly described in terms of a meditative Samadhi that is not a matter of the absorption of self, or attention, in the Divine or any emanation of the Divine, but which is nonetheless a Real Condition of Transcendental Bliss.

The entire Buddhist tradition is based on the supreme valuation of this Transcendental Realization (even in the case of schools that do not found themselves on the original materialistic realism of Gautama). Whether or not we say the world and the self emanate from the Divine or Transcendental Reality, all conditions are ultimately transcended if we Realize the Divine or Transcendental Reality. If we are not inclined to presume that self and world are caused (and thus, by implication, made necessary) <u>by</u> the Transcendental Reality, at least it is ultimately Realized that self and world, or all causes and effects, are arising, without necessity and without binding power, <u>in</u> the Transcendental Reality (or in such a fashion that Realization of the Transcendental Reality or Condition makes it obvious that all forms of conditional existence are unnecessary and even unreal in their apparent independence).

Conventional materialists, who are not disposed toward Transcendental Realization, tend to conceive of Gautama's materialistic realism in conventional terms. Thus, they interpret Gautama's denial of the existence of an immortal soul to mean that Gautama subscribed to a mortalist view of human existence. On the contrary, Gautama clearly believed in (and personally experienced the evidence of) personal existence before bodily birth and after bodily death. But he regarded human and all forms of conditional existence to be forms of suffering—always temporary and limited, always founded on the discomfort and deluding power of craven desires, emotions, and thoughts, and always ending in pain and separation. It was his will to transcend the automatic process of causes and effects that inevitably lead to embodiment that provided the basis for his view that human embodiment is not the expression (or emanation) of an immortal internal part (traditionally called the soul, or the atman). This view was simply consistent with his basic non-inclination to base his consideration of Realization on the conventions of ordinary language, animism, or the idea of Divine Emanation. He enjoyed an insight in which the world and the manifest self could be clearly seen to be <u>unnecessary</u>—and being unnecessary, they could be, must be, or inevitably would be transcended.

Gautama's view of no-soul is simply a form of radical "realistic" language that is free of the need to regard human existence as necessary or desirable for its own sake. Gautama's orientation was strictly in the direction of ultimate transcendence. The animistic idea of a soul is part of the ancient animistic philosophy of Divine Emanation, and it can, in the conventional mind, tend to support the idea of the necessity or inherent desirability of self and world. Gautama wanted to communicate the non-necessity of self and world, and so he was sympathetic to the unconventional language of the esoteric underground of materialistic realism, according to which the manifest self is not emanating from an internal soul and the world is not emanating from a Divine Cause. Both self and world are conditional, not Divinely Emanated, but unnecessary. This is the principal idea of Gautama. And on this basis he communicated his version of the Transcendental Way.

The original Buddhism of Gautama was free of the limitations of animism and Emanationism, but it was based on a problem-consciousness. Thus, his version of the Way is a progressive strategy of ultimate transcendence based on transforming the actions of the manifest self (in order to purify the self of bad karma, or negative future effects), until the desire to create more effects utterly ceases. Later versions of the Buddhist Way were attempts to avoid this limitation (which was based on the future transcendence or mechanical discontinuation of self rather than the present or inherent transcendence of self). Therefore, later versions of the Buddhist Way developed more along the lines of metaphysical idealism—or a direct appeal to Realization of the Transcendental Reality (or the Inherent Condition) rather than to the progressive elimination of manifest conditional existence.

The later schools of Buddhism tended in a direction that bears many similarities to the basic tradition of Divine Emanation, or at least the idealism of direct appeal to the Transcendental Reality. In the process, the tradition of Buddhism adopted many features of culture and practice that characterize the first five stages of life as well as the sixth and the seventh stages of life, whereas the original formulation of Gautama was a strictly sixth stage practice that could, if successful, lead ultimately to the seventh stage disposition of Realized Enlightenment (which indeed it did in the case of Gautama).

The Hindu school of Advaita Vedanta is based upon the traditional Vedic concepts derived from the original animistic tradition. It is, therefore, founded on the basic idea of Divine Emanation. However, it views self and world to be unnecessary, hence illusory, since all conditions are inherently Identical to (and, therefore, not separate from) the Divine or Transcendental Being, Self, Consciousness, Freedom, Happiness, Bliss, or Reality. The tradition of Advaita (or non-dualistic) Vedanta springs from the ancient Vedic culture and the schools of the Vedic Upanishads. But it is founded on an Intuition not at all different from that ultimately Realized by Gautama. It is the Realization of the Transcendental Reality, inherently transcending self and world (or conditional existence, in all its planes). Therefore, the ultimate Realization of Advaita Vedanta is no more attached to conceptions of necessity, soul, Creator God, Divine Emanation, or desire for this or any other world than is the ultimate Realization of Buddhism.

The only significant difference between the basic traditions of ultimate Realization according to the Vedic and the Buddhist (or non-Vedic) traditions is in the language of the Way toward Realization. The Upanishadic schools of Advaita Vedanta are the principal sixth to seventh stage schools of Vedic spiritual idealism. And the schools of Buddhism are the principal sixth to seventh stage schools of non-Vedic materialistic realism. But both traditions are oriented toward and originally based upon the same ultimate Transcendentalism.

It could even be said that both Buddhism and Advaita Vedanta develop their Ways based on one of the two basic options of ultimate consideration. In the simplest sense, two principles coincide in every moment of human existence: the self and the not-self (or the world of objects). The Way of Advaitic idealism is based on the consideration of the Source, Identity, Nature, or Condition of the manifest self, prior to the apparent emanation of the conditional body-mind-self and the world. The Way of Buddhism takes the alternate route. It is disposed to consider and transcend the whole process of conditions, differences, or the total cause and effect world (which includes the body-mind-self as only one of its conditional features). If we embrace the Great Tradition as a whole, then the Vedic Advaitism and the tradition of Buddhism can be understood simply to be the two principal traditional limbs of the sixth and seventh stages of life. There is no possible conflict between them once they are rightly understood in this manner.

In my own time and place, my own Realization and Teaching have appeared spontaneously and with characteristic and unique features. But I can now see my own Way in the perspective of the Great Tradition. My Way is a radical Teaching that enters into consideration of all the stages of life and the entire Great Tradition of the ancients and their modern representatives. But the Way that I Teach is ultimately most radical—an expression of the Intuition that is fundamental to the seventh stage of life itself. Even so, I enjoy great sympathy with the sixth stage traditions of Buddhism and Advaita Vedanta, since they ultimately transcended themselves in the seventh stage Enlightenment. The Buddhist Way ultimately goes beyond its problem-based views and its search to strategically bring an end to the conditional or karmic self. Likewise, the Way of Advaita Vedanta ultimately goes beyond its subjectivism and its search to strategically dissociate consciousness from conditional objects. When rightly understood and embraced as the two primary limbs of the sixth to seventh stage schools (and even accommodating the schools of the first five stages of life) of one Great Tradition, Buddhism (as a whole) and Advaita Vedanta (as the epitome of the entire Vedic or Emanationist tradition) may be described as a single and heretofore unacknowledged tradition. That tradition is now made evident and whole by my own Teaching. My own Teaching is the epitome of and the historical basis for the acknowledgment of this tradition, and my own Teaching provides a new structure of understanding which unifies and fulfills that tradition as well as the total Great Tradition. Therefore, the Way that I Teach may be called "Advaitayana Buddhism" (or the ultimate, unified or all-inclusive, but also radical tradition of both the Vedic, or Emanationist, and the non-Vedic, or non-Emanationist, schools).

That Way that I Teach is a complete view that makes it possible to understand the unity of the Emanationist and non-Emanationist views. My own Teaching is the basis for the proclamation of this new "yana" (vehicle or Revelation) of Buddhism. Earlier Buddhist yanas have arisen in India, China, and Tibet. This new yana stands in positive relation to each of the earlier three yanas—Hinayana, Mahayana, and Vajrayana—as well as to the world-wide Emanationist tradition, epitomized in the Upanishadic Advaitism of such sages as Ashtavakra, Shankara, and Ramana Maharshi, and it has arisen in the West, in America, thus fulfilling many long-standing prophecies that a Dharma-Bearer would arise in the West to renew the ancient Way.

The Way that I Teach is also the epitome of the entire Great Tradition. The consideration of the Way that I Teach may at first be expressed via disciplines that encounter the limits, conventions, and absorptive meditations of the first five stages of life (but free of the subhuman limitations of conventional materialism). Even so, all of that is eventually gone beyond via the critical intelligence and insightful meditations that consider the characteristics of the sixth stage of life, and even that process is ultimately transcended in the radically intuitive Realization or meditation-transcending Samadhi of the seventh stage of life.

The Way that I Teach is, like the Buddhist Way, realistic, since it is, in its mature form, expressed via free insight into the limiting mechanics of the self rather than via any process of strategic inversion of attention upon the self-essence or of contemplative absorption of the attention of the egoic self in the Divine Spirit or the Transcendental Other. But the Way that I Teach is also, like the Way of Advaita Vedanta, openly oriented toward ultimate transcendence of self and not-self in the Transcendental Reality, Being, Self, or Consciousness. Therefore, the Way that I Teach does not bear an exclusive affinity to either Buddhism or Upanishadic Advaitism (or non-dualism), but it acknowledges both as its most congenial ancient likenesses, and it acknowledges the entire Great Tradition, in all times and places, in all of the stages of life, and in the person of all true Adepts, to be its inherited Tradition.

The Way that I Teach stands on its own merits, and it has arisen freely and spontaneously, without fixed deference to the point of view of any part of the traditions, and without the benefit or the hindrance represented by a significant previous cultural training in the philosophies and practices of the traditions. Even so, the total Great Tradition is the true tradition of all of mankind, and the Way that I Teach is a complete fulfillment of that Tradition as well as a radical point of view that rightly and critically understands and values that Tradition as a whole. Therefore, the Way that I Teach can be called Daist, or Radical Transcendentalism, or the Way of Radical Understanding, or the Way of Divine Ignorance, or the Way of Advaitayana Buddhism.

II
Buddhas and Buddhism

Gautama was a philosopher who considered the Way of ultimate or Transcendental Realization in the terms of "phenomenal realism." He is not rightly called a "Buddha" because of this philosophy. He is rightly called a Buddha because he Realized the Samadhi of Awakening to the Nirvanic or Transcendental Condition.

"Buddhism" is not inherently associated with the philosophy of "phenomenal realism." It only tends to be considered in those terms because of the original association of traditional Buddhism with Gautama's philosophical consideration of the Way. Actually, much of historical Buddhism involves considerations of the Way in other terms than those of "phenomenal realism"—such as those of metaphysical and subjective "idealism."

Truly, "Buddhism" is a term that may rightly be applied to any sixth to seventh stage Transcendentalist philosophy or Way of Transcendental Realization, just as the term "Buddha" may rightly be applied to any Adept who has entered into the Realization or Samadhi that characterizes the seventh or fully Awakened stage of life.

III
The Spiritual Advaitism of Jesus of Nazareth

To paraphrase the Teaching of Jesus: "Don't you know that you are gods? God is Spirit. The Spirit gave birth to Man. That which is <u>born</u> of the Spirit <u>is</u> Spirit."

The Spiritual Advaitism of Jesus of Nazareth

The ultimate and secret (or "nighttime") Teaching of Jesus (such as he is reported to have given to Nicodemus, in the third chapter of the *Gospel of John*) goes beyond the traditional esoteric and mystical notion that we are each identical to an individuated immortal soul and need to identify with that soul inwardly and apart from the body in order to ascend to the non-physical spiritual or psychic world. Jesus Taught recognition of our total born bodily (or psycho-physical) being as soul, not merely in the sense of being an immortal subtle individual, but in the eternal sense, totally inhering in and thus totally identical to the Spiritual and Transcendental Divine. He Taught that we are utterly Spiritual (or eternal, and thus, in Truth, unborn), now and forever in intimate free Communion with God, Who is Spirit, or Radiant Transcendental Being—in (and thus as) Whom we live and move and exist.

According to Jesus, the Way is to embrace and participate in the Mystery of the "Kingdom of God." That Way involves (1) acknowledgment that we are inherently free, or of the nature of Spirit, and (2) awakening to the process of Spirit-Communion as a self-transcending exercise of the total body-mind, from the point of view that the total psycho-physical being and all its conditions and relations inhere in and are ultimately identical to the Transcendental Spiritual Divine.

The more public Teaching of Jesus is associated with the moral exotericism and animistic terrestrialism of the Emanationist religion of the first three stages of life. And he is also often quoted or depicted in the terms of traditional formulations that affirm the dualistic ideal of evolutionary soul-culture (or the fourth to fifth stage views of traditional Emanationism, which are concerned with mystical soul-travel, or ascent through the cosmic hierarchy to the "Throne" or "Heaven" of God). But Jesus' ultimate Confession of the Realization of his oneness with the "Father," or the Spiritual and Transcendental Divine Being, implies free and utter transcendence of the point of view and conventional independence of body, mind, self, and soul. By virtue of that Confession, we may consider Jesus of Nazareth to be an

Adept in the seventh stage of life, an Advocate of the point of view of Emanationist Non-Dualism, and thus, in Truth, an Enlightened "Buddha," "Bodhisattva," "Jnani," "Jivanmukta," or "Mahasiddha," Occupied with Transcendental Wisdom in the midst of a traditional culture of animistic spiritualism and Emanationist monotheism.

If we do not thus presume Jesus to have been a "Completed" or seventh stage Adept, the only alternative assessment that is also possibly legitimate is a spiritually less auspicious one, based on the evidence that suggests he was merely a typical figure in the moral and mystical traditions of the first five stages of life. According to that view, it is to be presumed that Jesus advocated the basically animistic doctrine that life is a struggle with unholy or daemonic "spirits" (which produce the symptoms of "sin," or denial of God's Help, in the form of disease, doubt, violence, hypocrisy, fear, anger, sorrow, defeat, and so forth). In that context, Jesus offered the "Holy Spirit" of God to believers (or those who would renounce "sin," or willful possession by negative spirits, and exercise the impulse of faith, or the will to be possessed by the Holy Spirit) as the means of salvation from the negative destinies that develop from daemonic possession. To be sure, this interpretation of Jesus is certainly a correct reflection of the general setting of his Work. The question is whether or not his Teaching, or at least his Realization, exceeded the limits of animism and monotheistic Emanationism in the context of the first five stages of life.

I would say that there is a basis (in the "Confessions" or self-descriptions of Jesus) for affirming that Jesus had himself entered into the Realization of the seventh stage of life, and there is some indication in the *New Testament* that he may have Taught the Non-Dualistic Wisdom to at least a few others (such as Nicodemus). In any case, Jesus of Nazareth has historically been more mythologized than remembered. And he has been blatantly transformed into a symbol for justifying worldly activity and social or political power, whereas he was a Spiritual Master who passionately called his hearers to repent of all worldly ambitions and follow him into the Mysterious Domain of Divine Being.

IV
God as the Creator, the Good, and the Real

Conventional religion originates in the consciousness that characterizes the earlier stages of life. Thus, it is ego-based and it serves the functional desire of the manifest or phenomenal self to be protected, nourished, pleasurized, and ultimately preserved.

The phenomenal self or egoic (self-centered) body-mind is the source of conventional religion as well as all of the other ordinary and extraordinary pursuits of born existence in the first six stages of life. Therefore, it is not God but the ego (perhaps gesturing conceptually toward God) that is the source and fundamental subject of popular religion as well as higher mysticism. Real spirituality, true religion, or Transcendental Occupation begins only when the egoic consciousness (with all of its mind, emotion, desire, and activity) is thoroughly understood and inherently transcended. For this reason, only the radical Teaching of the Wisdom of the seventh stage of life directly serves the process of actual God-Realization. All other forms of doctrine or instruction serve the purposes of the first six stages of life—all of which are founded on manifest egoity and conditional attention.

It is the culture of conventional religion that promotes the conventional ideas about God. The principal conventional God-idea is that God is the Creator (or intentional Emanator) of the worlds and all beings. Such seems an obvious idea to the bodily ego, trapped in the mechanics of the perceptual mind and the material or elemental vision. The ego is identified with embodiment, and the idea of the Creator-God is developed to account for this fact and to provide a conceptual basis (in the form of the idea of the ego as God-made creature) for the appeal to God to Help the ego in this world and in the yet unknown after-death state.

The difficulty with the Creator-God conception is that it identifies God with ultimate causation and thus makes God inherently responsible for the subsequent causation of all effects. And if God is responsible for all effects, then God is clearly a very powerful but also terrible Deity—since manifest existence tends to work equally for and against all creatures.

Therefore, the Creator-God idea is commonly coupled with the idea of God as Good (and thus both opposite and opposed to Evil). If the Creator-God is conceived to be Good (or always working to positively create, protect, nourish, rightly and pleasurably fulfill, and ultimately preserve all of Nature and all creatures), then the ego is free of the emotional double-bind and the anger and despair that would seem to be justified if God is simply the responsible Creator of everything (good, evil, bad, or in between). Therefore, conventional theology, most especially as it has tended to develop under the influence of the Semitic religions of the Middle East, is founded on the ideas of God as Creator and God as Good (or Good Will).

But if God is the all-powerful Creator (without whom not anything has been made), then how did so much obviously negative or evil motion and effect come into existence? The usual answer is generally organized around one or another mythological story in which powerful creatures (or one powerful creature, such as the Devil, now regarded to personify Evil) entered (on the basis of free will), into a pattern of "sin," or disobedience and conflict with God, which resulted in separation from God and a descent or fall into material consciousness, and so forth. Such mythologies are structured in terms of a hierarchical view of Nature, with various planes descending from the Heaven of God. Religion thus becomes a method of return to God.

Exoteric religion is generally based on an appeal to belief, social morality, and magical prayer or worship. The return to God is basically conceived in terms of this world and, therefore, exoteric or terrestrial religion is actually a process in which God returns to the ego and to this world (rather than vice versa), and it is believed that God will eventually reclaim mankind and the total world from the forces of Evil. But exoteric religion is an outer cult, intended for grosser egos and for mass consumption (or the culture of the first three stages of life). The ultimate form of conventional religion is in the esoteric or inner and sacred cult, which is a mystical society, open only to those chosen for initiation (and thus growth or evolution into the fourth and fifth stages of life). Esoteric religion is a process of cosmic mysticism, or the method of return to God by ascending as mind (or disembodied soul), back through the route of the original fall into matter and Evil, until the Heaven or Eternal Abode of God is reached again. The esoteric religious process goes beyond the conventions of exoteric religion to develop the psycho-physical mechanics of mystical flight and return to God via the hierarchical structures of the nervous system (ascending from the plane of Evil, or the Devil, or the "flesh," at the bodily base of the nervous system, to the plane of the Good, or God, or the Heavenly Abode, at or above the brain, via the "magic carpet" of the life-force in the nervous system).

Thus, the idea of the Creator-God leads to the idea that God is Good (or the Good Will), which leads to the idea that creatures have free will, which then accounts for the appearance of sin, suffering, evil, and loss of God-consciousness. And conventional religion then becomes the means (through structures of belief, sacramental worship, mystical prayer, yogic or shamanistic ascent, and so forth) for the re-exercise of creaturely free will in the direction of God, Good, the triumph over Evil and death in this world, and the ascent from material form and consciousness to spiritual, heavenly, or Godly form and consciousness.

All the popular and mystical religious and spiritual traditions of mankind tend to be associated with this chain of conceptions (or the characteristic ideas of the first five stages of life). It is only in the sixth and seventh stage traditions that these ideas begin to give way to different conceptions. It is only in the sixth stage of life that the egoic basis of the first five stages of life is penetrated. And it is only in the seventh stage of life that the ego is altogether transcended in the Real Divine.

The theological and general religious conceptions I have just described have always been subject to criticism (or at least simple non-belief) on the part of those who are not persuaded by religious and theological arguments. Atheism has always opposed theism. But atheistic ideas are the product of the same fundamental self-consciousness that otherwise produces theistic or conventional religious ideas. Atheism is the product of the ego (or the phenomenal self, grounded in elemental perception), and so also is theism. Atheism, like exoteric religion, extends itself only into the domain of the first three stages of life, whereas esoteric religion and theism provide a means for entering, mystically and spiritually, into the evolution of the fourth and fifth stages of life.

Atheism regularly proposes a logical view of life that has its own dogmatic features. It does not propose a God-idea but, instead, founds itself on and in the perceptual and phenomenal mind alone. Atheism concedes only a universal and ultimately indifferent (or merely lawful) Nature (not God), and so there is no need to create a religious "creation myth" to account for suffering. (And atheistic thinkers thus generally confine themselves to constructing a cosmology, based on material observations alone, that merely accounts for the appearance of the manifest events of Nature.) Indeed, just as conventional religion or theism arises to account for suffering, atheism arises on the basis of the unreserved acknowledgment of suffering. And if there is no idea of God, there is no idea of Man as creature (or Man as the bearer of an immortal or God-like inner part). Nor is there any need to interpret unfortunate or painful events as the effects of Evil. Therefore, the atheistic point of view is characterized by the trend of mind that we call "realism," just as the conventional religious or theistic point of view is characterized by the trend of mind that we call "idealism," but both atheism and theism arise on the basis of the self-contraction, or the ego of phenomenal self-consciousness, rather than on the basis of direct intuition of the Real Condition that is prior to self and its conventions of perception and thought.

The realistic or atheistic view is just as much the bearer of a myth (or a merely conceptual interpretation of the world) as is the conventional religious or theistic view. Atheism (or conventional realism) is a state of mind that is based in the phenomenal self and that seeks the ultimate protection, nourishment, pleasure, and preservation of the phenomenal self (at least in this world and, if there should be an after-life, then also in any other world). Therefore, it is simply an alternative philosophy to theism and conventional religion, based on the same principle and consciousness (the phenomenal ego), and seeking by alternative means to fulfill the manifest self and relieve it of its suffering.

Atheism, or conventional realism, is a state of mind that possesses individuals who are fixed in the first three stages of life. It is a form of spiritual neurosis (or self-possession), as are all of the characteristic mind-states of the first six stages of life. Esoteric religion and theism provide a basis for certain remarkable individuals to enter the fourth and fifth stages of life, but the commonly (or exoterically) religious individual is, like the atheist, a relatively adolescent (if not childish and even infantile) character, fixed in the egoic neuroses of the first three stages of life.

Atheism proposes a myth and a method for ego-fulfillment that is based on phenomenal realism, rather than spiritual idealism (or the culture of the conventional God-idea). Therefore, atheism is traditionally associated with the philosophy of materialism, just as theism is associated with spiritualism, animism, and Emanationism. And the realistic or atheistic view tends to be the foundation for all kinds of political, social, and technological movements, since its orientation is toward the investigation and manipulation of material Nature. Atheism is realism and materialism. It is about the acquisition of knowledge about Nature and the exploitation of that knowledge to command (or gain power over) Nature. And it is this scheme of knowledge and power (expressed as political and technological means of all kinds) that is the basis of the mythology and quasi-religion of atheism. The atheistic (or non-theistic) view of life is ego-based, organized relative to Nature as an elemental or perceived process, and committed to knowledge and power as the means of salvation (or material fulfillment of egoity).

In our time, this materialistic, realistic, and non-theistic philosophy of ego-fulfillment is represented by the world-culture of scientific, technological, and political materialism. The entire race of mankind is now being organized by the cultural movement of scientific materialism, while the alternative cultures of theism, mystical esotericism, sixth stage Transcendentalism, and the ultimate or truly radical philosophy of the seventh stage of life are tending to be systematically suppressed and propagandized out of existence. Scientism (or the culture of realistic or materialistic knowledge) and its two arms of power (technology and political order) are the primary forces in world-culture at the present time. And humanity at large is thus tending to be reduced to the robot acculturations of orderly egoism in the limited terms represented by our functional development in the first three stages of life.

Conventional and popular human culture has historically been limited to the conflicts and alternatives represented by theism and atheism, or egoic idealism and egoic realism. And the large-scale ordering of mankind has always tended to be dominated by the politics of materialistic knowledge and power. It is simply that in the twentieth century we are seeing that materialistic culture approach the achievement of a world-wide mass culture in which all individuals will be controlled by a powerful and materialistically oriented system of political and technological restriction.

The usual or most commonly remarked criticism of theism is based on the evidence of suffering and material limitation. Therefore, the common arguments against religion and theism are generally those proposed by the point of view of atheism. Likewise, the common arguments against atheism are generally those proposed by theism (or an appeal to egoic acceptance of the evidence of religious history, cultic revelation, mystical psychology, and psychic experience). For this reason, there may seem to be only two basic cultural alternatives: atheism and theism.

But theism and religion are, at base, the expressions of egoity in the first three stages of life, just as is the case with atheism and conventional materialism. Therefore, whenever theism or religion becomes the base for political and social order, it inevitably becomes the base for knowledge and power in the material world. And theistic regimes have historically been equally as aggressive in the manipulation and suppression of humanity as have atheistic regimes. Theism is, at its base, egoic and fitted to worldly concerns. Therefore, when it achieves worldly power, it simply adopts the same general materialistic means that are adopted by atheism. Knowledge and power are the common tools of egoity, not merely the tools of atheism. It is simply that theism and religion can, via the exercises and attainments of saints and mystics, apply knowledge and power to purposes that extend beyond the first three stages of life. But in the terms of the first three stages of life (or the common and practical social order), theism and religion are inclined to make the same demands for social consciousness and to apply fundamentally the same kind of political and authoritarian techniques for achieving obedience and order as are applied by atheism and scientism.

This is evident in the popular theistic (and now almost exclusively exoteric) cultures that have come out of the Semitic tradition of the Middle East. Judaism, Christianity, and Islam are the principal theistic religions (in terms of worldly power and numbers), and they are all based on similar idealistic conceptions of God and creature and salvation, but each of these cults has also historically sought and achieved the general power to command the social order. And, in the process, each of these cults became a political State, controlling the forms of knowledge and power. As a result, over time these religions developed more and more of a secular, materialistic, and worldly character. Each of the three cults claims absolute, independent, and exclusive religious and worldly authority, and the historical conflict among these three (and between their claims and the equally absolutist and absurd claims of other and atheistic or non-religious systems, such as communism, democratic capitalism, and technological scientism) has now become the basis for idealistic State politics and political conflicts all over the world. And the seemingly more important or esoteric matters of spiritual wisdom, mystical knowledge, and the magical power of sainthood or Adeptship are as much in doubt and disrepute in the common religious circles of theism as they are in scientific and atheistic circles.

All of this is to indicate that conventional religion and theism share a root error or limitation with atheism and worldly culture. That error or limitation is the ego itself, or the presumptions and the seeking that are most basic to the conception of an independent phenomenal self in a less than hospitable phenomenal world. What is ultimately to be criticized in religion or theism is the same limit that is to be criticized in atheism and materialism. It is the ego, the phenomenal self-base, from which we tend to derive our conceptions of God, Nature, life, and destiny.

It is only when the egoic root of our functional, worldly, and religious or spiritual life is inspected, understood, and transcended that self, and world, and God are seen in Truth. Therefore, it is necessary to understand. It is necessary to aspire to Wisdom, Truth, and Enlightenment. All occupations derived from the ego-base are necessarily limited to egoity, and all conceptions that feed such egoic occupations are necessarily bereft of a right view of self, world, and God (or the ultimate and Transcendental Reality and Truth).

When the mechanics of egoity are transcended in our understanding, then it becomes obvious that life (or manifest phenomenal existence) is simply a play of opposites. Neither "Good" (or creation and preservation) nor "Evil" (or destruction) finally wins. Nature, in all its planes, is inherently a dynamic. The play of Nature, in all its forms and beings and processes, is not merely (or exclusively and finally) seeking the apparent "Good" of self-preservation (or the preservation and fulfillment of any particular form, world, or being), nor is it merely (or exclusively and finally) seeking the apparent "Evil" of self-destruction (or the dissolution of any particular form, world, or being). Rather, the play in Nature is always in the direction of perpetuating the dynamics of the play itself—and, therefore, polarity, opposition, struggle, alternation, death, and cyclic repetition tend to be perpetuated as the characteristics of phenomenal existence. Therefore, the play of Nature is always alternating between the appearance of dominance by one or the other of its two basic extremes. And the sign of this is in the inherent struggle that involves every form, being, and process. The struggle is this dynamic play of opposites, but the import of it is not the absolute triumph of either half. Things and beings and processes arise, they move, they are transformed, and they disappear. No thing or being or process is ultimately preserved. But neither is there any absolute destruction. Nature is a transformer, not merely a creator or a destroyer.

To the ego (or present temporary form of being) self-preservation may seem to be the inevitable motive of being. Therefore, a struggle develops to destroy or escape the dynamic of Nature by dominating Evil (or death) with Good (or immortality). This ideal gets expressed in the generally exoteric and occidental or more materialistic efforts to conquer Nature via worldly knowledge and power. But it also gets expressed in the more esoteric and oriental or mystical efforts to escape the plane of Nature by ascent from materiality (or the Evil of the flesh) to Heaven (the Good God above the consciousness of Nature).

But when the ego (or self-contraction) is understood and transcended, then Nature is seen from the point of view of Wisdom. And, in that case, the egoic struggle in Nature or against Nature is also understood and transcended. Then the Way of life ceases to be founded on the need to destroy the dynamic of Nature via conventional knowledge, power, immortality, or mystical escape. The world is no longer conceived as a drama of warfare between Good and Evil. The righteousness of the search for the Good as a means of self-preservation disappears along with the self-indulgent and self-destructive negativity of possession by Evil. In place of this dilemma of opposites, a self-transcending and world-transcending (or Nature-transcending) equanimity appears. And in that equanimity there is an inherent

Radiance that transcends the egoic dualities of Good and Evil (or the conventional polarities of the self in Nature). It is the Radiance of Love. And in that Free Radiance, energy and attention are inherently free from the ego-bond, self-contraction, or the "gravitational effect" of phenomenal self-awareness. Therefore, dynamic equanimity, or the free disposition of Love (rather than the egoic disposition in the modes of Good or Evil), is the "window" through which God may be "seen" (or intuited)—not in the conventional mode of Creator, Good, Other, or Heavenly Place, but as the Real, or the tacitly obvious Condition of all existence.

The ultimate moment in the play of Nature is not the moment of egoic success (or the temporary achievement of the apparently positive or "Good" effect). The ultimate moment is beyond contradiction (or the dynamics of polarized opposites). It is the moment of equanimity, the still point or "eye" in the midst of the wheel of Nature's motions and all the motivations of the born self. The Truth and Real Condition of self and Nature is Revealed only in that equanimity, beyond all stress and bondage of energy and attention.

This disposition of equanimity (or free energy and attention) is basic to the conceptions of the sixth and seventh stages of life. In the sixth stage of life, it provides the functional base for the ultimate and final investigation of the ego and the dynamics of Nature. But in the seventh stage of life, fundamental equanimity is native and constant, expressing prior Transcendental Realization. It is in the seventh stage of life that God, Truth, or Reality is directly obvious, prior to every trace of egoity, dilemma, and seeking. Therefore, it is in the seventh stage of life that God is truly proclaimed, not in the conventional mode of Creator, or the Good, but as the Real. God is the Transcendental Truth, Reality, Identity, and Condition of self and Nature. In the seventh stage of life, That is tacitly obvious, and there is not anything that must be escaped or embraced for the Happiness of God-Realization to be actualized. It is inherently so. Therefore, the Way that I Teach is not any egoic means for attaining God-

Realization. The Way is God-Realization Itself (prior to the methods of the first six stages of life). God, or the Transcendental Reality, prior to self, world, and the conventions of religion and non-religion, exotericism and esotericism, is the Way, the Truth, and the Life.

V
Pain, Independence, and the Discovery of Consciousness

Manifest existence is association with the force of conditionality. The inherent circumstance of manifest existence is change, temporariness, limitation, struggle with opposites, search for happiness, motivation toward release, and attachment to what is neither ultimate nor necessary.

As a consequence of all of this, the manifest being tends toward bewilderment, stress, obsessive craving, frustration, anger, sorrow, fear, depression, disease, pain, unhappiness, inertia, and death.

In the midst of all of this, the mind tends to develop the psychology of the problem. Manifest existence tends to be conceived as a problem to be overcome. And thus the language of religious or spiritual consideration tends to be associated with this problem-consciousness, and religious or spiritual practice tends, therefore, to develop as a strategy for overcoming and ultimately eliminating pain, suffering, change, and even manifest existence itself.

We must understand and transcend this tendency to become grounded in the problem-consciousness of ordinary egoity. The proper or real consideration in the midst of manifest existence is not involved in this reaction to conditional experience. Enlightenment is not the elimination of phenomenal experience. Rather,

Enlightenment is the intuition of the Transcendental Condition of the phenomenal self and its objects and states. And that intuition is not predicated on the ascetical or yogic elimination of conditional states. Rather, it is inherent in the direct and most profound or radical understanding of the entire process of attention in relation to the self, its psycho-physical states, and its objects (or the not-self).

In the traditions of Transcendental Enlightenment, conditional existence is considered in terms of one or the other of its two fundamental characteristics. It is considered either in terms of its negative experiential impact (as pain, limitation, or suffering) or in terms of its status in relation to Reality. In the Buddhist tradition, conditional existence is named "samsara," and in the tradition of Advaitism conditional existence is named "maya." In both traditions, this leading conception is treated both as suffering and as a process to be understood in Reality. It is a characteristic of the beginner's (and particularly the sixth stage) consciousness in these traditions to consider manifest existence in negative terms and to make that consideration into the motivating principle of religious or spiritual practice. But it is characteristic of the advanced, spiritually mature, and, especially, the Enlightened consciousness of those same traditions to stand aside from the conventional egoic reactions to the manifest difficulties of life and to consider manifest existence simply and entirely as a process to be understood in the Context of Reality (or the Transcendental Condition of conditions).

The conventional or lesser approaches to religious or spiritual consideration tend to be based on a reaction to the difficulties of life. Such is the common basis of exoteric religion and even all of the worldly and esoteric pursuits that characterize the first six stages of life. To be sure, there is much useful knowledge, discipline, and ability that we can rightly learn and wisely apply to the conditions of manifest existence. Therefore, much of the culture of religious or spiritual life is naturally and inevitably associated with such learning and application. But all of that is nothing but ordinary wisdom. It is the human method for transforming the ego-crushing conditions of manifest existence into a creative process of ego-development, ego-salvation, and ego-release. The ultimate matter of Enlightenment or Transcendental God-Realization has nothing to do with the struggle between the manifest self and the pain of conditional experience.

The Way that I Teach is not based in the conventional mind or the negative reaction to conditional existence. The Way that I Teach is an expression of the free or radical consideration that characterizes the seventh stage of life. The conceptions of the Way that develop in the characteristic terms of the first six stages of life are all based on the problem of manifest (and thus egoic) experience. They are all a search for the fulfillment or the release of the manifest self or independent ego. I consider the Way in radical terms—not on the basis of the ego's problem or the ego itself, but freely, as a process of direct understanding and prior transcendence of the ego and its problem.

The traditions of Buddhism and Advaita Vedanta originally tended to be associated with concerns relative to the pain of manifest existence and the search for release from that pain via the escape from manifest existence itself. "Samsara," interpreted as the suffering of innumerable lifetimes of pain motivated and created by mere desire, was contrasted with "Nirvana," interpreted as the complete cessation of desire and its results (in the form of manifest or conditional existence). Likewise, "maya" was commonly interpreted to mean that manifest or conditional existence was an illusion that could, therefore, be seen through, overcome, and escaped via a kind of superior cleverness (much as one exercises in relation to the entertaining performance of a street magician).

The early tendencies of both Buddhism and Advaita Vedanta (or the ancient tradition of Upanishadic Advaitism) were, therefore, in the direction of a world-negating asceticism. However, both traditions developed from and via the Teaching of Great Adepts. Even though the common preaching of the two traditions tended from the beginning to appeal to the common reaction to the pain of living, the Realization of the Great Adepts in both traditions has, from the beginning, been associated with a most radical consideration—not merely of suffering (which is a convention or problem of the ego or manifest self) but of the status of conditional existence (or self and not-self) relative to Reality (or Transcendental Existence). And as the literatures of these two traditions developed over time, they began to develop the consideration less and less along the lines of appeal to the popular need to escape pain or find an ultimate egoic circumstance of manifest pleasure. The great literatures of Buddhism and Upanishadic Advaitism are, therefore, founded in the direct consideration of Reality, based not on a problematic reaction to egoic suffering, but on the intuitive understanding of the entire process of conditional existence or experience.

The ultimate (and thus more esoteric or non-popular) schools of Buddhism and Advaitism express themselves in terms that involve a radical (rather than a conventional or problem-based) consideration of self and not-self, and those schools are often associated with attitudes toward life that are ultimately non-conventional (or free of seriousness about egoic pain and pleasure). The advanced or seventh stage schools are often associated with Adepts who are not inclined toward the conventional method of asceticism, or the strategy of turning away from any of the basic features of this pleasure-pain world.

The Way that I Teach is like the Way conceived in these advanced schools of the Great Adepts. The likeness is due to the fact that I, like them, found the consideration of the Way on the basis of direct understanding of the ego and its problems and its goals of seeking, rather than on the basis of the uninspected motives created by the ego, its problems, and its search.

The radical approach to the consideration of manifest existence is not associated with self-based seeking for fulfillment within or release from the pleasure-pain world (or the total cosmos of Nature). Rather, the radical approach is to directly and constantly consider the <u>apparent</u> status of the manifest self and all conditional states and objects until the Real Condition of both self and not-self becomes Obvious.

Pain, Independence, and the Discovery of Consciousness

The apparent status of both self and not-self is that of independence. All objects appear to be independent or separate from the self and one another. The self appears to be independent or separate from all other selves and all objects. All states of the self appear to be both objects to the self (and thus separate from it) and also, since they are merely reflections of the phenomenal or objective world (made by the mechanics of perception via the nervous system), they appear, like illusions, to be separate from the "real" not-self of the objective realm of Nature. And, in their apparent independence, the self and its objects and states all appear to be inherently separate from any permanent, infinite, or Transcendental Reality, Identity, or Condition.

In one fashion or another, the radical or ultimate and seventh stage schools consider the appearance of independence or separateness that characterizes the self, the not-self, and the paradoxical states of the self that arise in contact with the not-self (including all other selves). When this appearance of independence, separation, or difference is transcended in Transcendental Awakening (to the Condition of all selves and every form of the not-self), that Realization (and not any mere development of physical, emotional, mental, or psychic states of the manifest self, nor any state that merely excludes such phenomena from awareness) is Enlightenment.

The Way that I Teach is founded on the radical consideration of the process of attention. It is a matter of direct and constant insight into the action that is the manifest or egoic self. That action is the expression of a consciousness that regards itself to be separate (based on conventional identification with the apparently independent body-mind). Therefore, the principle of the action that is the ego (or manifest self) is separative. This is first observed in the plane of common or ordinary relational existence. If there is true self-observation in the midst of functional relations, the self can be seen always to be operating in a separative or self-based manner. Insight into this common egoic separativeness is expressed via self-enquiry in the form "Avoiding relationship?" As this process of insight into the self-process develops further, it becomes expressed as the conscious process of re-cognition, or the observation and moment to moment transcendence of self-contraction. And such re-cognition and transcendence develops relative to all the possible conditions and orientations of the first six stages of life.

The Way that I Teach does not develop on the basis of attempts to solve the problem represented by conditional existence as self or not-self. Therefore, even the conventional problems and orientations of the sixth stage of life must be understood and transcended.

The conventional sixth stage point of view of Upanishadic Advaitism views all conditions (or the apparent not-self) as illusions of the self. Therefore, the method of approach tends to be to invert attention upon the self in order to locate its internal Source or Free Identity. In the Way that I Teach, this strategy of inversion upon the self-root (the ultimate locus of which is in the right side of the heart) must be observed, understood (or re-cognized as itself a form of self-contraction), and thus transcended before the characteristic disposition of the seventh stage of life can Awaken.

In contrast to the traditional method of Upanishadic Advaitism, the conventional sixth stage approach of classical Buddhism views conditional existence to be merely a chain of causes and effects. In that view, there is no self. There is only the vast not-self (made only of finite causes and effects, "dharmas," or the mechanical constituents of phenomenal Nature). Therefore, the method of approach tends to be to strategically focus attention on the conditions of existence and to see them all as not-self, until the tendency to conceive an independent self is utterly overcome (thus ultimately bringing an end to the arising of conditional states). In the Way that I Teach, this strategy of cognition of the not-self (and knowing the self as not-self) must be observed, understood (or re-cognized) as itself a form of self-contraction, and thus transcended before the characteristic disposition of the seventh stage of life can Awaken.

Pain, Independence, and the Discovery of Consciousness

In the case of either of the two basic traditional approaches I have just described, the ultimate Goal of the practice is the elimination or transcendence of conditional awareness (or the awareness of self and not-self) and the restoration of the Realization of the Condition that is prior to the awareness of self and not-self. The fundamental Argument of the Way that I Teach stands in most positive and radical relation to that Realization which is the Goal of the sixth stage traditions. That which is to be Realized and affirmed is That which stands forth as the Obvious when the characteristic forms of contraction that are the principal orientations of sixth stage Buddhism and Upanishadic Advaitism are understood and transcended.

The ultimate form of the Way that I Teach (and the Enlightened stage of the traditional forms of the Way) involves the understanding and inherent transcendence of the strategy of seeking to overcome and eliminate the self and/or the not-self. Therefore, the transition to the ultimate stage of the Way involves the understanding and inherent transcendence of the conventional approaches I have just described. If this is done, the Real or Transcendental Condition of conditions stands out as the Obvious. Then self and not-self no longer stand out independently, as a binding process separated from Transcendental Bliss, Happiness, Truth, Reality, Being, or Consciousness. And when this seventh stage Awakening occurs, all conventional doubts and limiting presumptions (based on the egoic problems of the first six stages of life) are inherently transcended. The conventional Buddhist reluctance to positively admit the Existence of Transcendental Being is thus transcended, as well as the conventional Upanishadic tendency to conceive of the Transcendental Reality in exclusively inward and even personal terms. That which is ultimately Obvious as Reality is Radiant Transcendental Being or Consciousness—the Identity and the Condition of all beings and conditions, in which all beings and conditions are only apparently (and without necessity or ultimate binding power) arising as spontaneous and merely apparent modifications of Itself. The Awakening of the seventh stage of life is thus the Great

Discovery—the Sublime Discovery of the Nature of Consciousness and the Condition of self and not-self.

In the sixth stage of life (and the conventional approach represented by the lesser tendencies of Buddhism and Upanishadic Advaitism) there is a subtle effort to exclude awareness of the separate self and its objects. This subtle effort is the final contraction to be understood, re-cognized, and thus inherently transcended before the radical or seventh stage process of the Way can begin.

Samsara or maya or conditional existence is not in itself a problem to be systematically eliminated. The traditional names or terms are nothing more than descriptions of the characteristics of the un-Enlightened view of life. They do not indicate substances. Samsara is not a something. Maya is not a something. Conditional existence is not a something. Rather, these terms simply indicate or describe the characteristics inherent in the un-Enlightened view, which is the notion or presumption that whatever arises is indeed a something—a substantial or merely independent entity or thing. This same un-Enlightened view tends to regard Realization of Nirvana or the Transcendental Self to be a something independent of conditional existence, whereas such terms as Nirvana or the Self are meant simply to indicate or characterize the Enlightened (rather than the un-Enlightened) view of whatever appears to be the case.

Therefore, in the ultimate literatures of the Buddhist tradition, the Enlightened view is presented via such declarations as "Nirvana and samsara are the same." And in the ultimate literatures of Advaitism, the Enlightened view is presented via the declaration that to seek to escape from maya is absurd, since there is only Brahman, or the Transcendental Self, and, therefore, nothing separate from or other than the Transcendental Condition can be found, even in the conditional worlds.

When samsara, or maya, or conditional existence (in the form of self or not-self), viewed as a configuration or a condition that is apparently independent and separate from the Transcendental Condition, is recognized in and as the Transcendental

Condition, that is Transcendental Self-Awakening, Enlightenment, or ultimate God-Realization. That recognition is the ultimate fulfillment sought or considered in all forms of the Great Tradition, including the traditions of Buddhism and Upanishadic Advaitism. Likewise, it is such recognition that is the real, fundamental, and ultimate context of the Way that I Teach. Therefore, I Teach a Way that from the beginning considers conditional existence via a disposition that is priorly established in this ultimate or seventh stage view.

At first there must be the consideration of my Argument until true hearing or real understanding develops. This understanding (or the process of observing, re-cognizing, and inherently transcending the self-contraction) then becomes the basis of a continuous consideration in the midst of daily life. The degree of attention available for that consideration is increased via various disciplines in this "yoga of consideration"* by which devotees approach fully Awakened maturity in the Way itself. Therefore, the practice of the conscious process of understanding is also associated with various forms of functional self-discipline, devotion to life as service, and spiritual conductivity (or the cultivation of psycho-physical equanimity). But all of this is finally transcended in the full Awakening of the seventh stage disposition.

The seventh stage disposition is nothing else but tacit intuitive Identification with the Transcendental Condition of self and not-self—or That which is Obvious when self-contraction (or the appearance of the independence, separateness, and necessity of self or not-self) is recognized in the Condition (or Consciousness) that is the case prior to contraction itself (or the noticing of self or not-self). Enlightenment is simply the native, intuitive Realization of the Condition (or Real Status) of whatever is presently the case. Enlightenment is Transcendental Consciousness, inherently Radiant and Free.

* The practitioner of the Way that Master Da Teaches observes the stages of life on the basis of the Master's critical Argument and to the point of understanding, rather than practice the stages of life for their own sake, as in the traditional paths. This "yoga of consideration" is a preparation for the Way Taught by Master Da, which is the Way of the seventh stage of life, or the tacit recognition of what arises in the Transcendental Reality.

The Enlightened Realization is free of the limiting or binding presumption that is inherent in the conventional view of conditional existence. Therefore, the Enlightened view is not one that sees conditional existence as samsara or maya. Rather, the Enlightened view sees conditional existence as (or in the context of) Nirvana, or Brahman, the Self, or Radiant Transcendental Being.

Those who have not yet Awakened into the Fullness of such Transcendental Realization tend to imagine they are Enlightened on the basis of superficial thinking. They are yet ego-bound and they may even tend to imitate the non-ascetical conceptions and behaviors of the Great or seventh stage Adepts.

The seventh stage point of view is often lived out in the form of unconventional behaviors by true Adepts. In the Enlightened Condition, free of the egoic views and implications of samsara, maya, or the problem of self-contraction, Adepts act in a spontaneous, inherently free manner, communicating the Enlightened view directly, without humorless bondage to the social and religious conventions of the first six stages of life. Even those seventh stage Adepts who are characterized by the apparently conservative habits of a renunciate are inherently free of the conventional motives of asceticism and world-denial. But some tend to act in an utterly unconventional, even bizarre and offensive, manner. Such behavior in the case of Great Adepts is traditionally called "Crazy Wisdom," and it expresses the freedom from negative views and egoic preferences. Therefore, such behaviors have a role in the Teaching Work of some Adepts, and it is all intended to draw devotees into the radical Awakening of Transcendental Consciousness.

It should not be presumed that Enlightenment necessarily expresses itself through "Crazy" behaviors, nor are such behaviors any more than self-indulgence in the case of un-Enlightened individuals. Enlightenment is simply Awakened Consciousness, or native Realization (Sahaj Samadhi) of the

Transcendental Condition or Real Status of self and not-self. Some who thus Awaken may tend to behave in the "Crazy" fashion, particularly if they have the Teaching or Awakening Function of the Adept, but most generally behave in a relatively conservative or ordinary manner. In any case, there is always inherent freedom from binding presumptions about conditional existence. And since, in the seventh stage of life, every moment of conditional existence is inherently recognized in the Real Condition, all those who are thus Awakened tend, at least gradually, to motivelessly relax from the flow of action. This is not due to any conventional preference to withdraw from conditional existence. Rather, the continuous recognition of self and not-self (or conditional events) in the Transcendental Being or Consciousness is ultimately expressed as the Outshining of all phenomenal noticing (or attention). Thus, the Realization of the Nirvanic or Brahmanic or Transcendental Condition of samsara, or maya, or conditional existence, or self, or not-self ultimately and motivelessly Outshines and Transcends the arising of conditional states of attention. And, therefore, the seventh stage of life inevitably becomes Nirvanic (or Bhava) Samadhi, or Translation into the Transcendental Condition. In the case of some individuals, Enlightenment becomes Translation or Nirvana only after many lives of Spiritual Play and compassionate service to living beings. Some pass in and out of Bhava Samadhi, to Play many roles of Spiritual Demonstration in the planes of manifest existence. In any case, there is only the Realization of Truth.

VI
Ancient and Traditional Buddhism and Upanishadic Advaitism Seen in Relation to the Radical Way of Advaitayana Buddhism

1.

The central orientation of all the traditional schools of Buddhism is toward the transcendence of conditional existence (samsara).

The central orientation of Upanishadic Advaitism (finally epitomized in the tradition of Advaita Vedanta) is toward Identification with That which inherently transcends conditional existence (samsara or maya).

The Way that I Teach (which may also be called Advaitayana Buddhism) is not strategically oriented toward either the transcendence of conditional existence or Identification with That which inherently transcends conditional existence. It is not founded in the view of conditional existence as a problem, nor, therefore, does it pursue any form of Identity (or Identification with Reality) as a solution to that problem. Rather, the Way that I Teach is the natural process of intuitive understanding of conditional existence. In that process, all conditions of existence (in the apparent form of either self or not-self), all subject-object states, or all distinctions, are simply observed to be forms of self-contraction (or contraction and differentiation or individuation of the subject-consciousness). And this understanding is <u>naturally disposed</u> (rather than strategically oriented) to the intuitive Realization of inherent and free Identification with That in which all distinctions, all forms of self and/or not-self, or all forms of contraction and differentiation or individuation are apparently arising.

Therefore, the Way that I Teach effectively Realizes the Buddhist ideal of the transcendence of conditional existence as well as the Advaitic ideal of Identification with the Transcendental Reality. But it does so naturally or inherently rather than strategically (as a form of problem-solution) and, therefore, it does not depend on the more conventional Buddhist and Advaitic arguments to verify either the practice or the Realization. And this Way of Advaitayana Buddhism is inherently free of the exclusiveness that tends to be associated with the classical Buddhist and Advaitic goals. (That is, it does not argue itself into the corner of either denying the existence of the Transcendental Identity or the natural association between that Identity and the conditional or phenomenal process of manifest existence.)

2.

The original or "Hinayana" school of Buddhism begins with the problematic presumption that the phenomenal self (or existence as a phenomenal or conditional self in a phenomenal or conditional world) is inherently a form of suffering (or, indeed, is the very definition of suffering). The unique view of original Buddhism is that the ego (or the conditional phenomenal self) is only phenomenal. That is to say, what is conceived to be a self is only a temporary composite of phenomenal or conditional constituents (even as everything that is considered to be not-self—or every phenomenon related to the presumed self—is also only a temporary composite of phenomenal or conditional constituents). Therefore, both self and not-self have the same status. They are both part of a single flow or eternally changing pattern of causes and effects. The self or ego is not more or other than conditional phenomena. (It is not independently emanating from an unchanging core or soul.) And all that is not-self is not more than conditional phenomena. (None of it is emanating from an unchanging Super-Core or Super-Soul.)

The original tradition of Buddhism proposes that, since there is no unchanging self, the self is only conditional or phenomenal, and is, therefore, rightly viewed as not-self. The import of this presumption is that self and not-self are not necessary. They are not held in place by Divine Will, but they are originating conditionally and without necessity. Therefore, the presumed problem of conditional existence can be solved by observing and reversing the chain of causes that lead to the arising of the phenomenal self. And the classical or original Buddhist method is to strategically uncause the caused or born self. The ultimate success of this method is what defines the original Buddhist concept of Nirvana (which Gautama declares is not annihilation but the indescribable attainment of the "unborn," the Condition that is previous and prior to birth, previous and prior to self and not-self, or previous and prior to all causes and effects).

3.

The later or more philosophically developed schools of Buddhism (in the traditions called Mahayana and Vajrayana) develop the original phenomenal and ascetical logic of Gautama into a process of metaphysical consideration. Instead of proposing that the phenomenal self is inherently a form of suffering, the later schools propose that the phenomenal self is merely a false idea (and suffering is the result rather than the inherent nature of the self-idea). Therefore, instead of proposing that the phenomenal or conditional self is only phenomenal (and thus can be uncaused by ascetical efforts in the phenomenal plane), the later Buddhist schools propose that the phenomenal self (or the total phenomenal not-self, which includes the apparent self and all of its states and relations) is inherently egoless, or no-self (a mere pattern of changes without an unchanging base that emanates it or makes it necessary).

The later Buddhist tradition builds its argument on the base of a logic that is at least partially suggested in the original argument of Gautama. It was a matter of extending the conception of the Way on the basis of the original idea that phenomenal existence is not emanated from a permanent base but caused via the chain of previous conditions. The consistent idea is the presumption of manifest existence as mere and ultimately unnecessary change. But whereas Gautama developed his consideration of the Way on the basis of phenomenal observation, insight, and subsequent ascetical (or phenomenal) effort, the later schools developed their consideration of the Way on the basis of insight (or conceptual and intuitive logic) alone. Therefore, whereas the classical school was devoted to the solution of the phenomenal problem of phenomenal existence by uncausing phenomenal existence, the later schools were devoted to the solution of a metaphysical problem (the false idea of an existing self, or an existing "entity" of any kind, rather than a beginningless and endless pattern of apparent changes). And that solution was not a matter of the development of ascetical non-causation (or non-desiring of self and not-self) and conventional ascetical Nirvana. It was a matter of the development of Wisdom—or the transcendence of the false ideas of self and not-self as entities. Therefore, the later tradition is not directly or necessarily associated with the attainment of acausal Nirvana (or the cessation of phenomenal states), but it is uniquely associated with the primal Intuition or Wisdom-Realization that samsara (or conditional existence) is itself Nirvana (or <u>inherently Nirvanic</u>)—inherently free of self, necessity, or binding power. The Nirvanic Realization that characterizes the later traditions of Buddhism is thus associated with prior or Transcendental Freedom (or prior and inherent transcendence of phenomenal limitations) as well as with the free orientation toward continued personal existence as a compassionate and spiritually powerful being in the phenomenal worlds. And it is also in the later traditions that Realization began to be described or pointed to in positive terms as a substantial or Really or Self-Existing Transcendental (or non-phenomenal) Condition (called by such terms as the "Buddha-Mind").

4.

The tradition of Upanishadic Advaitism had an ancient, pre-Buddhistic basis in the culture of Vedic and Upanishadic Emanationism, but it developed its ultimate form (as Advaita Vedanta) both on that ancient basis and on the basis of the cultural dynamics that included the non-Vedic traditions (and thus Buddhism). It appears that both the later or more metaphysical schools of Buddhism and the later or more formal and academic tradition of Upanishadic Advaitism (in the form of Advaita Vedanta) developed side by side and in play with one another. And the ultimate exposition of Advaita Vedanta (via Gaudapada and Shankara) actually appeared only after the basic development of Mahayana Buddhism and with full awareness of its arguments.

Therefore, the school of Advaita Vedanta may rightly be seen as a stage in the progression of Buddhism as well as Upanishadic Advaitism. Its arguments provide a Vedic or Upanishadic (and thus Emanationist) basis for the orientation toward ultimate transcendence that was championed earlier by the Buddhists and other non-Vedic schools (who themselves developed the ultimate implications of non-Vedic as well as Vedic and Upanishadic philosophies of Transcendental liberation). And the stages of the school of Advaita Vedanta also extended the metaphysical considerations of the Mahayana to embrace a more direct orientation to the positively conceived Transcendental Reality.

In the tradition of Advaita Vedanta we see a synthesis of Vedic (or Upanishadic) and Buddhist considerations, just as the Mahayana and Vajrayana schools of Buddhism may rightly be seen to be a synthesis of non-Vedic as well as Vedic or Upanishadic tendencies.

Certain aspects of the arguments of Advaita Vedanta may rightly be seen to be an advance upon (or a later and synthetic stage of) the metaphysical implications of the logic of Mahayana Buddhism. This is evident in the positive orientation toward

Realization of the Transcendental (and thus non-egoic and non-phenomenal) Condition, Reality, Being, Consciousness, or Self, which is inherently beyond the categories of phenomenal eternality or phenomenal annihilation. In proposing the Realization of the Transcendental Identity, the Advaitic sages were developing a consideration that was inherent in the original Buddhist presumption of the "unborn" and which was implicit in the later Buddhist conception of the Buddha-Mind. And by developing a full positive conception of the Transcendental Reality they gave voice to the silence of Gautama (who was committed to avoid metaphysical language) and also released the tradition of Transcendentalism (of which Buddhism was a dominant part) from the tendency toward merely phenomenalistic, materialistic, and even nihilistic views. Indeed, the advance represented by Advaita Vedanta was most specifically a release of Transcendentalism from the apparently nihilistic associations and tendencies inherited from original Buddhism. Truly, Gautama was not a nihilist but a Transcendentalist. Even so, his language was limited to the address of phenomenal conditions, and from this the tradition of Buddhism inherited not merely silence in relation to the demand to speak about the Condition Realized in Nirvana but a tendency (particularly in the Hinayana schools) to deny the existence of the "unborn" Condition Itself. Thus, even when Buddhism began to develop a metaphysical philosophy, it tended to make Gautama's silence into a metaphysical proposition that is often reluctant to admit the existence of the "unborn" to which Gautama himself referred. It is this tendency, inherited from the sixth stage phenomenal language of Gautama, that represents one of the basic limiting tendencies (even tending toward the status of a false view) in traditional Buddhism. What should have occurred at the time Buddhism made the turn toward metaphysical language is the free abandonment of the reluctance to speak of the Transcendental Condition in positive metaphysical terms. Indeed, a change in that direction occurred, but it was in the tradition of Advaita Vedanta that the language of that reluctance was fully conquered.

Even so, the arising of the schools of Advaita Vedanta also marks the introduction of a new scheme of limitations into the tradition of Transcendentalism. Certain limitations of the Buddhist language were overcome in the language of Advaita Vedanta, but Advaita Vedanta also introduced certain limitations of Vedic and Upanishadic language into the stream of the Transcendentalist movement. Thus, the Emanationist orientation toward subjectivism (or exclusive inversion upon the internal self as if it were an eternal individual or soul-entity) is reflected in the characteristically sixth stage method of Advaita Vedanta. In this tendency, the viewpoint of Advaita Vedanta suffers from the limits of the sixth stage point of view of the Emanationist tradition, just as the Buddhist tradition has suffered from the sixth stage limits of the non-Emanationist tradition.

This having been said, let me pass on to consider the unique features of the argument of Advaita Vedanta in contrast with (or, truly, in extension of) the early and later schools of Buddhism.

5.

Whereas the original Buddhist view was that the phenomenal self is inherently a form of suffering and the later Buddhist view was that the phenomenal self (or ego-entity) is only a false idea about phenomenal existence, the Advaitic view was that the phenomenal self (or ego-entity) is indeed, when seen in itself, a form of suffering, but it is to be understood as a false idea—not merely <u>about</u> phenomenal existence, but <u>within</u> a <u>noumenal</u> Condition of existence. Thus, while original Buddhism concentrated on the phenomenal self and saw it to be <u>only phenomenal</u>, and the later Buddhist tradition concentrated on the phenomenal self and saw it to be <u>inherently egoless</u> (or without a permanent or underlying phenomenal entity), the Advaitic tradition concentrated on the phenomenal self and saw it to be <u>only noumenal</u> (or an unnecessary process that, while it can be conventionally seen to be arising as a phenomenal effect of previous phenomenal causes, is always presently or priorly arising as a play upon Transcendental Consciousness).

The Advaitic tradition appealed directly to the Realization of the Status of phenomena in relation to their <u>noumenal Ground of origination</u> rather than their <u>phenomenal chain of origination</u>. The phenomenal self was viewed (as in the original tradition of Buddhism) to be inherently a form of suffering—as long as it is seen in itself, as an independent phenomenal process. But when viewed in its Ground of origination, the phenomenal self was seen to be un-Real, or an illusion or false idea, in its independence. The Ground Itself was presumed to be the Reality, and only that Ground could grant Reality to any phenomenon.

Therefore, the Advaitic solution to the egoic suffering of phenomenal existence was to see it as unnecessary and un-Real in its apparent independence (as mere phenomenon) and to locate it in the Real (or the Self-Existing Transcendental Being or Consciousness). According to this view, it is only when the Self or prior Consciousness is Realized to be the Transcendental Ground and Substance or Status of all origination that the un-Reality, illusion, necessity, and apparent independence of the phenomenal self and/or not-self is overcome. Therefore, the proposed solution to the problem of phenomenal existence was, in the Advaitic tradition, to Realize and radically Identify with the prior or Transcendental and Self-Existing Source-Ground of all phenomena. In that case, neither the phenomenal self nor the phenomenal not-self is seen to be Real as an independent or merely phenomenal condition. In this view, the merely phenomenal self of original Buddhism is seen to be un-Real, and the phenomenally based orientation of all traditional Buddhism is seen to be a mere convention—unnecessary to presume, unnecessary to solve, and simply to be understood. The original Buddhist view sees the phenomenal self to be unnecessary and reversible. And the Mahayanist view was that the phenomenal world is inherently selfless. In contrast, the fundamental Advaitic proposition is that the phenomenal world and the phenomenal self are not the

Context of existence, but the Real Condition is noumenal and Transcendental. There is no independent self, not-self, or no-self. There is only the Transcendental Self (or Brahman, or the Nirvanic Condition of Transcendental Being).

6.

The original Buddhist or non-Emanationist and non-Vedic view is grounded in the conventional view of phenomenal perception and conception. It is from this conventional "realism" that the great tradition of Buddhism gained and inherited its limitations as well as its virtues. And that original Buddhist view is focused on the basic proposition that the phenomenal self is unnecessary and thus inherently transcendable. Even the later Buddhist schools maintain the tendency toward analysis of the phenomenal self (and all phenomenal events) as <u>merely</u> or exclusively phenomenal events (or merely phenomenal ideas). Thus, the ultimate Buddhist conception is flavored by this conventional phenomenal context of consideration. All apparent entities are ultimately viewed to be not-self, non-entities, Void of self-essence.

Some Buddhist schools (such as the Vijnanavada) tended to give positive metaphysical status to that phenomenal Void (calling It Mind, Consciousness, and so forth), and such Buddhist schools bear the greatest affinity to the ancient Emanationist tradition of the Vedas and the Upanishads as well as the philosophical tradition of Upanishadic Advaitism and Advaita Vedanta. Even so, all characteristically Buddhist conceptions are, to one or another degree, founded in phenomenal realism, and, therefore, traditional and conventional Buddhist orthodoxy tends to feel uncomfortable with the affirmation of an ultimate noumenal Reality.

The Advaitic tradition, however, is based on the conception of the noumenal Emanation of the world and all selves. Therefore, it is openly comfortable with the affirmation that the phenomenal self and the phenomenal not-self are not merely Void of a permanent phenomenal essence but Full of the Transcendental Essence, Consciousness, or Self-Existing Being. This freedom of ultimate affirmation is an advanced stage of what Buddhism contains implicitly (i.e., the philosophy of the "unborn") and the tradition of Transcendental Advaitism may thus rightly be regarded as an advanced stage of the Transcendentalist consideration that is the Great Occupation of Buddhism.

7.

Buddhism and Advaitism represent the two basic and ancient traditional approaches to Transcendental Realization. As such, these two traditions are really streams of one tradition. That single tradition is the ultimate stage of religious and spiritual philosophy. It is a tradition that is principally associated with the orientations of the sixth and seventh stages of life. Therefore, the total tradition of Transcendental Realization stands either in contrast to or as an advancement beyond the traditions that pursue the various goals of the first five stages of life.

However, this tradition of Transcendental Realization itself bears certain historical limitations. And those limitations originate in the conceptual orientations of the sixth stage of life. My own Work is the ultimate development of the tradition of Transcendental Realization. My Teaching stands in positive but critical relation to the entire Great Tradition, including all the schools of the first six stages of life. I view the traditions of Buddhism and Advaitism to be the ultimate, most advanced, or sixth to seventh stage dimension of the Great Tradition. But my Work is also to reconsider and purify what we have inherited from the Great Tradition as a whole, and, therefore, my Work stands in critical relation even to the Buddhist and Advaitic traditions themselves.

What we must understand and overcome are the peculiarly sixth stage expressions that are the historical limitations of both Buddhism and Advaitism. An aspect of my Argument is devoted to a purifying criticism of those very expressions and tendencies. Just as Buddhism and Advaitism stand in critical relation to the traditions and stages of life that precede them, and just as each advancing stage of Buddhism and Advaitism stands in critical relation to its precedents, my own Work also develops a form of Argument based on criticism (positive and creative rather than merely sectarian and destructive) of the entire Great Tradition that is our Treasured Inheritance and all of the developing stages of life that are our school of transcendence. Therefore, I Teach a Way that epitomizes the Great Tradition and that stands entirely on the base that is the Free Transcendental point of view of the seventh stage of life.

In relation to the traditions of Buddhism and Advaitism, I must especially criticize the limitations on Transcendental Realization that represent the sixth stage of life. (Truly, those traditions have, over time, also assimilated traditions of orientation and practice that pertain to the first five stages of life, but I criticize those tendencies primarily in my discussions of the Great Tradition as a whole.)

The principal limitations of the sixth stage type that have become identified with traditional Buddhism are the tendency to consider existence exclusively in the terms of phenomenal realism and the tendency to view manifest existence as a problem to be solved. Thus, Buddhism has tended to develop its considerations and its practice on the basis of ordinary conventions of perceptual and conceptual attention, rather than on the basis of the prior presumption of the "unborn" Reality or Truth. And this same conventional realism is responsible for the tendency to conceive of manifest existence in terms of a problem and, therefore, to conceive of the Way as a strategic method for advancing toward Realization on the basis of the problematic or egoic presumption.

Buddhist sages have made many attempts to reconsider the Way in a manner that somehow or other avoids the effects of these limitations, and so the various schools and "yanas" have developed over time. My own Work is to make plain the nature and import of what Buddhism itself is always working to purify in itself.

The principal limitations of the sixth stage type that have become identified with traditional Advaitism are a consequence of the Emanationist logic of ancient animism.

The Advaitic tradition stands on the base of a noumenal conception of Reality (or the Transcendental Being) rather than on the base of a phenomenal conception of un-Reality (such as generally characterizes traditional or conventional Buddhism). Therefore, it is able to appeal directly and positively to Transcendental Realization rather than to the struggle with the problematic un-Reality. In this manner, the Advaitic tradition represents both an ancient precedent (in the form of Upanishadic Advaitism) for and a later historical development (in the form of Advaita Vedanta) of the Buddhist (or general non-Vedic) philosophy of Transcendental Realization. It is simply that Buddhism developed a seventh stage tradition on the basis of sixth stage phenomenal realism and Advaitism developed a seventh stage tradition on the basis of sixth stage noumenal idealism.

In terms of providing a base for positively considering or describing the "unborn" Reality Itself, Advaitism is an orientation superior to traditional or conventional Buddhism (even though Buddhism can just as well, if not more directly, point to that Reality). This is because Advaitism is able to by-pass the limitations of the language of phenomenal realism.

However, Advaitism not only inherited the Emanationist orientation toward the noumenal Divine or Transcendental Reality (which is the fundamental Realization of the seventh stage of life), but it also inherited the subjectivist tendencies of animistic spiritual culture. Thus, the Way proposed in the schools of Advaitism may be generally free of the problematic and phenomenalistic limitations and motivations of conventional realism, but it works toward the Realization of the Real via the technique of subjective inversion.

The classical and conventional approach of Advaitism is to invert attention away from phenomena and toward the noumenal core of the manifest self. This produces a sixth stage type of subjectivism that is released only once the ego is finally transcended in the transition to the seventh stage of life.

The subjectivist orientation is inherently egoic or Narcissistic. It is disposed to dissociate the self from phenomena and to propose a noumenal Reality that is separate and different in kind from phenomenal existence. Therefore, in the sixth stage method of conventional Advaitism, Brahman (or the Transcendental Being) tends to be conceived as the "atman" (the noumenous self) exclusive of objects. It is only in the Awakening of the seventh stage Realization that the consciousness that is the noumenous root of the manifest self is Realized not to be an internally based and non-phenomenal atman (or a soul) but Brahman (the Transcendental or Self-Existing Reality). And it is only when the atman is transcended in Brahman (rather than Brahman reduced to atman) that the phenomenal world is recognizable in Truth.

Therefore, if the tradition of Buddhism tends to suffer or struggle with the sixth stage limitations of phenomenal realism, the tradition of Advaitism tends to suffer or struggle with the sixth stage limitations of subjective idealism (which is rooted in the noumenous ideas of the soul that are part of the ancient traditions of animism and Emanationism).

The Buddhist vision in the sixth stage of life is concentrated in the merely phenomenal self (free of the false idea or implication that the manifest self is built upon a permanent or eternal and non-phenomenal individual being or soul). The idea of such a soul is based on the conventions of animism and Emanationism, and it is presumed on the basis of the sense of a noumenous and undying force of being underneath the mechanics of the body-mind. The original virtue of Buddhism was to see that this idea is only an uninspected implication of the phenomenal self, and it is neither necessary nor Real. However, the Buddhist logic then went on to apply the attitude of phenomenal realism to the extreme, so that the noumenal Reality that is the Ground and Context of phenomenal existence tended to cease to be logically admissible.

The characteristic limitation of traditional Advaitism is the disposition to invert upon the manifest self to locate its Transcendental Core. Until there is emergence into the seventh stage of life, this method of attention is limited by the un-Enlightened exclusiveness of self-meditation, or exclusive inversion upon the self or soul (to the exclusion rather than the recognition of other selves, souls, or the entire not-self of phenomenal Nature).

In the sixth stage mode, Buddhism sees self as not-self (or only phenomenon rather than noumenon), and so it by-passes the false view of soul (or a permanent non-phenomenal self) and the implied necessity of phenomenal existence. But it also is bound to a problematic struggle with phenomenal existence and a reluctance to admit the always present Reality that always already Outshines self and world.

And Advaitism in its sixth stage mode sees the phenomenal self and the phenomenal world as not-Self (or only as non-noumenous un-Reality). In doing so, it by-passes the conventional bondage to phenomenal perception and conception, but it is also bound to the Narcissism of exclusive inversion and the identification of the Transcendental Reality exclusively with the noumenous ground that is behind the individual body-mind.

Truly, the great sages in the traditions of both Buddhism and Advaitism ultimately Awaken to the Transcendental Condition beyond the sixth stage of life. The Buddhist Adept Awakens to the "unborn," and the Advaitic Adept Awakens, beyond inversion, to the "natural" (Sahaj) Realization that the world of not-Self (or all selves and phenomenal conditions) is Really only Self (and thus it is inherently or always already transcended, prior to any act of inversion or attention to the interior of the individual self).

The Way that I Teach is based upon the "viewpoint" inherent in the Realization of the ultimate or seventh stage of life. Therefore, I acknowledge the ultimate or seventh stage

Realization of Adepts in the traditions of Buddhism and Advaitism. But I also criticize the sixth stage limitations that tend to be made the traditional basis of Argument and practice in the Transcendentalist schools. One of the names I have given to my own Way is Advaitayana Buddhism, in acknowledgement of the ultimacy of Buddhism and Advaitism in the Great Tradition, but this Advaitayana Buddhism is in fact a new tradition or Way that is consistently based on criticism and transcendence of the propositions of the sixth stage of life as well as each of the first five stages of life.

The Way that I Teach is, therefore, a radical Way, or a Way that is based entirely and freely on the understanding and the Awakening that characterize the seventh stage of life. In contrast with the conventional language of Buddhism, and in a likeness to Advaitism, the Way that I Teach is Argued in terms of positive intuition and affirmation of the "unborn" Transcendental Reality, the Radiant or Divine Being, Consciousness, or Love-Bliss that is the Identity and Condition of all beings and things, or all that is manifest as self and/or not-self. However, in contrast with the conventional language of Advaitism, and in a likeness to Buddhism, the Way that I Teach is not Argued or practiced in terms of the method of exclusive inversion upon the noumenous or independent and internal conscious ground of the manifest self. Rather, in response to my Argument, practice first develops as a total psycho-physical discipline of consideration or understanding of the phenomenal self in the midst of all of its relations and states of knowledge and experience. The Narcissism of subjective inversion as well as the conventionality and inherent contractedness of phenomenal attention in any form is thus thoroughly inspected, understood, and transcended. In this manner, the noumenous Reality, or the Real Status of Consciousness, ultimately becomes simply, naturally, and tacitly obvious, free of any taint of limitation engendered by conventional phenomenalism or subjectivism. And it is only when the Radiant (unborn or not contracted) Transcendental (not phenomenal or individual) Reality, Self, Being, Consciousness, or Happiness is simply obvious that the Way that

I Teach can actually begin.

The Way that I Teach is the seventh stage Way of natural, inherent, or always prior Abiding as the Radiant Transcendental Being, free of the self-based or inherently contracted tendency toward phenomenal extroversion or noumenal introversion. In that natural State (Sahaj Samadhi), all arising conditions, whether phenomenal or noumenal, conceived as self or as not-self, are transparently obvious (or tacitly recognized) as merely apparent or unnecessary and non-binding modifications of the Transcendental Being (or Consciousness). That very Being is the Ground or Identity of self and/or not-self as well as the Substance or Condition of self and/or not-self. It is the Real Status of the Energy and apparent Creative Will that moves the phenomenal flow. All of that inheres in the Transcendental Being without qualifying the Bliss or Radiance of Consciousness even to the slightest degree.

The Way that I Teach is to Abide in this Awakened Realization of the Transcendental or unborn Being or Consciousness, recognizing all that arises in It, tacitly allowing the manifest world and self to be spontaneous expressions of the Radiant Self, until that very Divine Self or Reality Outshines all noticing of conditional existence.

8.

The Way that I Teach stands in natural harmony with the Enlightened or seventh stage disposition of Buddhist and Advaitic sages in all schools. It stands in critical relation to the sixth stage orthodoxies of those traditions (as well as the orthodoxies of the earlier stages of life represented elsewhere in the Great Tradition), but Enlightenment Itself always stands free of any conventions of approach that preceded It.

I agree with the original Buddhist view that the manifest self is only an unnecessary and apparent phenomenal process (made up of "dharmas," or the phenomenal constituents of the cause and effect universe). Therefore, self is not ultimately different from not-self. And this is why the "I" (or manifest self-consciousness) does not know what anything is. The "I" (or phenomenal self) is not ultimately different from the not-"I" (or the phenomenal not-self). Therefore, "I" cannot inspect the existence of anything (or itself) from a position different from or outside existence itself. "I" is not Transcendental but phenomenal. "I" is the body-mind-self, and its right or native disposition is, therefore, not contraction, differentiation, and dissociation from the not-self (or the phenomenal world) but surrender to the degree of no-self, no-contraction, or self-transcending equanimity. And it is only in that disposition of psycho-physical equanimity (or free energy and attention) that the Transcendental Reality is obvious.

The self and the not-self are thus rightly perceived only in Ignorance (or the awareness corresponding to the view "I do not know what anything is"). Such is equanimity, freedom from self-contraction, or the state of free energy and attention. And such is the basic disposition that develops in the "yoga of consideration" that is the initial form of response to my Argument.

The phenomenal self and not-self are arising in a universal flow of causes and effects that is, rightly conceived, without beginning or end or independent necessity. (This corresponds to the original Buddhist conception of dependent origination.) But this phenomenal flow is merely un-Real as an independent (or exclusively phenomenal) process. It is a convention of the perceptual mind to conceive of the phenomenal world of selves as a merely independent mode of existence. Therefore, I agree with the Advaitic contention that the phenomenal cycle of self and not-self is not independent, or merely dependent on phenomenal causes, but priorly dependent upon and always inhering in the noumenous Transcendental Conciousness or Radiant Being (the "unborn" that is obvious in the seventh stage of life and which was obvious in the ultimate Samadhi of Gautama and that of all other Great or Completed Adepts of the Buddhist and Advaitic traditions).

Therefore, I propose that we simply and directly inspect and understand this process of born or phenomenal existence. In this manner, we see that the self is indeed of the same stuff or in the same plane of causes, effects, and dependency as the not-self. "I" is the body (or the total phenomenal self or body-mind-self), and "I" does not know what anything is. "I" does not transcend the world. "I" is not other than the world. "I" is contraction from the world. Therefore, all conceptions or perceptions of "I" or not-"I" (or the not-self) are themselves forms of self-contraction.

Simply practice this understanding and the basic beginner's disciplines of expansion beyond self-contraction until there is a basic equanimity of the body-mind-self in Ignorance (or Divine Communion). In that equanimity (rather than in any form of belief or concentration of attention in experience or knowledge) there are free energy and attention. Therefore, when there is such basic equanimity, use the freely available energy and attention to inspect and re-cognize all the forms of self-contraction. In this manner, transcend each stage of life. Do not merely invert upon the self or the "I" as if it had independent Reality or independent intimacy with Reality. Rather, simply re-cognize the self-contraction as all forms of phenomenal (or bodily, emotional, and mental or psychic) awareness. Even re-cognize the "I" (or the self-contraction) in the form of the tendency toward meditative inversion upon the self (or its noumenous root). Do this until the Transcendental Self or Consciousness is simply and intuitively obvious, prior to contraction as or upon the personal self or "I"-consciousness and prior to all the apparent forms of the not-"I" or not-self (or all the phenomenal states of self-contraction). And when the Transcendental Self (or the Real Status of Consciousness) is obvious, thereafter simply and intuitively (prior to acts of mind) Abide in and as That, tacitly recognizing all arising conditions of self and/or not-self as merely apparent or transparent, unnecessary, and non-binding modifications of That.

The ego is, as Gautama proposed, only phenomenal, and thus, merely as itself, it is unnecessary. And, as the Mahayanists, such as Nagarjuna, proposed, the idea of self as an entity or soul is merely a false idea or implication superimposed on the flow of conditional existence in the midst of all the temporary moments of the body-mind. Therefore, the self as ego-idea is inherently transcended if the self as action (in the form of self-contraction) is understood, and even the self as a phenomenal event (or body-mind) disappears in the Nirvanic Bliss of Bhava Samadhi. But between the understanding that transcends the clinging to the self-idea and the transcendence of phenomenal existence in Bhava Samadhi there must develop a profound understanding and practical transcendence of the self-contraction. Between Wisdom (which is intelligent self-transcendence) and Nirvana (or the Outshining of attention or phenomenal noticing) there must be tacit or native (or Sahaj) Samadhi (or sublime and prior Realization of the Radiant Transcendental Identity and Condition of the phenomenal self and not-self). Such Realization or Samadhi is the ultimate substance of the Teaching of the Way. It transcends the conventions of the phenomenal self, the not-self, the no-self, and all the presumed logic, knowledge, practice, and experience of the first six stages of life. If this Samadhi is Realized, then the phenomenal self and/or not-self (or no-self) are not a problem, but phenomenal existence is obviously a Divinely Transfigured and Eternally Free Process that is always and ultimately Outshined in Divine Bliss. This Samadhi is the ultimate substance or import of the Way that I Teach, and it is likewise the ultimate substance or import of the Teachings of all Great Adepts in all traditions. This Samadhi is the basis of the Work of all Great Adepts, Bodhisattvas, and Jivanmuktas. It is Itself the Origin of the spontaneous Siddhi or Power to Teach, Help, and Awaken others to the Truth.

VII
The Three Views of Consciousness and Light

1.

There are three views or orientations relative to consciousness that have historically been adopted by the schools of the Great Tradition. Each of these views is justified as a mode of orientation under one or another circumstance of attention, but each view is only one alternative way of characterizing the same subject. Even so, the historical application of these three views has tended to represent one or the other of them as the only correct view. It is this tendency that has caused the general historical conflict among the schools or traditions that represent the point of view of one or the other of the first six stages of life, and, in particular, it has caused the schismatic conflict among the separate schools of Buddhism and between the traditions of Buddhism and Advaitism.

These three views of consciousness are similar to the views that have been historically proposed (in both scientific and spiritual traditions) relative to the subject of light, or energy. Light or energy is often used as a metaphor for consciousness in the considerations of philosophy. And, ultimately, the subject of light or energy is identical to the subject of consciousness. Consciousness, it will be Realized, is the ultimate Identity or Real Condition of light or energy (and thus all phenomena).

If we can appreciate the considerations of the advanced physics of contemporary science, we can see how the scientific investigation of matter ultimately yields to a description of Nature as light (or energy), transcending matter (which is only a temporary appearance or transformation of energy). And if we can understand that _all_ of phenomenal Nature (subjective and objective) is a complex of energy, then we can transcend the dualism of matter and consciousness. Consciousness, then, is not merely reducible to matter (or material processes) but it is at least a distinct form of the single principle (or energy) that is also appearing as matter (or form). This understanding sets us free to investigate consciousness and mind as dimensions of existence that are equally as real or viable as matter. The investigation of consciousness and of mind (or psyche) is thus just as direct a means for entering into the depths of reality as the investigation of matter. And, therefore, there is just as much justification for the spiritual discipline of self-knowledge and the exploration and transcendence of matter, mind, and self as there is for the scientific discipline that explores the perceptible or material world alone. Indeed, the ultimate philosophical or spiritual process is directly oriented to considerations of greater significance than is the process engaged by merely materialistic investigators. But materialistic science can ultimately go beyond itself into the paradoxes of space-time and light-energy. And when science leads to such profundity, it is at the threshold of the ancient Ways of spiritual and Transcendental philosophy.

2.

In the considerations of Transcendental philosophy, consciousness is the primary and ultimate subject. But such considerations cannot truly begin until the conceit of egoity and mere materialism has been transcended in the practical intuition of the energy, light, or "Spirit" that is the underlying Matrix of phenomenal appearances. Therefore, energy, light, or Spirit, the manifest Matrix of material or phenomenal Nature, is commonly used as a metaphor for consciousness itself. And the viewpoint toward consciousness tends to be determined by the particular orientation to matter, phenomenal events, energy, light, or Spirit that is preferred by the tradition (and the stage of life) in which the consideration of consciousness develops.

Because of the differences in approach to the consideration of the subject of consciousness, differing conclusions have been achieved (derived from the original premise, logic, or stage of life that provided the basis for the consideration). And those differing conclusions may all be seen to represent one or the other of three basic propositions:

1. Consciousness is always and only conditional and phenomenal (arising temporarily, and never independently, but always in mutually dependent relationship to a vast system of other temporary phenomenal and conditional causes and effects).

2. Consciousness is a noumenal absolute, appearing either as a unique phenomenon (unlike and ultimately independent of all other phenomena) or in a state of inherent identification with the Energy, Light, or Spirit-Power that is the universal Matrix of all phenomena.

3. Consciousness is ultimate Transcendental Being, the Identity of all apparently separate consciousnesses and the Condition of all phenomena and of the Energy, Light, or Spirit-Power that is the universal Matrix of all phenomena.

These three propositions correspond to three distinct views (or modes of inspection) of consciousness. The first proposition is based on the inspection of consciousness of (or consciousness in the mode of extroversion, or the awareness of objects of all kinds). The second proposition is based on the inspection of consciousness as (or consciousness in the mode of introversion, or the awareness of itself as the principle or subject that is the necessary and prior basis for all objective awareness). And the third proposition is based on the native view, or consciousness is (which is consciousness prior to all modes of introversion or extroversion, and all modes of limiting identification with self or not-self).

Each of these three propositions and their unique views or modes of inspection of their subject is valid in its own terms. Therefore, each proposition can be consistently applied as the basis for a complete and self-contained philosophical system. Indeed, this has in fact been done in the various schools and cultural systems of the total Great Tradition of human consideration.

The first proposition is the basis for all materialistic and "realistic" philosophies. Thus, it is the common basis for the perceptually based logic of the first three stages of life. It is the basis for atheism and the doctrines of scientific materialism. And it is also the basis for the "realistic" philosophies of the sixth stage of life, such as is reflected in the original or Hinayana school of Buddhism.

The second proposition is the basis for all "idealistic" philosophies. Thus, it is the common basis for those esoteric schools and traditions that express the "idealistic" point of view in the terms of the fourth, fifth, or sixth stages of life. It is the basis for fourth and fifth stage Emanationist mysticism (in which consciousness is raised to a state of contemplation of and then unity and identity with the Energy, Light, or Vibratory Spirit-Power and Life-Consciousness that is felt to be the Substance of all phenomena. And this same "idealistic" view of consciousness is otherwise made the basis for the sixth stage Advaitic philosophy of exclusive inversion upon the principle of consciousness.

The third proposition is the ultimate basis for Transcendental philosophy. It is the spontaneous expression or Confession of Realization in the seventh stage of life. In its true form, this unique proposition is made only in the case of Transcendental Realization, wherein the propositions of the first six stages of life are inherently and tacitly transcended. This is the basic proposition of the Way that I Teach, and it is to this ultimate proposition that all Great Adepts Awaken, even if they approach that Awakening via the two lesser propositions and the six conventional stages of life. Therefore, this same proposition may be found in the midst of all traditions that achieve Completeness. It is evident by implication (rather than concrete description) in the Teaching of Gautama (and Hinayana Buddhism), even though the language of that Teaching is basically confined to the "realism" that characterizes its particular form of the sixth stage approach to life. It is also evident in the Teaching of Advaitic sages of the highest type (such as Ashtavakra and Ramana Maharshi),* even though the language of Advaitic Teaching

---

* The sage Ashtavakra, or Aṣṭāvakra, is referred to in the *Mahābhārata* (III. 132 and

tends to confine itself to the "idealism" that characterizes its particular form of the sixth stage approach to life. And this same proposition may here and there be found in the expressions of great fourth and fifth stage mystics, who have at least in moments glimpsed the ultimate Condition of self and world.

There does, however, appear to be a problem reflected in the exclusive and absolutist claims of advocates and practitioners of the various traditions. Those advocates and practitioners who have not yet entered into the disposition of the seventh stage of life often imagine that their appropriate task is to conceive of their own path in absolute terms and to conceive of the differences between their path and other paths in such terms that no reconciliation or common ground can be admitted. For this reason, the Great Tradition may seem to be a mixed bag of absolutes and absolutists, as if hundreds of lunatics were all claiming to be independent God with the right of rule over all others.

It is in our unique moment in history, when all traditions and all propositions are equally visible (due to a world-wide communicativeness that is making all provincialism obsolete) that we must consider the apparent differences among traditions with a new kind of wide intelligence. And my Work is devoted, in part, to provide the critical means for understanding and transcending these differences, so that the mass of traditions may rightly be comprehended as a single and dynamic Great Tradition.

3.

The third of the three propositions is the proposition based on ultimate Realization, whereas the first two propositions are the expressions of "realistic" and "idealistic"

XIII. 19–21). His name became associated with the *Aṣṭāvakra Gītā*, a Vedānta text which Master Da Free John has identified as a "seventh stage" document.

Sri Ramana Maharshi of Tiruvannamalai was one of the few seventh stage Adepts of this century. He lived from 1879 to 1950.

orientations of egoic (or phenomenal) awareness in the first six stages of life. However, the first two propositions are not merely false. They are simply conventional. From the point of view of the Transcendentally Realized or seventh stage disposition, the orientations represented by the first two propositions are understood and accepted as conventions of the phenomenal self. Adepts in the seventh stage may even at times Teach via conventional descriptive language that is based on the viewpoint of the first two propositions. But such is only a Teaching device, applicable in the setting of instruction, and used for the sake of serving individuals who are yet practicing (or qualified for practice) in the lesser stages. Even so, the ultimate language of the Way is necessarily radical, or an expression of a "point of view" that transcends phenomenal egoity and the first six stages of life. And the logic of that ultimate language corresponds to the third of the three basic propositions.

4.

The metaphor or analogy of light is a useful tool to serve our understanding of the three propositions. If consciousness is conceived as a kind of light, then the three propositions can be seen as descriptions of three ways in which light (or consciousness) can be observed (rather than as three exclusive interpretations or definitions of light, or consciousness, each standing in contradiction to the other two, and all together demanding that we choose one or the other as the only correct idea).

The first proposition is based on the observation of objects in the light (of consciousness). It is a matter of seeing light (or consciousness) only as it is reflected from objects. In this view, light (or consciousness) is observed in the form of objects—or the visibility, perceptibility, or knowability of phenomena.

The context of the first proposition is the ordinary observation of phenomena. Light makes objects visible (or observable), and this first view is based on the observation of phenomena. Here consciousness is observed as consciousness of objects (or phenomenal events). It is a matter of observing the phenomenal event of consciousness extroverting, or reflecting on (or being aware of) objects. And this view of consciousness is then used as a means for describing and defining consciousness from the "realistic" point of view.

The "realistic" point of view is simply a convention based on confinement of the observation of consciousness to the circumstance of objective or phenomenal awareness. This confinement results in the idea that consciousness (or light) is only manifest as (or in the context of) objects in space and in moments of time. Thus, from the "realistic" point of view, neither consciousness nor light is conceived to be a continuous independent medium behind (or in front of) phenomenal objects, or space-time, but consciousness or light is conceived to be merely one of the phenomenal events of space-time dependently arising with all of the other elements, objects, forms, and forces that are observed by consciousness or via the light.

This view has provided the basis for the philosophy of materialism (in which consciousness and light are interpreted in exclusively materialistic or phenomenal terms). Materialism reduces all quantities to its own status. Therefore, materialism is the natural basis for atheism and conventional scientism (which tends toward reductionist and materialistic views).

And this same phenomenal "realism" has been made the basis for the sixth stage arguments of conventional Buddhism. In that view, consciousness is considered only in the context of the phenomenal or born personality. It is contemplated only as one aspect of a complex or composite phenomenal entity. Therefore, it is not described in any other terms (or as it might be Realized to be in the Nirvanic Event of utter transcendence of the conditional mode of being). Therefore, in the original language of Buddhism, consciousness is conceived to be only one among many "dharmas" or constituent elements of phenomenal existence— none of which is absolute and prior to the others, and all of which arise in mutual dependence on all the others in a beginningless and endless flow of causes and effects. Therefore, consciousness, like all other conditional states or processes, is temporary and discontinuous (or always arising on the basis of a present cause and effect circumstance, rather than as a continuous phenomenal or noumenal reality that transcends and always stands behind the flow of observed events). In this view, consciousness is not regarded as a permanent, continuous, or independent reality. And, therefore, the sixth stage view of Buddhism does not conceive of the self (even in its most profound depth) as a soul, or a permanent continuous reality. There are simply moments of phenomenal existence, each arising as a result of the moment before, and all of which is a plastic of mutually dependent causes and effects. It is this "realistic" conception that provides the basis for the Buddhist view of the non-necessity of phenomenal existence, self, or consciousness. It is all seen as an unnecessarily caused process, perpetuated by the arising of desire, and capable of being uncaused by the cessation of desire.

The limitation of this "realistic" philosophy, whether it is used to express the viewpoint of conventional materialism (or the materialistic consciousness typical of the first three stages of life) or the viewpoint of Transcendentalism (as in the case of Buddhism) is that it provides no basis for any larger view than phenomenal "realism." Therefore, if the end of life or the end of philosophy is the cessation of phenomenal existence, the ultimate proposition of this point of view is necessarily nihilistic. The conventional materialists are satisfied with this implication, although they still seem to want everyone to live this dying life with great orderly enthusiasm. But the Transcendentalists are not satisfied with this implication. Gautama was not a materialist but a Transcendentalist. He argued for a Way toward Transcendental Realization that progressed on the basis of criticism of the limitations of the necessarily "realistic" (or merely phenomenal, limited, dying, repeating, and ultimately pleasureless) life of the ego. He was not, like the conventional materialists, arguing for the vigorous embrace of phenomenal existence. And he did not see the cessation of phenomenal existence as annihilation.

The Three Views of Consciousness and Light

Rather, he saw it (and Realized it) as an Awakening into perfect and "unborn" Freedom, Bliss, or Happiness. Gautama's language of argument was intentionally limited to the "realistic" proposition, and he was, therefore, silent (or intellectually unwilling and logically unable to offer descriptions) relative to the ultimate Transcendental Reality. Gautama could point the Way to that Reality, but he did not offer language to describe It (since he was strategically unwilling to use metaphysical language, which always suggests a kind of phenomenal eternalism rather than utter Transcendentalism). Clearly, what Gautama Realized and pointed toward is That which is suggested in the third (or seventh stage) proposition relative to consciousness—or the proposition of the utterly Transcendental Reality that is Realized in the case of perfect transcendence of the limitations of phenomenal egoity.

5.

The second proposition is based on the observation of consciousness in a fashion that is the most obvious conventional alternative to the form of observation that is the basis of the first proposition. Using the metaphor or analogy of light once more, the viewpoint that is the basis of the second proposition is the observation of light (or consciousness) at its source rather than in the context of the illumination of objects. It is as if, when standing in a room, one looked at the light bulb in the ceiling rather than at the objects in the room and the visible room as a whole. The second proposition focuses on light (or consciousness) itself rather than on the objects illuminated by the light (or known to consciousness). Thus, if the first proposition is based on consciousness of (or consciousness reflecting on physical and mental, or gross and subtle, objects), the second proposition is based on consciousness as (or consciousness self-aware, inverted on itself, seeing itself distinct from all its possible phenomenal objects).

This proposition corresponds to the "idealist" (as opposed

to the "realist") view of existence. It is the basis of all conventional religious or spiritual language, all of which is based on the idea of a noumenal Source (light or consciousness) that is eternal (or always behind, or in front, or outside the flow of phenomenal changes). This view is specifically intended to counter "realistic" phenomenalism and nihilism.

As is the case with the argumentation of Buddhist "realism," the argumentation of this "idealistic" view may also make use of the idea of "dharmas"—or the idea that phenomenal existence is composed of distinct phenomenal constituents. The "idealist" view considers consciousness as one of the constituents (or "dharmas") of the phenomenal world and as the basic constituent of the phenomenal self. The "idealist" method is to analyze the self in terms of its apparent hierarchy of constituent elements and functional parts (or "sheaths").* On the basis of this analysis, consciousness is located as the basic or root component. But the "idealist" view considers that if we examine (or invert upon) consciousness itself (which is the knower or witness of all the extended functions and objects of the phenomenal self, or body-mind), that very orientation toward consciousness permits and determines a different awareness of consciousness and a different presumption about consciousness than is permitted and determined by the "realistic" orientation (which sees consciousness indirectly, only in the context of the moment to moment awareness of objects and states). To observe consciousness as itself (as the witness, or the "light" that illuminates and knows all phenomenal objects) is to observe and know it in an altogether different mode than is made evident in the context of objects.

From this "idealist" point of view, consciousness as a "dharma" or constituent of phenomenal existence is not rightly understood if it is seen in the context of objects rather than as

---

* Vedānta generally recognizes five "envelopes," viz. the "sheath made of food," i.e., the gross body (*annamaya-kośa*); the "sheath made of vital energy" (*prāṇamaya-kośa*); the "sheath made of mind" (*manomaya-kośa*); the "sheath made of awareness" (*vijñānamaya-kośa*); and, lastly, the "sheath made of bliss" (*ānandamaya-kośa*). The transcendental Self (*ātman*) is said to be beyond these covers.

itself (as a direct source of "visible light" rather than an indirectly viewed "light" source, seen only as its reflection in the form of a field of illuminated objects). Therefore, when the "dharma" of consciousness is viewed directly, it is not seen to be merely one among many dharmas, arising in dependence on, as an effect of, and with the same status as all of its objects. Rather, the "light" (or consciousness) that otherwise shines on and illuminates or knows phenomenal objects (or objective "dharmas"), and which, in that context, takes on the dependently arising form of moments of mind (or conditional awareness), is a discrete "dharma," or absolute and independent element of existence. If consciousness inverts directly on itself, it intuitively discovers that it does not arise discontinuously, by causes that are arising successively, moment after moment. Rather, it discovers itself to be an unbroken, unqualified reality, continuous, without any necessary reference to objects, states, or outside causes. The "idealist" (inverted upon consciousness) asks the "realist" (extroverted via consciousness): If phenomenal existence is composed of discrete "dharmas" or constituents, and if, at the point of death (or disintegration) of any phenomenal being or composite form, each of the constituents returns to its own elemental or "dharmic" state (so that the previous individual being or form no longer exists), then where does consciousness go? What difference could death make to consciousness since it only returns to consciousness and thus remains as consciousness, even as the watery part returns to water and remains as water (or in a purely inert or insentient condition)? If consciousness is examined in and as itself (and thus effectively as it would be after the disintegration or death of the present body-mind), it shows itself to be an inherently continuous and indestructible absolute, always prior to and independent of (or not dependent for its existence on) objects and moments of space and time. Therefore, when death occurs, consciousness is not and could not be changed or ended, but always remains continuous as itself, free of the conditioning or binding power of space-time processes. From the "idealistic" point of view, consciousness, known in and as itself, is not dependently arising with all other phenomenal constituents, but it is the ultimate essence or primal element of phenomenal existence. It is the ultimate principle in the midst of phenomenal existence. It is that which grants sentience (and thus both reality and apparent necessity) to phenomenal existence. It is that which is involved in and apparently limited by phenomenal existence. It is that which must be Realized, in itself, to transcend phenomenal existence. And it is that which must thus be disentangled from dependence on, limitation by, and dependent arising with the lesser "dharmas" (or insentient parts) of phenomenal existence.

6.

The orientation of "idealism," or the second of the three propositions relative to consciousness, does indeed provide a logical and consistent and experientially verifiable means for transcending the nihilistic tendencies in the materialistic and phenomenalistic arguments of "realism," or the point of view organized on the basis of the first of the three propositions. However, it is not without its own inherent limitations. And if we could say the root error of "realism" is nihilism (or the idea that there is nothing left over when phenomena come to an end), we could say that the root error of "idealism" is eternalism (or the idea that there is a phenomenal essence that never comes to an end).

The "idealist" tradition tends to develop on the basis of the exoteric and esoteric philosophies of the religious and spiritual culture of Emanationism. Therefore, the ultimate "idealist" arguments (which appear in the sixth stage language of the various schools of Upanishadic Advaitism) tend to be built upon the religious and spiritual conceptions of the Emanationist tradition and the first five stages of life. It is for this reason that the "idealist" tradition, even in its sixth stage form, is associated with the idea of the eternal soul (or the inner self as a permanent, independent, and even phenomenal entity or "atman"). And that sixth stage tradition is also often associated with God-ideas, traditional religious cultism, and even yogic processes of contemplation that develop the conventional mysticism of psychic ascent via the mechanics of attention in the nervous system (toward the ascended "nirvikalpa samadhi").

The cultural tradition associated with the second proposition is also commonly aligned with a conceptual philosophy in which consciousness is conceived as one of two principal manifest forms of the ultimate Divine. The other of the two is contrasted with consciousness and is evident as all that is insentient, or not consciousness. In this view, consciousness is, in the Hindu tradition, commonly called "Purusha," and all that is not consciousness is called "Prakriti." And the ultimate goal of the fourth and fifth stage mysticism of this view is to attain a form of contemplative absorption (or trance "samadhi") in which the distinction between consciousness and all that is not consciousness is transcended in the Realization of the Consciousness/Energy (or "Purushottama") that is the Source and Substance of the phenomenal worlds.

The sixth stage schools of this "idealist" tradition generally continue to make use of the conventional concepts of soul (or "atman"), God (or "Purushottama"), "Purusha," and "Prakriti" as the basis for the description of a Way of ultimate liberation that finally Realizes an utterly Transcendental Condition. Therefore, the ultimate argumentation of the second proposition goes beyond the exoteric and esoteric conceptions and mysticism of the "idealistic" culture of the first five stages of life. And it proposes a method or a path that cuts through the ideas of soul and God and the Heavenly Abode. Therefore, that same method cuts through the esoteric yogic techniques of mystical ascent to higher cosmic planes (or states of mind) and "nirvikalapa samadhi" (or the trance-ecstasy, dependent on the mechanics of the egoic body-mind, in which there is a temporary vision of Unity).

The ultimate traditional schools of the second proposition are the sixth stage schools of Upanishadic Advaitism (including the tradition of the *Yoga Vasistha* and culminating in the tradition of Advaita Vedanta), and although the traditions of

Samkhya and Jainism were originally built upon a materialistic or non-Emanationist view of phenomenal existence, they too were clearly founded on the "idealist" point of view of the second proposition. These schools or traditions are also the inheritors and, to one or another degree, the bearers of the Emanationist and animistic language of the cultural and yogic traditions of Shaktism and Shaivism as well as Vaishnavism (as represented in the *Bhagavad Gita* and the *Bhagavata Purana*), but it must be understood that the sixth stage schools always stand in critical relation to the traditions of the first five stages of life. Therefore, it is in these specifically sixth stage traditions of "idealism" that the second proposition relative to consciousness is developed in its purest form, free of the more conventional religious and spiritual associations of the first five stages of life. And it is in the sixth stage arguments of "idealism" that the fundamental limitations and conventionality of the second proposition are made most clear in philosophical terms.

7.

The second proposition, like the first, is founded on a conventional (or phenomenal) view of consciousness. Therefore, like the first proposition, it contains an inherent error (or conventional prejudice) that prevents it from describing or representing its subject simply and ultimately, as it is. It can be said that the first proposition represents a materially phenomenal conception of consciousness, whereas the second proposition, in contrast with the first, represents a noumenal and absolutist conception of consciousness. Even so, the second proposition still represents a relatively phenomenalistic approach to the subject of consciousness—and this is the root of its inherent error or prejudice.

The ultimate or sixth stage philosophy based on the second proposition considers consciousness as an absolute noumenal phenomenon, or as one of the constituents of conventional or phenomenal reality. It views consciousness in the context of

The Three Views of Consciousness and Light

phenomena and from the point of view of the phenomenal self. It conceives of a path or method for Realizing a state of exclusive identification with consciousness. That Realization is considered to be liberation or Truth, since it separates consciousness from the phenomenal not-self and thus effectively solves the apparent "problem" of egoic suffering. And that Realization is based on meditative inversion of the phenomenal being, or the concentration of attention on consciousness rather than on any insentient phenomenal object.

The ultimate or sixth stage cultures of both the first and the second propositions suffer from the limitations of a phenomenally based logic. That phenomenally based logic may, in each case, provide a practical means for approaching Transcendental Realization, but in neither case does the base proposition provide a viable conceptual structure for describing the Transcendental Reality Itself (or the Transcendental Condition or Status of consciousness). And, in both cases, the method and the concepts of the original path of practice must be utterly transcended before the transition to actual Realization (or the seventh stage of life) can be made.

Clearly, then, the philosophies and practices of the sixth stage of life are based on limiting conventions (as are the philosophies and practices of the first five stages of life). And it would seem altogether preferable to consider the Way of Realization directly in terms of a proposition that represents the point of view of the seventh stage of life while yet providing a structure of practice for those who are yet involved in the psycho-physical cycles of the first six stages of life. This is in fact the basis for my own Teaching Work, and it is the third proposition that provides the conceptual basis for the ultimate descriptions of this seventh stage point of view.

The second proposition is limited by its phenomenal orientation toward consciousness. It views consciousness as a noumenal absolute, but it contrasts that noumenal absolute with all other constituents of phenomenal existence. Therefore, the second proposition is based on the conception of a contrast between consciousness and all that is not consciousness. And this requires that the point of view toward consciousness be limited to the plane of phenomenal events. That is, consciousness is not conceived in ultimate or truly Transcendental terms but always at base in phenomenal terms. Like the sixth stage traditions of the first proposition, the sixth stage traditions of the second proposition are limited by the conception of "dharmas," or phenomenal constituents. The difference between the two is simply that the sixth stage schools of the first proposition (such as those of the early Buddhist tradition) conceive of consciousness as a dependent constituent of phenomenal existence, whereas the sixth stage schools of the second proposition (such as those of Samkhya, Jainism, and of Upanishadic Advaitism) conceive of consciousness (or the ultimate essence of the conscious being) as a noumenal but nonetheless phenomenal absolute.

As I have already indicated, the distinct and, to some degree, mutually contradictory conceptions of schools separately based on either the first or the second proposition are due simply to the arbitrary selection of one or the other of the two principal conventional orientations that may be adopted relative to consciousness. I have used the metaphor of light to help make it clear that these two propositions are not based on two absolutely unrelated and inherently contradictory conceptions of their subject. Rather, they are simply based on two different orientations to the same subject. Each of those orientations is a legitimate alternative in the context of phenomenal experience (just as one may either look at a room full of illuminated objects or at the lamp that is illuminating them). But when either of these two conventional (or merely phenomenal) alternatives is embraced exclusively and rigorously applied as the basis for a logic of ultimate Realization, then the paths separately designed by each focus inevitably begin to contradict (and, historically, even oppose) one another.

I am trying to demonstrate that these contradictions are merely conventional and of no ultimate consequence, and the historical oppositions are of course absurd, unnecessary, and merely destructive. In any case, when either of the two primary

The Three Views of Consciousness and Light

approaches is exhaustively applied to the point of actual Transcendental Awakening, the conventional or merely phenomenal point of view is itself utterly transcended. Then the conceptual and meditative apparatus of the first six stages of life loses all utility and falls away in Transcendental Wisdom, or Transcendental "Samadhi" (free of all the egoic and psycho-physical limitations of the phenomenal "samadhis" of the stages of life previous to the seventh).

Gautama entered into that Transcendental "Samadhi" in the moment of his Enlightenment. And so also did Advaitic sages such as Ashtavakra. And in such "Samadhi" (which is "Sahaj Samadhi," or natural, native Transcendental Awakening) the propositions that may have provided the original path of approach no longer apply—because such propositions are founded in a purely phenomenal and egoic or un-Enlightened context of mind rather than in the Transcendental disposition of Enlightenment. Therefore, those Adepts who have actually completed (and thus gone beyond) the "sadhana" or practice based on either of the two conventional propositions begin at last to express themselves in different terms about the matter of Realization and Reality. They may prefer silence (or non-verbal transmission, as in the case of Ramana Maharshi), or they may engage in the strategy of denial of the applicability of conventional language to the description of That which is Realized (as was the case with Gautama), or they may behave strangely and speak in paradoxes or in the form of apparent nonsense (as in the case of certain individuals in the Ch'an or Zen tradition and in the Crazy Wisdom tradition), or they may try to construct a language of philosophy that is compatible with ultimate Realization (as in the cases of Nagarjuna and Shankara). Even all of these forms of communication and transmission may be used by Awakened Adepts, and my own Teaching Work is an example of the use of all such possible means.

All "Completed" or seventh stage Adepts are faced with the fact that the conventions of language and behavior (even of traditional philosophical language and the prescribed behavior of traditional religious and spiritual practice) are all based on the phenomenal, psycho-physical, and thus necessarily egoic point of view. And what the Adept would and must communicate or transmit is the Transcendental Reality, or Awakened Realization of the Transcendental Condition of all phenomenal conditions.

The philosophies and the cultures of practice that are based on the first two propositions relative to consciousness are based on the conventions of the phenomenal, psycho-physical, and egoic point of view. They are intended to motivate and lead practitioners beyond the phenomenal (or "dharmic"), merely psycho-physical, and egoic point of view, but they do not provide a base for the ultimate description (or even the direct intuition) of That which is to be Realized. Therefore, another language and logic is needed to describe the Transcendental Reality and the ultimate Way of Its Realization. And it is the third proposition relative to consciousness (as Transcendental Reality rather than phenomenal event) that provides the basis for that language and logic.

The philosophies of both the first and the second proposition tend to organize themselves around the idea of a "problem" to be solved. That "problem" is the phenomenal point of view or context of existence itself. The philosophy of the first proposition tends to conceive of a path based on the "uncausing" of the phenomenal process. And such can lead, in itself, to the ideal of mere nihilism. The philosophy of the second proposition tends to conceive of a path based on inversion upon consciousness to the exclusion of all that is apparently not consciousness. And such can lead, in itself, to the ideal of the isolation of consciousness as an exclusive, absolute, and eternal phenomenon. The ultimate philosophy, which is founded on the third proposition, is inherently free of the "problem" and the conventional logic of phenomenal egoity. Therefore, it is not organized around the language of phenomenal existence. Rather, the ultimate philosophy is an expression of the always prior and inherently free Realization of consciousness as it _is_ (as Transcendental Consciousness, rather than as consciousness in the context of either association with or separation from phenomena).

The Three Views of Consciousness and Light

In the disposition represented by the third proposition, consciousness is Realized in Its Real Status, not as one of the "dharmas" or constituents (whether absolute or conditional) of phenomenal existence, but as the "Dharma" or Truth or Real Condition or Transcendental Identity. It is not a matter of consciousness extroverting toward objects or introverting upon itself. It is a matter of consciousness directly and intuitively Realizing Itself as the Transcendental Condition of all phenomenal conditions. Consciousness thus Realized is the Condition of that consciousness which is described either in the form of proposition one or proposition two. It is Consciousness as it is, always and already, whether or not phenomenal conditions arise in the form of apparent self and/or not-self. Consciousness as Reality is not merely appearing in the form of phenomena, as the knower of phenomena, or as a phenomenon exclusive of or unlike other phenomena. It is simply Itself, always and already—and all phenomenal conditions are appearances or merely apparent, unnecessary, and non-binding modifications of Itself.

Consciousness Realized in the terms of the third proposition is not viewed by or in contrast to any other or phenomenal condition. It is the Condition and ultimate Substance of self and world. It is not merely Spirit-Energy (which is the phenomenal Matrix of the phenomenal world). It is the Condition or Truth and Reality of the Spirit-Energy, of Light, and of all lights and sounds and heavens and hells and worlds and embodied beings. It is the Condition or Truth and Reality of all of Nature, of all "dharmas," of the phenomenal self (or body-mind), of the presumed soul (or "atman"), of phenomenal consciousness (or "Purusha"),* of all that is phenomenal but not consciousness (or "Prakriti"), and of all the forms and ideas that are called God, or "Purushottama," or the Eternal Creative Other. Consciousness is ultimately Realized and Proclaimed to be Transcendental Being, the Condition of all phenomena and even of the All-Pervading

---

* In the systems of classical Yoga and Sāmkhya, both *puruṣa* and *prakṛti* are treated as noumena. But from the point of view of Radical Transcendentalism they are eclipsed and thus relativized by the Total Field which is the Radiant Being. From the ultimate "point of view," therefore, they are phenomena.

Energy that is the Creative Matrix and Mover of all phenomena. Consciousness is to light (or Energy) what light (or Energy) is to forms or phenomenal conditions of all kinds. It is the Transcendental Context of phenomena, even as light (in its ultimate form as the Creative Energy behind and within all phenomenal forms and processes) is the phenomenal Context (or Matrix) of all phenomena. (Therefore, light is a useful metaphor for phenomenal consciousness, and Energy may be a conventionally useful object of contemplation or psycho-physical submission, but light and Energy are, in Reality, nothing more than phenomenal appearances of and in Transcendental Consciousness.)

The Realization expressed via the third proposition is not dependent on either extroversion or introversion of attention. It transcends the phenomenal mechanism of attention itself. It is the tacit, motiveless, free, and prior Realization of the Obvious, or That which is always already the case. It is the free Realization of the Condition that is Consciousness. That Consciousness is not an object to us, nor is It merely within us. It has no necessary relationship to phenomena. It is simply the ultimate or Real Context of the phenomenal self and world (in any of the gross or subtle planes of cosmic Nature).

The tacit Realization of Transcendental Consciousness as the Obvious Condition is the natural or native Realization of Reality, Self, Being, Love-Bliss, or Radiant Happiness. It is not dependent on any state or conception in body or mind, but it may be apparently obstructed by the various phenomenal states and relations of body and mind. Therefore, until the Obvious is Realized, there is utility in the conceptions and practices that release energy and attention from bondage to the context of phenomenal egoity. But in our "natural" or native state of profound equanimity (or free energy and attention), Consciousness is tacitly Obvious as the Transcendental Condition of self and not-self.

Therefore, the ultimate Realization of Consciousness (as expressed in the third proposition) makes possible a Transfigured or inherently Enlightened phenomenal existence in any phenomenal world. Just so, the Enlightened disposition is such that, without seeking to seclude Consciousness from phenomena, It will ultimately Outshine (and always already inherently Outshines) all phenomenal worlds and self states.

Therefore, this third proposition is the basis of the conception of Consciousness in the Realized, Enlightened, or seventh stage of life. The traditions of the first six stages of life generally seek to Realize that Radiant Transcendental Consciousness on the basis of arguments and practices based in the phenomenal and thus inherently egoic point of view of the born being. Therefore, the leading or conventional arguments of the traditions are based either on the first or the second of the three fundamental propositions I have described. However, all traditions that achieve Completeness ultimately transcend their own original propositions and practices in the Transcendental Awakening of the seventh stage of life, and that Awakening can only be expressed (if it is to be described at all) via the ultimate language of Transcendentalism (and thus via the language of the third proposition).

My own life and Realization confirm this, and I have, therefore, argued for a Way of understanding and practice that immediately transcends the phenomenally based and egoic "problems" and propositions of the first six stages of life. The Way that I Teach is founded on the Realization of Consciousness (or Radiant Transcendental Being) in the seventh stage of life, and I argue for a consideration and a practice that make the radical understanding (rather than the conventional practice) of the first six stages of life (and their phenomenal or egoic propositions) into the basis for direct Awakening into the Realization of the Truth of the seventh stage of life.

VIII
The Great Principle

Energy (Prakriti or Shakti) is not the Great Principle. Energy is not the Ultimate Domain of the conscious self. Energy is simply the manifest Matrix or Substance of all objects and conditions of the conscious self. To Realize that Energy, even in its Primal Form or State (prior to differentiation into particular objects and states) is not to Realize Reality, Truth, Freedom, or Perfect Happiness. It is simply to be absorbed in the Substance of all objects, without necessarily Realizing the Identity of the conscious self and without necessarily recognizing Energy in its Ultimate Source or Domain. Therefore, none of the various possible states of Energy or of knowledge and experience (subjective or objective), including savikalpa samadhi and nirvikalpa samadhi, is itself the Fulfillment of the Way.

Consciousness (Purusha) is the Great Principle. Consciousness is the Ultimate Domain of the conscious self. Consciousness is also the Ultimate Domain of the world, all objects and states of the conscious self, and Energy (the Ultimate Object and Substance of all conditional objects). To Realize that Consciousness in which the conscious self, its objects and states, and the Substantial Energy of the world are presently arising is to Realize Reality, Truth, Freedom, or Perfect Happiness.

But that Consciousness is not merely (or as a matter of fact rather than Realization in Samadhi) the interior or essential consciousness that is basic to the manifest self. That essential self-consciousness is presumed to be separate from other consciousnesses, all objects, and the Substantial Energy. Therefore, jnana samadhi and any other form of strategically exclusive inversion upon the essential self-consciousness is not the Fulfillment of the Way.

Consciousness is the Transcendental Being or Domain (Brahman or Purushottama) in which the conscious self, all other consciousnesses, all objects and states, and the Substantial Energy are arising as apparent modifications or limitations of Itself. Therefore, only that Realization (Sahaj Samadhi) in which the conscious self, all other consciousnesses, all objects and states, and the Substantial Energy are tacitly and inherently recognized (rather than strategically excluded or embraced) as transparent, non-binding, merely apparent, and unnecessary modifications of Consciousness is the Fulfillment of the Way.

Transcendental Consciousness is Radiant. That is, Reality is One, not exclusive, not divided, and not Other. All conscious selves and their objects and states are made of It and recognizable as It. The Substantial Energy is nothing but the Radiance (or Fullness) of Consciousness perceived as Object to Itself. When even the Substantial Energy is utterly recognized in and as the Transcendental Consciousness, there is only Consciousness (Bhava Samadhi). And when Consciousness is so Realized, It is Obvious as Reality or Truth. And that Realization, in Its Perfection, is Freedom, Happiness, or Translation into the Divine or Transcendental Domain, which is Obviously Consciousness and not apparent as any thing or any one that is not Simply and Fully that very Consciousness.

IX
The Three Ways of Buddhism

In the Buddhist tradition there are three primary Ways—the Hinayana, Mahayana, and Vajrayana (or the Ways of the Arhat, the Bodhisattva, and the Mahasiddha).

The Hinayana Way of the Arhats is the Way of the transcendence of sympathetic (and, ultimately, sorrowful) attachment to conditional self, its relations, and its worlds of experience. It is the "masculine" Way of uncompromising abandonment or transcendence of the motives of sympathy or desire.

The Mahayana Way of the Bodhisattvas is the Way of the transcendence of angry rejection of the conditional self, its relations, and its worlds of experience. It is the "feminine" Way of self-surrender and compassionate service.

The Vajrayana Way of the Mahasiddhas is the Way of the transcendence of both sympathetic attachment and angry rejection, or all the positives and negatives relative to the conditional self, its relations, and its worlds of experience. It is the magical Way of the powers inherent in the male-female unity (or the unity and equanimity of polarized opposites).

Behind and beyond these is Enlightenment Itself, or Realization of the Transcendental Priority that is, under one Name or another, the Ultimate Goal of all the Wisdom traditions.

X
Nirvana and Samsara Are Not the Same

1.

The earliest literature of Buddhism describes a Way of Transcendental Liberation (or Nirvanic Realization) that is based on a "realistic" (or phenomenalistic) rather than an "idealistic" (or noumenalistic) analysis and evaluation of manifest existence. It describes the method of approach to Realization, but it does not directly describe Realization Itself (or That which is ultimately Realized). Therefore, that literature stands in contrast to the literatures of the first five stages of life, since such literatures base themselves either on idealistic and ego-based methods of absorptive meditation and mystical ascent to higher worlds (as is the case in the paths of the fourth and fifth stages of life) or on materialistic ideals of personal and collective human fulfillment in the context of embodiment in this world (as is the case in the paths of the first three stages of life). And the language of the earliest Buddhist literature also stands in contrast to that of the literatures of the seventh stage of life, since such seventh stage literatures are founded on and expressive of prior Enlightenment, Transcendental Realization, or Inherent Freedom, rather than on the progressive search for such. All of this indicates that the earliest Buddhist tradition (or the Pali tradition, commonly called the Hinayana or "lesser vehicle") is a Transcendentalist tradition of the sixth stage type.

Mahayana and Vajrayana Buddhism (which are the traditions or "yanas" that appeared most immediately after the original or Hinayana tradition) generally represent syncretistic developments of the original tradition. In those later traditions there is an accommodation to the cultural orientations that precede the sixth stage of life, and there is also the development of descriptive considerations of Enlightenment, Reality, or Truth that represent the disposition of Enlightenment or Transcendental Realization Itself (rather than the consciousness that is only seeking such Enlightenment). Therefore, the later literatures of Buddhism contain direct representations of the seventh stage Realization Itself, but the later literatures also contain syncretistic and conventional representations of the points of view that characterize the stages of life earlier than the sixth. The later Buddhist literatures that communicate cultural and practical means of the type that characterize the first five stages of life represent at best the adaptation of religious and mystical or yogic means that may, at the beginning, serve the approach toward radical Awakening, but when those means are promoted as an end in themselves, or when they are otherwise permitted to become the very basis for the characterization of Enlightenment itself, then those literatures simply represent an abandonment of the radical Transcendentalist position of true Buddhism.

My own Teaching, or the Way that I Teach, may, for all the reasons I have already given, be rightly named "Advaitayana

Buddhism," since it may be seen to be a rigorous application of the seventh stage or ultimate point of view of Transcendentalism, and it may also be seen to be a critical epitome of the entire Great Tradition of the progressive stages of life, which is itself epitomized in the sixth to seventh stage points of view of traditional Buddhism and Advaitism.

As was the case with each of the previous "yanas" (or "vehicles" or "Ways") of Buddhism, the fundamental or original culture of Advaitayana Buddhism has arisen on the basis of an original contact with the spiritual culture of India, after which it has gone on to develop in another geographic and cultural region (America) before the development of its final or ultimate phase, which is world-wide or universal expansion. Hinayana Buddhism arose in India and then passed on to develop in the broad cultural milieu of southern Asia. Mahayana Buddhism arose in India and then passed on to develop in China and Japan (or northern Asia in general). And Vajrayana (or Tantrayana) Buddhism arose in India and then went on to develop in regions north of India, primarily in Tibet.

Advaitayana Buddhism is now developing in the West. My life and Work are uniquely and originally Western or Occidental, rather than Eastern and Oriental. Therefore, this Advaitayana Buddhism is the true "Western Buddhism." The Buddhisms of the three earlier yanas expanded successfully in the East in earlier centuries (during their creative phase), but they did not pass to the West via a process of real cultural transformation. The earlier yanas have only recently passed to the West, via books and airplanes rather than through Western Adepts. Therefore, the Buddhisms of the three earlier yanas have indeed been passed on to Westerners—by Orientals, and in the form of Oriental mind and culture.

Even so, Advaitayana Buddhism is an epitome of Buddhism as a whole, and it is, therefore, neither Occidental nor Oriental, but suited to the unified world-wide culture that is the inevitable future of collective mankind. And, like all previous forms or yanas of Buddhism, Advaitayana Buddhism also has its roots in India.

My own sadhana was a spontaneous process that involved spiritual transmission from Indian yogis, saints, and sages (as well as from Western-born sources). And the fulfillment of my sadhana was followed by the recognition of the separate languages of the Advaitic tradition and the Buddhist tradition as clear precedents for the description of what is also my own Realization. Therefore, Advaitayana Buddhism has its roots in India, and it has developed as a unique and new consideration because of its association with a cultural environment that is different from those which provided the base for the unique development of each of the previous yanas of Buddhism.

This Advaitayana Buddhism does not stand in direct line with the Buddhist traditions alone, but with all previous sixth and seventh stage traditions (which are primarily represented by the various schools of Buddhism and Advaitism). And it stands in critical relation (as well as rightly positive alignment) to all schools and points of view that represent the stages of life previous to the seventh. Therefore, it stands in right critical relation to the exclusively sixth stage conceptions of Buddhist "realism" and Advaitic "idealism," and it also stands in right critical relation to the lesser orientations (representing the first five stages of life) that have been traditionally associated with the cultures of Buddhism and Advaitism.

2.

In previous essays I have specifically and critically considered the sixth stage limitations of traditional Buddhism and Advaitism. And I have also criticized the conceptions and practices of the first five stages of life as they appear in the Advaitic tradition (or the Emanationist tradition as a whole). In this essay I want to address the specifically Buddhist conceptions and practices that represent the orientations of the first five stages of life, and also those that represent the seventh stage of life.

The literatures of Mahayana Buddhism (or the so-called "greater vehicle") represent the first movement beyond the original written tradition of Buddhism. They also represent a tendency to make a transition from strictly "realistic" language to the generally "idealistic" language of metaphysical conception. (And, therefore, the later Buddhist tradition represented by the Mahayana and Vajrayana schools is always characterized by a synthesis of "realistic" and "idealistic" conceptions.)

The original Mahayana tradition represents a dynamic stimulus-response encounter between the "realistic" sixth stage tradition of early Buddhism and (1) the "idealistic" metaphysical and Emanationist traditions that represent the ancient exoteric and esoteric cultures of the first five stages of life as they are conceived in the traditions of Hinduism, (2) the sixth stage idealism of Upanishadic Advaitism, and (3) the cultures of the first six stages of life outside the domain of Hinduism (especially the Taoist and naturalistic traditions of China and Japan). In that dynamic encounter, Buddhism developed literatures of consideration that represent the seventh stage of life as well as the stages of life previous to the sixth.

The Mahayana tradition most especially added to Buddhism the dimensions of seventh stage consideration and the devotional and practical religious "idealism" of the fourth stage of life. The seventh stage consideration was at first developed by Nagarjuna, who conceived of phenomenal existence in terms of an inherent Nirvana, or "Shunyata," in which each phenomenal event is seen to be completely dependent upon, or without the slightest independence from, all other phenomenal events, and thus Void or Empty of separateness, or of an invisible, independent, or permanent internal core, and of any Cause that is outside or independent of the phenomenal flow of causes and effects. After Nagarjuna (or the Madhyamika school), the seventh stage consideration of the Mahayana was further developed by the basically "idealistic" schools of the *Lankavatara Sutra* and of Yogacara (or Vijnanavada) Buddhism.

These philosophical schools of Mahayana Buddhism extended the original "realistic" logic of Buddhism into the framework of metaphysical "idealism" and the positive or direct description (and equally direct or unmediated Realization) of Ultimate Reality or Nirvanic Realization. Therefore, they represent an orientation to a conception of Buddhist Realization Itself, and to a conception of manifest existence in the Context of Ultimate Reality, or in the terms of inherence in (rather than separation from) the Nirvanic or Transcendental Condition. This orientation may be contrasted (argumentatively but not absolutely) with the original Buddhist orientation, which was based on conventional and problem-based conceptions of conditional existence as a non-Nirvanic or inherently un-Enlightened state, and which conceived of the Way as a necessarily progressive conventional effort to escape conditional existence and so finally achieve Nirvanic or Transcendental Realization as an alternative to conditional existence. Because of their willingness to describe the Ultimate Condition in positive and thus necessarily ontological terms, and also because of their presumption of the point of view of inherence in rather than separation from the Transcendental Condition, the Mahayana philosophical schools represent an orientation that can be seen in terms of the seventh or Enlightened stage of life.

The original phenomenal realism of Gautama was centered around the proclamation that the ego is only phenomenal (or the conventionally inevitable product of unnecessary conditional causes) and thus capable of being uncaused (or transcended in the acausal disposition of Nirvana). The later or Mahayana schools proclaimed, in contrast to Gautama, that phenomena are inherently egoless. This attitude was expressed in the Madhyamika view that "Nirvana and samsara are the same." The same view was later expressed (in the *Lankavatara Sutra* and in the Teachings of the Yogacara or Vijnanavada school) via the "idealistic" Buddhist view that "Consciousness," or the Transcendental and Unconditional "Buddha-Mind," is the Source and Condition and Truth of all conventional, conditional, and conceptual "dharmas" or apparent "realities." And the persuasions associated with this original Mahayana tradition provided the basis for the Vajrayana conception of Enlightenment as

"Coemergent Wisdom," or the unconditional Samadhi that is inherent in the transcendence of the idea of a difference between Nirvana and samsara.

The central thrust of these philosophical trends in later Buddhism is in the direction of conceiving a path that is most basically about the transcendence of concepts, or the conditional mind. And the Mahayana method (epitomized in the techniques of Ch'an and Zen Buddhism) is based on direct appeal to Awareness beyond mind (or thought constructions). All of the Mahayana schools tend to be associated with the ideal of Enlightened or mind-transcending (and thus phenomena-transcending) Wisdom, or the transcendence of egoity and phenomenal limitation as if it were all an illusion or false idea within an ultimate Transcendental Condition. That condition was not conceived as an alternative Reality—or a Reality outside, merely inside, or in any sense independent of phenomena (and thus related to phenomena as a cause relates to an effect). Rather, that Condition was conceived to be the inherent Condition of conditions (or all causes and effects, great or small in the scale of Nature). Therefore, the Mahayana path is based on an "idealist" conception in which conditional or phenomenal existence (or samsara) is understood to inhere in (or not to be separate from or causally related to) the Transcendental Reality (or Nirvana). And that path stands in contrast to the original Buddhist path which was based on a purely "realistic" analysis of phenomena (or self and not-self), and which viewed Nirvana as an utterly independent and relationless Transcendental Realization (not related to phenomena via causation, not at all coincident with phenomena or phenomenal consciousness, and, therefore, attainable only in the event of the utter cessation of phenomenal arising).

As I have said, these ideas of the philosophers of the Mahayana school should not be presumed to stand in stark contrast to the ideas of the original or Hinayana school. Rather, these ideas of the Mahayana should be understood to be truly Buddhist or Transcendentalist conceptions, rooted in the Realization and basic disposition of Gautama, but they consider the

Way in terms of the Wisdom of inherent Transcendental Realization (or in the seventh stage mode) rather than in the terms of conventional mind, the inherent problem of phenomenal egoity, and the progressive tactics of transit from the reality of bondage to the "Alternative Reality" of acausal Bliss (all of which characterize considerations in the sixth stage mode).

In my own descriptions of the seventh stage of life, I have indicated that there are two primary and unique but equal modes of Transcendental Realization. "Sahaj Samadhi" is the "natural" mode of Realization, in which all phenomenal, conditional, contracted, or samsaric states are inherently and tacitly recognized (and thus transcended and even transformed but not eliminated) in and as the Transcendental Condition or Being. And "Bhava Samadhi" is the same Realization, but in that case recognition has achieved such a degree or quality of transcendence that all phenomenal, conditional, contracted, or samsaric states are inherently and motivelessly Outshined. And such is the Nirvanic Samadhi beyond all noticing.

Gautama's original sixth stage consideration of the Way points toward seventh stage or Nirvanic Realization in the mode of Bhava Samadhi, whereas the Mahayana (and later Vajrayana) consideration of the Way points toward Nirvanic Realization in the mode of Sahaj Samadhi. If this is understood, then there is no need to see any conflict between the views of the original school and the later schools. And my own Teaching of the Way (or Advaitayana Buddhism) no longer considers the ultimate or seventh stage Realization exclusively in terms of one or the other of the two primary modes, but in terms of the equality of the two modes (as Realization) and of the inevitable progression from Sahaj Samadhi to Bhava Samadhi. Therefore, Bhava Nirvana may be Realized either as a terminal Event (at death), or as one of the two primary Poles of Nirvanic Realization (so that there appear to be cycles of transition from Sahaj Samadhi to Bhava Samadhi and back to Sahaj Samadhi, repeated again and again within the same lifetime or from lifetime to lifetime).

If we understand rightly, then all modes of human endeavor

become obvious as expressions of one or another of seven stages in a natural progression of Wisdom. Advaitism and Buddhism represent a number of different considerations that belong to the sixth and seventh stages of life. And Advaitayana Buddhism comprehends, epitomizes, and inherently transcends the entire Great Tradition of human endeavor, which culminates in Transcendental Wisdom, Freedom, Love, and Bliss.

3.

I must emphasize the fact that the conceptions of Enlightenment developed in the Mahayana and Vajrayana traditions are radical expressions of the Realized or seventh stage point of view. They are not to be considered as conventional propositions of the mind of the first six stages of life. However, there is a current trend to popularize Buddhism (as well as all Transcendentalist and esoteric traditions), and in the mode of "pop" Buddhism formulae such as "Nirvana and samsara are the same" are reduced to slogans that justify the conventions of egoity in the lesser stages of life.

The equation (or "sameness") of "Nirvana" and "samsara" is not factually the case. It is not a conventional truth, nor is it in any sense obvious to the egoic mind. In the un-Enlightened condition, Nirvana and samsara are the ultimate opposites. The declaration (or Confession) that they are the same is truly made only by those who have transcended the limits of ego and phenomenal appearances. The Buddhist conception of the sameness of Nirvana and samsara is like the Hindu Advaitic conception of the sameness of the self-essence (or "atman") and "Brahman" (or the Transcendental Reality, Condition, or Being). Each of these two great traditional formulae indicates a Transcendental Condition to be Realized. Therefore, neither formula represents a conventional truth, and neither one is a principle intended or suited for popular belief. Each one is a formula that Confesses the Truth in terms that transcend all differences and that recognizes the conditional world and self in Truth rather than apart from Truth (or apart from the Realization of Truth).

Those who are not thus Enlightened or perfectly Awake must clearly understand (and take heed of the fact) that Nirvana and samsara are not the same. A conventionally worldy life, egoically attached to the merely apparent or perceptual "realities" of phenomenal existence, is not in any sense Nirvanic. Indeed, such a life is truly nihilistic (since it constantly reduces Transcendental Being to a cycle of limitation and death).

Even so, there is a trend, both modern and traditional, to use the great Mahayana equation of Nirvana and samsara (as well as the great Hindu or Advaitist equation of the atman and Brahman) as a basis for the promotion of popular techniques of living that substitute worldly, religious, and ego-based (or merely psycho-physical) yogic or mystical practices, consolations, and attainments for the Way and the Realization of Transcendental Enlightenment. And this same trend can be seen in the worldwide effort to reduce the Way of Transcendental Realization, epitomized by the Buddhist and Advaitist traditions, to egoic paths of mere materialistic worldliness, conventional social consciousness, exoteric religious consolation (or mere anxiety-reduction), and magical-mystical aspiration (which may bear the characteristics of the fourth and fifth stages of life, but which basically serve the childish or adolescent social ego of the first three stages of life). In the domains of "pop" Buddhism, the Enlightened Confession "Nirvana and samsara are the same" is reduced to the idea that discipline and transcendence are unnecessary, or the ideal of the ego with a quiet mind, or the benighted and merely consoled feeling that everything is OK as it seems—as if one could achieve a state of fear that is free of anxiety! The same tendencies are evident in "pop" Hinduism, where, according to the conventional belief in the sameness of atman and Brahman, the ego is regarded to be Divine, the Truth is reduced to the mortal patterns of psycho-physical inwardness, and the Spiritual Master is abandoned for the "Inner Guide" (or the ego as Master). These conventions of "street wisdom" are combined with bits and pieces of all traditions (such as the Confession of Jesus that "the Kingdom of God is within you") to create the absurd movements of "pop" spirituality (or "pop" esotericism), and these popular movements constantly clash in the streets with the equally absurd "pop" religions (or the "pop" exotericism of all the righteous absolute State religions) and their cultic Idols made of arbitrary beliefs and conventional mythologies about Jesus, Krishna, and all the other half-imaginary Prophet-Gods of the past. And all of these street wars of religion against religion, dull idea against dull idea, are nothing but the muscle of stupidity, sheeplike ego clashes (socking macho hornheads as if competing for a rut), the separate junk piles of the past all hurled at one another for the angry sake of power, whizzing between minds that are mucked in self, hardened by fear, defined by the resident passions of birth, and utterly oblivious to the Truth and the Wide Wise significance of our bleeding worried lives.

In the popular un-Enlightened mind, the ego is eternal, good, Divine, and even very God. And mind is sufficient Heaven, or else this mortal Earth-life is the ultimate goal of conscious being. Such views are not only false, they are the very substance of un-Enlightenment, fear, cruelty, and madness. There are countless numbers of angry people and angry "religious" groups willing to do great harm to anyone or any organization that does not subscribe to the popular views of salvation. And, therefore, it is not only the message of worldly people but the message of ordinary and even extraordinary religious people that must be confronted by Wisdom. The righteous egoic "bite" of "pop" religion (and "pop" politics, "pop" science, and the "pop" mind cults of psychiatric vintage) must be tempered and transformed by unrighteous love, tolerance, and intelligent understanding.

The great ideas of the Adepts and philosophers who stand at the origin of all popular exoteric, esoteric, and Transcendentalist movements are, as I have been explaining, expressions of a different level or dimension of being than the popular usage of those ideas tends to suggest. Therefore, the popularization of such great ideas is in the direction of the falsification or false interpretation and misinterpretation of those ideas—and the primary error of the often well-intended popularization of the great ideas associated with the Way of Truth is that the great ideas are promoted as mere ideas (capable of being believed and asserted as Truth by the ordinary or un-Enlightened mind) rather than as ideational expressions of higher mind or a mind-transcending Enlightenment.

The central problem with conventional or popular religion and philosophy is the substitution of systems of affirmative belief about Truth for the self-transcending practice of devotion to the Realization of Truth. The usual man or woman tends to be less than human—human only in the gross technical sense, but reduced by the influences of this world to a robot of personal drives, conventional ideas, and social motives, all of which characterize the first three stages of life, and all of which are kept under control by the locally standard social propaganda and its closed system of stimulus-response educational techniques. The social influences that are generated to "educate" and control human beings in every part of the world are all basically of the kind that is now popularly declaimed as "brainwashing" whenever the educational propaganda of "others" is being criticized or mocked. People whose bodies, minds, and selves are under the control of the basic machinery of the State collective are not generally involved with the free pursuit of Truth in any ultimate sense. And popular religion is one of the primary instruments that is commonly used to organize their minds away from socially destructive self-indulgence and toward socially useful participation.

"Pop" religion and philosophy are basically tools of the gross social order. They consist primarily of systems of propagandized belief. And the practice associated with such popular belief systems is, at its worst, nothing more than the continuous affirmation of those beliefs and, at its best, the embodiment of those beliefs in the form of socially benign or materially productive behaviors. Thus, popular movements (of both a religious and a non-religious variety) tend to be associated with a conception of "salvation" by mere belief (or affirmation of concepts and the believer's state of mind and emotion), and "practice" in all popular movements is generally associated with conservative (and even suppressive) disciplines relative to personal pleasure, taboos against exclusive commitments to the asocial subjective life, and intense demands for productive and enthusiastic social action. In this manner, the merely social ego (developed only in the terms of the first three stages of life) is mechanically reproduced in the form of millions of people in each generation, much in the same manner (and for the same basic purpose) as "worker" bees in a hive. Conventional or "pop" religion is tailored to serve such social functionaries, and the standard "gospel" is that social existence and salvation are the same. The basic purpose of such religion is to guarantee the social order through the development of altruism and the propagandizing of anxiety-reducing messages.

The Way that is expressive of profound commitment to the Realization of Truth is another order of existence than the common path of the ordinary social personality. That Way is not even very interesting to the usual individual, since the usual individual does not have (or represent) sufficient free energy and attention for the consideration and practice of ultimate self-transcendence. Therefore, the great Teachings of the Way generally develop outside the common marketplace (that is, in the meetings of those who are seeking beyond the popular context of human existence).

However, over time the great Teachings generally expand outward from their point of origin—as a result of the general increase in the numbers of individuals of the "beginner" type who somehow or other come into contact with those Teachings. At some point in this process of expansion, beginners (or lesser aspirants), rather than individuals of an already advanced type, become the focus of address. And once this occurs, it is inevitable that the world in general will soon become the focus of the "call" of the Teaching.

Once a Teaching movement enters the sphere of the common world, it begins to look for "converts" rather than true beginners (or those who would seek out the Teaching on their own). Therefore, the tendency of all such movements is to move toward a greater and greater accommodation of people who have no basic inclination or ability for the great discipline of the Way of Truth. And it is that accommodation that is the basic source of lesser and false representations of the Way.

There is nothing inherently wrong with the motive of communicating the Way to the general or immature gathering of humanity. Indeed, it is necessary for this to be done, or else the karmas of un-Enlightenment will rule the world. But it is necessary for the Way Itself, in all of its traditions, to be constantly purified of the limitations and false representations that are added to the Way in the process of its accommodation of all the kinds of individuals who are yet bound to the point of view of any of the first six stages of life.

In my own life of Teaching I have been moved to submit myself to ordinary people in a time of great confusion and doubt relative to life in general as well as to the Way of Truth. There have been no superior individuals for me to address. Therefore, I have often Taught in the "Crazy Wisdom" manner, exaggerating and satirizing the usual Man, mocking the conventions of social and religious behavior and belief, and in general taking on and transforming all of the tendencies of humankind that are abroad in my time and place. This Crazy Wisdom method of Teaching is one of the traditional options used by Adepts, and it does not involve a "fall" or an embrace of un-Enlightened views. Indeed, it is a means for expressing and maintaining the difference between the conventional point of view and the Enlightened or Transcendental "point" of view. Therefore, through all of the "theatre" of my Teaching Work, I have always maintained an absolute commitment to the Way Itself, and it is to this most profound and radical Way that I have brought all of those who have found me and held on to me in these Teaching years.

Just so, all of the traditions need to embrace the Way for its own sake if they are to retain the integrity of Truth. And this requires continuous self-purification in all institutions, as well as a periodic purification of all institutions through the Work of Great Adepts. Therefore, it is a part of my Work to criticize and purify the Great Tradition and realign all traditions to the Truth.

An aspect of my purification of the Great Tradition is my criticism of popular religious and philosophical movements of all kinds (exoteric, esoteric, and Transcendental). And, therefore, I must say again that the popular movements of salvation by the social and/or psychological affirmation of belief are nothing but expressions of the un-Enlightened social order of the first three stages of life. Such movements do not truly even demand or finally produce great positive and free social changes, but the best they do is control and ceaselessly modify personal and social behaviors. The practices involved in such movements do not require or produce ultimate change or ultimate transcendence, because they represent an accommodation to (or a compensation for) an already un-Enlightened and worldly (or ego-fulfilling rather than ego-transcending) habit of existence.

There is no sufficiency in mere belief—no matter Who or What is the Object of such belief. There is no sufficiency in mind (which is the domain of mere believing and knowing), just as there is no sufficiency in the experience of the body or of the world (since body and world are always encountered in the context of the believing and knowing mind). The mind, the body, the world, and the God-idea that supports them are all nothing but the environment and expression of the ego, Narcissus, who is the essence of un-Enlightenment. Unless there is a profound understanding of self, mind, body, world, and the usual God-idea, there is no movement that is self-transcending and oriented toward Enlightenment or God-Truth. The Way of Truth is just such self-transcendence, founded on profound understanding of every feature of conventional existence. And there is no sufficient substitute for the Way of utter self-transcendence. Popular movements are at best reflections of the Way within the domain of our collective and basically immature (or lower human) social order. But they have no proper claim to righteousness, nor do they possess any more Truth than the ego can entertain. Therefore, it is time for all traditions within the Great Tradition to be aligned again to the Realizable Truth that is the matter of value in all schools and all religions. And this realignment to Truth (and the self-transcending Way of practice in the Company of authentic practitioners and Adepts) must humble all traditions, all advocates, and all the separate institutions of this world.

4.

An example of how popular usage transforms the original meaning of a great idea can be seen in the case of the Mahayana Enlightenment Equation (or the equation of Nirvana and samsara). The original idea expressed in the form "Nirvana and samsara are the same" is an expression of Enlightened freedom from egoic and phenomenal bondage. Therefore, in that formula, "samsara" simply means "phenomenal existence." It does not mean "bondage." (That is to say, the equation does not mean Nirvana, or Enlightenment, and bondage are the same.) It is only in the original or Hinayana concept of "samsara" that the term means both "phenomenal existence" and "bondage." (Therefore, in the Hinayana view, Nirvana is absolutely not samsara.) The Mahayana formula views "samsara" (as a general term for phenomenal existence) from the Enlightened or seventh stage point of view, whereas the Hinayana formula criticizes "samsara" as a general term for the conventional, egoic, or pre-Enlightened point of view in the midst of phenomenal existence.

However, the popular or exoteric usage of the Mahayana Enlightenment Equation is itself inherently conventional, egoic, or un-Enlightened. It is an idea intended for the general use of ordinary people who are seeking the Truth. Therefore, for such people, "samsara" is in fact still "bondage" and not merely "phenomenal existence." Clearly, they stand in the "Hinayana position," in which it should be understood that Nirvana and samsara (or Enlightenment and bondage) are not at all the same. And the Mahayana Enlightenment Equation should be regarded as the expression of a point of view that will be possible for them only in the event of their spiritual maturity.

The justification of the popular usage of the Mahayana Enlightenment Equation has traditionally been related to the "Bodhisattva" ideal. The origin of the idea of the equation between Nirvana and samsara was in the ultimate or seventh stage consideration of Enlightenment (as Sahaj Samadhi), but that same equation has otherwise traditionally been used to justify the popular idea of "preventing" one's Enlightenment in order to devote one's present life (and all future lifetimes) to the Enlightenment of all other beings. This popular idea of the "Bodhisattva" is a conventional social and cultural ideal that belongs to the first four stages of life. It is an ideal offered up in the later and more popular phases of Buddhist culture as a counter to the ancient Hinayana ideal of ascetical withdrawal from social and phenomenal relations for the sake of one's own Enlightenment or release from bondage. And it is this more popular and conventional social and cultural motive that reduced both the great Mahayana Equation and the idea of the Bodhisattva (which was originally intended to describe an individual who is profoundly involved in the pursuit of Enlightenment for Its own sake rather than for the ego's own sake) to the level of conventional beliefs and ideals in the lesser stages of life.

The true Bodhisattva is not one who in any sense prevents his or her own Enlightenment in order to first Enlighten others. How can an un-Enlightened being Enlighten anyone else? Rather, the true Bodhisattva is either pursuing ultimate Enlightenment (and perhaps doing so in the context of service, or positive social and cultural relations with others) or else he or she is already fully established in the Awakened Wisdom of true Enlightenment while still alive. The Enlightened Bodhisattva is a true Buddha or Transcendental Siddha. And such an individual may intentionally remain in the phenomenal worlds through

Nirvana and Samsara Are Not the Same

countless rebirths in order to Awaken others—but this does not involve the prevention of his or her own Enlightenment. The Buddhas or Enlightened Bodhisattvas or Awakened Siddhas that constantly or periodically reappear in the phenomenal worlds for the sake of Helping un-Enlightened beings always reassert their Enlightenment (as Sahaj Samadhi) in each lifetime. What they prevent (or have not yet permanently entered into) is not Enlightenment but the Hinayana form of Nirvana (which is the complete cessation of phenomenal existence, and which is basically equivalent to what I call "Bhava Samadhi," in contrast to "Sahaj Samadhi," or the Condition of Enlightenment while yet alive and active). And even such Enlightened Ones are at least periodically (during life and at death) entered into the Nirvanic Samadhi or ultimate Bhava of unqualified Transcendental Being, Consciousness, and Bliss (wherein all phenomenal conditions are perfectly Outshined).

It should be clear, then, that both the ultimate Mahayana idea (of Enlightenment as the equation of Nirvana and samsara) and the ultimate Mahayana ideal (of the Enlightened Bodhisattva) are conceptions born of the Transcendental Wisdom of the seventh stage of life. But both of these great conceptions have frequently been reduced to popular ideas or beliefs and conventional ideals of the beginner's mind and the earlier stages of life. Indeed, the larger tradition of the Mahayana was specifically oriented toward this popular reductionism, because it intended to be a popular religion rather than a "hard school" reserved exclusively for those who were capable of the most mature and advanced kind of practice. It is this aspect of the Mahayana that represents a tendency to decline from the original attitude of the Buddhist tradition, and it is this will to popularize Buddhist institutions that is the seed of the false views or conventional reductionism I have just described. Indeed, the pressures created by the needs of a popular institutional system are what have created the greatest problems for all esoteric and Transcendentalist traditions. The will to "save" everyone (or to reduce the profound disciplines and intuitions of the Way of Truth to a path that is acceptable even to those who have neither the time nor the inclination to submit themselves to the Truth) is the cause of all the most devastating compromises in philosophy. Of course, the intention to serve and Help others also has undeniable merit, and so all Teachers and traditions must struggle to serve humanity and yet retain the authenticity of confinement to Truth. The Mahayana Buddhist tradition has, like all other traditions, suffered from compromises between Truth and the un-Enlightened demands of humankind. But it has also retained its original purity in the form of its great philosophical literatures and in the form of many schools that continue with an uncompromised devotion to Transcendental Awakening.

5.

The third of the three traditional yanas of Buddhism was built upon the Mahayana tradition (and, therefore, at least some of the original seeds of the Hinayana tradition), and it added tantric and Taoist yogic and mystical techniques (as well as magical religious ceremonialism and devotional practices) to that basic Mahayana tradition. The Vajrayana tradition basically extended the list of "means" whereby Enlightenment could be pursued. The Mahayana schools also added ceremonial and devotional practices to their lists of means whenever they expanded their influence into the popular domain. Therefore, whereas the original Buddhist tradition generally limited its list of means to those that were compatible with the strictly sixth stage orientation, the Mahayana tradition extended those means in order to provide a framework for practice in the terms of the first four stages of life. And although there was some development of fifth stage yogic means in the Mahayana tradition, it was largely the Vajrayana tradition that grafted the mystical yogas of the fifth stage of life onto the traditional list of means associated with Buddhism. Therefore, it is with the Vajrayana tradition that we see the Buddhist tradition return full circle to the shamanistic, animistic, and Emanationist orientation from which Gautama originally recoiled. Even so, the Vajrayana Adepts were able, with the help of Mahayana conceptions, to make a rational synthesis of the fundamental "realism" of original Buddhism and the basic "idealism" of both the Mahayana religious philosophy and the mysticism of Indian tantrism and Chinese Taoism. And, at its best, the Vajrayana represents a true development of Buddhism, although, as was the case with the Mahayana, the popular institutionalization of the Vajrayana as well as its fifth stage mystical tendencies have also produced a range of limitations and false (or at least conventional) views.

The principal contribution of the Vajrayana tradition was to develop a more esoteric and complete conception of the Bodhisattva (or at least to propagate a view of the Bodhisattva that was emphasized more as a myth and less as a reality in the popular Mahayana tradition). The Mahayana tended to support a popular idea of the Bodhisattva as the bearer of an ideal attitude toward the world. Thus, the Mahayana Bodhisattva ideal tends to align itself toward the popular motives of the social ego rather than toward the radical Realization of Transcendental Enlightenment. The Vajrayana schools continued this line as part of their popular Teaching, but they otherwise promoted the idea of Bodhisattvas as Enlightened Siddhas who intentionally remain in the phenomenal planes of existence in order to Help un-Enlightened Beings.

The Vajrayana Bodhisattvas are already Enlightened beings who have spontaneously Realized the Transcendental Condition of phenomenal existence and have, either as a spontaneous result of that Realization or as an end-product of esoteric yogic practices, achieved various super-normal freedoms and powers that enable them to be uniquely effective in Helping others toward Enlightenment. Such Bodhisattvas are what I call seventh stage Adepts (or "Bodhisiddhas").

The principal examples of such true Bodhisiddhas in the Vajrayana tradition are the Indian Mahasiddhas and the Crazy Wisdom Adepts of Tibet. (And their likeness may also be seen in the Awakened Adepts and "Avadhoots" of Advaitism—such as may be sometimes found in the "Devi" school, the Siva school, and the Dattatreya school—who, like the Buddhist Siddhas, have transcended both the subjective and the objective tendencies of mind). Such individuals behave in an unconventional fashion as an expression of the true understanding of Enlightenment. They are frequently non-ascetical and non-celibate masters of yogic tantrism, and they are also frequently associated with supernormal powers of the fifth stage yogic variety. However, the significance of the Crazy Wisdom demonstration of Enlightenment is not self-indulgence or attachment to subtle powers and states. Rather, its significance is the spontaneous communication of the attitude of transcendence (in the form of non-preference).

This expressed attitude of non-preference is, in the Vajrayana tradition, the equivalent to the acausal (or Nirvanic) disposition that is the basis of the original Teaching of Gautama. It is different in appearance from Gautama's demonstration of acausalism, which was associated with what I call "Bhava Samadhi," or the Realization of no-desire (or no-contraction) to the point of the cessation of phenomenal consciousness. The Vajrayana demonstration of the ultimate acausal disposition is, by contrast, associated with what I call "Sahaj Samadhi" (or Transcendental Awakening in the midst of phenomenal states). Therefore, the Vajrayana demonstration is expressed in the terms of phenomenal existence (rather than in the terms of the non-phenomenal or phenomena-transcending State). And the content of that demonstration is not the exclusion of any particular category of existence, nor the exclusive embrace of any particular category of existence, but no-preference for any particular category of existence—no-preference for any phenomenon or phenomenal state (pleasurable or painful, positive or negative, "yang" or "yin," low or high, vulgar or saintly), no-preference for phenomenal existence itself, and no-preference for the cessation of phenomena or phenomenal existence.

The philosophical origins of the Vajrayana demonstration of Enlightenment are in the Mahayana Enlightenment Equation (or the Realization of samsara, or phenomenal existence, in the context of Nirvana, or the Transcendental Condition, rather than in the context of egoic bondage). Thus, the Vajrayana philosophy is basically that of the Mahayana schools of "Mind Dharma" (or the Transcendental Idealism expressed in the Mahayana equation of Nirvana and samsara). But the Vajrayana tradition of <u>practice</u> has its roots in the tantric tradition of India and the Taoist tradition of China, both of which traditions are basically oriented toward the psycho-physical yogism of the fifth stage of life. And it is this fifth stage connection (as well as the motives toward institutional popularization and social power) that are the source of the unique characteristics and the lesser or limited formulations of the Tibetan Vajrayana tradition.

The techniques of the Vajrayana schools are typically either fourth stage devotional and exoteric disciplines (intended to purify and concentrate the mind) or fifth stage yogic disciplines comparable to the psycho-physical yogas of India and China) intended to develop powers or "siddhis," visionary and other forms of super-sensory contemplation, and, ultimately, a Nirvana-like samadhi that is virtually identical to the ascended "nirvikalpa samadhi" of all the ancient schools of shamanistic "sky-magic" or mystical ascent). Therefore, the Vajrayana system of means is generally mapped out along the lines of the contemplative phenomenal mysticism associated with the goals of the fifth stage of life. But these means are, in the best of the Vajrayana schools, considered to be secondary or "helping" yogas, preliminary to the ultimate or "Mahamudra" yoga of mind-transcendence (rather than mind-development).

The greatness of any Vajrayana school, as of any school, is to be measured in terms of the degree to which the motives and means of the first six stages of life are ultimately sacrificed into the seventh stage Realization of Truth. The interpretation (or conventional "picture") of Vajrayana or Tibetan Buddhism that is popularly held (both by the Tibetan people and all non-Tibetans, including Westerners) is one that associates the Vajrayana with the magical-mystical romance of cosmic hierarchies and powers over Nature. The native Tibetan schools developed institutional organizations (both of the ascetical and the non-ascetical variety) that were designed to maintain ordinary social order and political power in the period before the recent grossly destructive Chinese invasion of the closed society of Tibet. Therefore, the "Bodhi-siddhas" of the traditionally organized Tibetan culture came to be identified more or less exclusively with endlessly reincarnating magical "tulkus" and high Adepts who were said to be always embodied in the ecclesiastical authorities of the traditional Vajrayana organizations. This more or less exclusive identification of Enlightened Adepts with ecclesiastical hierarchies is an ordinary or popular device of social, cultural, and political power. Even though it may have made some kind of sense in the context of the pre-invasion culture of Tibet, it is not a necessary feature of the Vajrayana system. The Free Adepts, or those who are moved to Truth and Awaken by whatever trial of means, are the real heart of the Vajrayana tradition of Bodhisattvas (as well as all other traditions), and even though such beings may have also appeared in the form of authorities in the traditional Tibetan hierarchy, it is the tradition of spontaneously appearing Adepts that grants fundamental authenticity to the Vajrayana Way, just as it is the Transcendental philosophy (expressed in the "Mahamudra" version of the Mahayana philosophy of mind and Enlightenment), rather than the magical-mystical yogic philosophy, that is the reason why the Vajrayana is an authentic form of Buddhism rather than merely a species of fourth to fifth stage yogism.

Institutions are inevitable and necessary for the orderly transmission of philosophical Teachings, practices, and cultural structures for practice in the larger world of any generation, and from one generation to the next. Therefore, each of the three earlier yanas of Buddhism as well as the newly arising Advaitayana Buddhism are associated with unique institutions. But all such institutions must be regarded as creative processes rather than as fixed entities, and they must constantly be purified of the dross of accumulated limitations that temporarily develop through accommodation to the outer or popular domain, or that arise whenever the lesser (or exoteric and esoteric) conceptions (belonging to the first six stages of life) begin to dominate or obscure the greater or ultimate Teaching of the seventh stage of life. Therefore, the great institutions are self-purifying. And Adepts continually appear to purify, realign, or redirect their own institutional traditions. Likewise, from time to time, Great Adepts appear to purify, realign, and redirect all institutions and all traditions, and so also to produce a new tradition that is built upon the foundation of all that came before. My own Work is of this last kind.

XI
Gautama's Problem

Gautama defined cônditional or "born" existence in the terms of a problem, and he described the Way of Transcendental Realization in the terms of a solution to the originally presumed "problem" of born existence. He declared that conditional existence in any form (or as any individuated being) is (1) necessarily temporary (or always changing), (2) only the product and expression of conditional causes (rather than of some Divine Cause or of some immortal internal and personal essence), and (3) inherently, always, and ultimately disturbed, frustrated, confounded, bewildered, deluded, and summarized as suffering.

On the basis of this analytical summary of the status of conditional existence as a problem, Gautama built his program for release. Once he was able to define conditional existence in the terms of a problem with specific features, he could indicate the process and the state of release as a logical solution that followed inevitably once the specific original problem was accepted as a factual description of the status of born existence. In fact, Gautama's intention to motivate his hearers (and himself) toward the state of release was the principle that caused him to consider and describe conditional existence in the terms of a problem and the Way in the terms of a solution to that problem.

For Gautama, the matter of ultimate importance was the Samadhi or unconditional Realization of the Transcendental (or Nirvanic) Condition. And it is the Realization of That that is the common Truth of all Great Adepts. What distinguishes such Adepts from one another are (1) the characteristic limitations of the first six stages of life that may yet affect their thought and communication, and (2) motives and tendencies in their Teaching to Argue the Way toward Realization rather than simply express ultimate Realization Itself. Therefore, what distinguishes Gautama from other Buddhist and Advaitist Adepts is his sixth stage "realist" orientation toward descriptions of existence and his intention to Argue for Realization on the basis of a description of existence that implies release as the only appropriate or rational goal of human endeavor.

I have already criticized the content of Gautama's "realism." In this brief essay I simply want to indicate that Gautama's motive for considering the Way of Transcendental Realization in the terms of "realism" was simply his commitment to motivate people toward Realization via a rational consideration (or a logic of inevitability). "Realism" was Gautama's tool of motivation. Above all, he wanted to motivate people toward release, and the logic of "realism" seemed to him to be the most direct means.

The language of "realism" did not provide Gautama with the means to describe Realization or the Transcendental Condition Itself. Therefore, his commitment to "realism" (and to the role of motivator or cause of the Way toward release) made it necessary for him to be silent when asked to describe the Transcendental Condition. There is no doubt that he had Realized that Condition and that he wanted all beings to Realize that Condition. But his language of Argument was not equipped or intended to describe the very Condition that was the ultimate import of his life and

Teaching. This is the surest indicator that Gautama's "realism" and Gautama's "problem" are simply devices of mind developed for the sake of motivating beings toward release via the logical force of certain basic mental propositions.

Gautama is reported to have been reluctant to Teach after his Realization. He felt that the matter of Realization was too subtle or profound to be grasped by people generally. His reluctance was primarily based on his feeling that most people are not (and could not easily be) motivated toward ultimate Realization. He was eventually persuaded to Teach, based on an altruistic commitment to at least those few who would be ripe for "hearing" the Truth. But, clearly, Gautama's principle concern was directed toward the inability of people to be changed in their minds to a sufficient degree to be moved toward Transcendental Realization rather than mechanical ego-fulfillment. And Gautama's Argument of the Way may thus be seen as a creative result of his will to motivate as many people as possible toward Realization.

The "realist" Argument must, therefore, be seen not simply as a patently or exclusively true conception of conditional existence but as a kind of method or device—a kind of yogic means, which may be called "Buddhi Yoga,"* or the exercise of the discriminative and intuitive faculty of mind in order to understand the process of conditional existence and, on that basis, Awaken to the Transcendental Condition. Such Buddhi Yoga is a sixth stage yoga that focuses on the exercise of the processes of the abstract or discriminative mind in relation to all the internal and extended aspects of the body-mind. In this manner, it stands in contrast with the lower functional yogas (of the types that characterize the first five stages of life), which exploit the comparatively grosser mechanisms of sensory mind, emotion, nervous system, body, and so forth for the sake of mystical states of contemplative absorption.

---

* The term *buddhi-yoga* appears for the first time in the *Bhagavad Gītā* (X. 10 and XVIII. 57), though it is used there in the context of an "emanationist" philosophy. The *buddhi* is the mental faculty of discernment.

This Buddhi Yoga also stands in contrast with the sixth stage yoga of traditional Advaitism, which is the "idealist" yoga, usually called "Jnana Yoga." The method of such Jnana Yoga is, like that of Buddhi Yoga, to exercise the faculty of discriminative and intuitive mind, or what is traditionally called "vijnanamaya-kosha," the "intellectual sheath," which is the fourth most subtle of five functional layers that are observed to compose the human individual. (The three preceding layers are the gross body, then the functional energies that move the gross body, followed by the lower or sensory mind. And even subtler than the "sheath" or faculty of discriminative and intuitive mind is the core of individual existence, the "anandamaya-kosha" or sheath of individuated bliss, which corresponds to the "immortal" or transmigrating soul, or the "atman," the essence of individuality.) The exercise of Jnana Yoga is directed first to the analytical differentiation of the "knowing" consciousness from the grosser faculties or structures of self (represented by the three lower or grosser sheaths). And this is followed by the ultimate exercise, which is the inversion of the mind upon its even subtler root (anandamaya-kosha, the innermost sheath or blissful and essential core of self). This ultimate exercise of inversion upon the atman is done until the individuated character of the self-essence is transcended in Transcendental Awakening.

Buddhi Yoga specifically avoids the "idealistic" gesture of the inversion of mind (or attention) upon anandamaya-kosha in order to develop a state of absorptive identification with the atman. Instead, it rigorously maintains the position of vijnanamaya-kosha (the fourth most subtle) itself, and thus works to observe, understand, and directly transcend the inner atman (the fifth or most subtle sheath of the conditional self) as well as the three lower sheaths. Jnana Yoga also eventually transcends the limits of the anandamaya-kosha or atman, but it does so only after submitting vijnanamaya-kosha to anandamaya-kosha and thus entering attention into a process of absorptive internal contemplation.

It is simply this specific difference in technique of <u>approach</u>

to Realization that distinguishes Buddhi Yoga (or the yoga of "realism") from Jnana Yoga (or the yoga of "idealism"). But both of these sixth stage techniques ultimately pass beyond themselves to Transcendental Awakening (to the Condition of self and not-self), or the seventh stage of life. Therefore, neither the philosophies (of "realism" as opposed to "idealism") nor the techniques (of Buddhi Yoga as opposed to Jnana Yoga) of the sixth stage schools should be regarded as ultimately or exclusively true. Each simply represents a different but characteristically sixth stage approach to the same Transcendental (or seventh stage) Realization. And as sixth stage philosophies and methods of approach to Transcendental Realization, both the "realist" and the "idealist" yogas contain inherent limitations.

The most basic limiting convention of Advaitist "idealism" is its orientation toward inversion upon the individuated self-essence (or internal atman). It is that very self-essence and that very tendency toward self-absorptive inversion that must be transcended before the seventh stage Awakening can occur in the Advaitist Way. And the process whereby absorption in the independent self-essence is transcended is enacted via vijnanamaya-kosha, the understanding that characterizes the free "buddhi," or the intelligence of free attention. Therefore, even the Advaitic sage must admit the ultimate superiority of the faculty of vijnanamaya-kosha over the three lower sheaths as well as the innermost sheath—although all of the sheaths or functions of self (including vijnanamaya-kosha) are ultimately transcended in radical intuition of the Transcendental Identity or Condition of conditional existence.

In contrast to the Advaitist Way, the most basic limiting convention of Buddhist "realism" is its orientation toward concentration of attention on the totality of phenomenal existence as a problem (or a merely conditional process). It is that very problem and the very tendency toward fixation of attention in the conventional or merely phenomenal condition (rather than the Transcendental Condition of all conditions) that must be transcended before the seventh stage Awakening can occur in the original Buddhist Way. The Buddhi Yoga exercised in the "realist" tradition rightly avoids the illusions and merely temporary or conditional attainments associated with contemplative absorption in the various parts of the self or in the play of the not-self. But that very faculty which is engaged merely to observe (rather than become absorbed in) the phenomenal conditions of existence must ultimately and radically transcend itself via intuition of the Transcendental or Real (rather than conventional) Condition of mind, or attention, or all that is self and not-self.

Both Buddhism and Advaitism Realize and proclaim an ultimate Truth or Real Condition that transcends the world, the body-mind-self, the conventional ideas about God (or the Transcendental Reality), and the sixth stage conventions of "realism" and "idealism." I Teach a Way that is founded from the beginning in that Truth and Condition that is Realized in the seventh stage of life by all Great Adepts. The Advaitayana Buddhism that I Teach is not founded on the conventions of "realism" or "idealism" but on the Transcendental Truth or Condition of conditions. I Argue in modes of consideration that express that Realization and that specifically avoid any appeal to the sixth stage conventions of "realistic" and "idealistic" views of existence. I simply call attention to the direct understanding of whatever is presently arising. Since I call simply for such understanding (or discriminative insight), rather than for the absorptive inversion of mind or attention in any part of self or not-self, the practice of the Way that I Teach may rightly be viewed as a form of Buddhi Yoga (rather than Jnana Yoga). However, I do not call attention merely to notice that the arising conditions of self and not-self are merely phenomenal and thus problematic (or demanding to be escaped or eliminated). I do not call for understanding in the conventional mode of "realism." Rather, I call for direct observation of all modes of self (or all five "sheaths"), in the terms of all of its relational states of association, in combination with whatever is conventionally presumed to be not-self (rather than in the terms of its exclusive or essential interior, separate from all relations). And I call for the observation that all the modes of the self/not-self process (including the very conceptions of "realism" and "idealism") are forms of self-contraction, or the gesture of differentiation, separation, limitation, and individuation. Whenever this self-contraction is directly and presently observed and understood as a process, there is a simultaneous intuition, a feeling beyond, in which the Condition within which and from which the self-contraction is arising stands out as the Obvious. And, in likeness to the spirit of Jnana Yoga (and in contrast to the spirit of the Buddhi Yoga of conventional "realism"), the radical intuition that is the heart of the Way that I Teach is fully equipped to make positive reference to That which is Realized. It transcends the body-mind-self, or all of the conditional modes of attention. It is not merely an inner essence or consciousness. It is not merely the negation of phenomenal states. It is Radiant Transcendental Being. It is the Transcendental Self or Identity of the apparently individuated consciousness (not in the sense that the self-contraction or ego in itself is Transcendental, Divine, Nirvanic, or Free, but in the sense that the self-contraction can be observed to be a direct contraction from or within the Condition of Radiant Transcendental Being, and in this manner the conditional and also internal self is inherently transcended in the Transcendental or Divine Self, wherein all other selves and the world are also arising). The Consciousness that is Realized when self-consciousness is re-cognized (or known again exactly in the form in which it happens) and thus transcended is Transcendental Consciousness, or Consciousness prior to differentiation, separation, individuation, or limitation. It is the Radiant Love-Bliss of which all apparent conditions (or all that is self and not-self) are merely apparent, transparent, unnecessary, and nonbinding modifications. And when this Realization is most profound (so that there is native Identification with Radiant Transcendental Being rather than with the phenomenal self or the independent and individuated noumenal self), the Way is simply to Abide as That, recognizing and inherently transcending all conditions in That, so that self and not-self are Transfigured,

Transformed, and ultimately Outshined in That Radiant Divine Being.

We may say, then, that the direct intuition of the Radiant Transcendental Being is my "method" or Way. And the Ways of "realism" and "idealism" (as opposed to my Way of radical Transcendentalism) are relatively indirect methods for Realizing the same Radiant Transcendental Being. The Advaitist's "atman" (or the philosophy and technique of ultimate inversion, which is the sixth stage development of the animistic tradition of Emanationism) is the "idealist's" method. And Gautama's "problem" (or the description of conditional existence based on his "realism") is Gautama's method. We may rightly say that the Arguments for the Way that are developed in all traditional or conventional schools (of "realism" or "idealism" or whatever) are in fact forms of method rather than simple or patently or exclusively true descriptions of what is. (Therefore, the differences among the various traditional schools of the first six stages of life are nothing but differences in method. The differences are not absolute—such that only one school can represent the true description of what is. Rather, all the schools point toward the seventh stage Realization, and in the seventh stage of life all the schools are ultimately resolved and unified in the Only and One Truth.)

According to Gautama, conditional existence is suffering—necessarily and inherently. This view may be useful to motivate the mind toward release, but it is not patently, factually, inherently, necessarily, or exclusively true. From the point of view of Transcendental Realization, conditional existence is not merely conditional existence (nor is it, in itself, a condition of present or potential happiness, and thus a condition to be embraced for its own sake). Rather, conditional existence is, in Truth, an inherently transparent or merely apparent, unnecessary, and non-binding modification of the Real Condition (or Radiant Transcendental Being). Because of this, even philosophers in the Buddhist tradition other than Gautama were moved to consider conditional existence in terms that are not at all framed in the "realist" mode. And it is because of their convergence in the singularity of Realization in the seventh stage of life that both "realistic" and "idealistic" modes of consideration of the Way toward Realization are independent but equally adequate (or inadequate, or conventional) designs for consideration in the stages of approach toward Realization.

Just so, since it is the case that only the ultimate Truth is the Truth—or only the Realization that characterizes the seventh stage of life is the Realization of Truth—I have been moved to consider the Way strictly in terms of the direct observation and understanding of moment to moment existence and in the terms of Realization Itself, or the ultimate Reality or Truth of the seventh stage of life. The Ways of the "realist" schools and the Ways of the "idealist" schools represent Arguments for Realization that are based either on the conceptions of the sixth stage of life exclusively or on the conceptions of the sixth stage of life plus those of the stages of life earlier than the sixth. The Way of Radical Understanding or Divine Ignorance—or the Radical Transcendentalism of Advaitayana Buddhism—is a consideration of the Way based on conceptions that reflect the disposition of the seventh stage of life. Therefore, in my most fundamental Argumentation of the Way, I do not make use of the argumentative devices (or the problem/solution logic) of "realism," nor do I appeal to the metaphysical arguments and conventional belief systems of traditional "idealism." I simply call attention to the always present context of awareness, so that its precise features may be observed.

If this is done, the unnecessary activity of contraction is found to be obvious (even in the form of any kind of mental conception—whether "realistic," "idealistic," or whatever). And if the self-contraction is obvious (and seen to be a secondary and unnecessary feature of awareness), then every form and moment (and concept) of such contraction can be so observed, understood, and transcended. And when every form of contraction that is superimposed on every present moment is thus observed, understood, and transcended, the Radiant Transcendental Condition of

Being stands free as the Obvious (Its Status self-evident prior to all categories, conceptions, and persuasions of mind). Such is the unique process of the Way that I Teach. And when the Real Condition (rather than the conditional and independent self) is most profoundly Realized, then the Way is simply and tacitly and always presently to recognize all conditions of apparent self and not-self in That (rather than embracing or avoiding or escaping any conditions whatsoever), until all noticing of conditional states is Outshined in Radiant Transcendental Divine Love-Bliss.

In my Teaching Work I have, like all other Adepts before me, encountered and suffered the absence of interest and intelligence (or free attention) as well as the absence of motivation (or free energy) in those who have come to me. Such is the perennial limitation of un-Enlightened egoity. My basic "method" for dealing with all of that does not involve resort to "realistic" and "idealistic" arguments. My fundamental "method" is simply to persist in (1) directing the attention of everyone to the radical process of understanding, and (2) making the setting of Good Company, "Satsang," or self-transcending Transcendental Communion with the Spiritual Master and the Radiant Divine or Transcendental Being, into the one and constant context of existence (rather than any other presumption based on the conventions of the merely egoic mind).

XII
Three Fires

1. Gautama's Fire

Gautama's principal and most concrete image of born existence was that of fire or heat. His philosophical conceptions are feeling-conceptions (rather than merely intellectual or verbal-mental conceptions). His philosophy has its concrete basis in a profound feeling-sensitivity to the status of born existence. He felt that born existence (or every form of psycho-physical process) is literally on fire. That fire is the concrete feeling-context of all desire. And desire, in Gautama's view, is the prime mover or creative cause of all forms of motion, effect, thought, experience, birth, self, and death.

Gautama's entire philosophy is devoted to convincing us of the existence of this fire and motivating us to put it out. Therefore, his Argument is first of all devoted to waking us up to the fact that we are on fire (much as one would try to call someone's attention to the fact that a burning coal had fallen into his or her clothing). His first effort is devoted to the establishment of the conviction in his hearers that they are on fire—which is to say that born existence is inherently painful, burning, or driven by desire.

Gautama's second great effort is devoted to those who have heard his "Fire Sermon"*—or who are attentive to their actual condition and who are thus convinced that they are on fire. Therefore, the second great aspect of Gautama's Argument is the description of the Way (or Method) whereby this fire can be quenched. And that Way is associated with another principal concrete image. It is the image of coolness, or a cooling air that ultimately blows out the fire. That coolness is the central meaning of "Nirvana" in Gautama's philosophy. And the Way of Gautama's Buddhism is simply a practical effort to cool (or truly understand) and finally quench (or transcend) the fire that is born existence.

In Gautama's view, born existence is on fire, but the fire is not necessary, and it can be cooled (or relieved) and ultimately quenched (or transcended). The fire is originally ignited and also continually reignited by desire (or a motion and a departure from an original tranquility, which is Transcendental Bliss). Therefore, the fire can be cooled and eventually snuffed out by simply cancelling the ignition or initiation of self (or all the kinds of independent and individuated psycho-physical states).

* See *Mahāvagga* I. 21.

Gautama's Method for cooling the fire took the form of a number of instructive arguments and techniques. The state of the individual would determine which instructive argument would seem convincing and, therefore, which technique would be applied in practice.

The lesser "hearers" would devote themselves primarily to conservative personal and moral disciplines. But such disciplines are not sufficient for ultimate quenching, since they are themselves ego-based and desire-based (and would thus cause the practice to be perpetual rather than temporary and finally conclusive). Personal and moral disciplines are generally necessary aspects of the daily practice of serious practitioners, and they do indeed have a "cooling" effect, but they are only a beginner's practice, or a rudimentary aspect of the general practice. The cooling effect produced by disciplines and absorptive meditations eventually becomes <u>desirable</u> for its own sake, and the enjoyment of it reinforces the bondage to self (and the illusion that the self is not on fire). Therefore, there is an ultimate form of practice in Gautama's Way (and in any true form of the Transcendentalist Way). That practice transcends the egoic body-mind, its desires, its states, and its attainments. And that ultimate form of practice required (and still requires) ultimate or most radical "hearing" or understanding of the principal Argument of the Teaching. Therefore, only those who achieved great maturity on the basis of the original disciplines, or who were otherwise naturally equipped with a profoundly free intelligence (or with energy and attention free of the profound burdens of gross and also subtle personality limitations) could understand Gautama's more radical instructive arguments and so practice his more radical technique of quenching.

Gautama's most radical instructive argument is simply that the born ego (or psycho-physical self) is an utterly and entirely painful and unnecessary process. Those who could "hear" this argument would not be moved merely to improve or gradually to purify themselves. They would be utterly and directly Awakened to a free disposition, unconcerned with born existence. And the

Awakened Way (or natural process that transcends all motivated and self-based techniques) they would be moved to practice would follow inevitably and naturally from this original understanding and dispassionate freedom from all the implications and states of apparent or born existence. That Way is Samadhi Itself, or native Abidance in the Transcendental (or Nirvanic) Condition that becomes Obvious when attention is no longer fixed upon conditional motives and states. It is Sahaj Samadhi, the Native Condition (prior to desire, fire, and cooling), in which there is utter indifference to the body-mind and its states and relations, but in which there is also profound Awakeness to the Transcendental or Nirvanic Condition.

Gautama's Teaching developed spontaneously from his own Samadhi. (Such is also the case with my own Teaching and the Teaching of all Great Adepts.) His Great Argument is not merely a call to discipline, or to blow cool breaths on the fire of self. Such is only a lesser aspect of his Teaching—or that part that first attracts the gross personality. Gautama's Great Argument is basically a call to Samadhi, or Nirvana Itself, which is Oblivious to the born self and all conditional possibilities, but Awake to the Inherent Bliss of the Transcendental Reality (or That which is Obvious in the Samadhi of utter self-transcendence).

I do not Argue the Way on a basis that depends on negative images or on the problem-categories of conventional self-awareness. Nor is practice of the Way that I Teach limited to self-discipline and the search for meditative or mystical absorptions of attention, since the pursuit of such means or ends for their own sake is self-based, inherently Narcissistic, and bereft of real understanding. I call for direct or radical understanding of self in every moment. Those who "hear" me most profoundly understand that the self (and thus the entire process of conditional attention) is only and entirely an unnecessary contraction. And this understanding (or most subtle meditation) ultimately allows That in which the contraction is always occurring to be Self-Revealed as the Obvious. Sahaj Samadhi is simply Awakeness to That which is Obvious when all forms of conditional or egoic attention are recognized as unnecessary instants of self-contraction (or separation from the prior or Transcendental Condition and into an illusion of limitations). And such Samadhi is beyond all forms of meditation (since meditation is an act of conditional or egoic attention in relation to one or another kind of object or Object). Therefore, my own Way, like the Way of Gautama, is a call to the Samadhi (or free conscious Realization) of the Real, which is Transcendental, beyond all differences, and thus beyond all descriptions.

2. Vedic Fire

Gautama's Teaching developed as a consideration outside the traditional and popular culture of his time. Gautama and his Teaching were part of the anti-Vedic and non-Vedic "underground" of India, twenty-five hundred years ago. (The traditions of Jainism and Samkhya also developed in that same milieu.) Therefore, the most characteristic features of Gautama's Teaching represent trends of consideration that are the polar opposites of the even more ancient traditional conceptions of Vedic culture.

As I have already indicated, the ancient Vedic tradition of India was, like the traditions that appeared everywhere in the ancient world, a development of the basic or most primitive "philosophical" consciousness of mankind. That "philosophy" (or primitive psychology) is best represented by the concept of "animism." And animism is the basis of all primitive religious and spiritual "technology" or craft—which technology or craft is generally called "shamanism."* The root-idea that developed from the primitive animistic and shamanistic culture was that of the Divine Emanation of the living world of events and beings

---

* This reading of the relation between animism and shamanism differs markedly from the interpretation given, for instance, by Mircea Eliade, who regards the two as exclusive of one another. However, this anti-evolutionistic interpretation is due to Eliade's overevaluation of the significance of the shamanistic motif of the soul's ascent (which he does not consider in "emanationist" terms).

(all of which are conceived to be inhabited and controlled by an invisible "spirit-force" or life-force, which is conceived either to be individuated as specific and independent entities or else to be all-pervading as an Ultimate Entity). And this primitive religious and spiritual culture is the origin of all forms of polytheism, monotheism, ritual cultism, magical practice, yogic mysticism, and so forth.

This great Emanationist tradition is associated with a number of primary ideas that describe existence in the Emanated worlds, but the principal idea is that of <u>sacrifice</u>. The Emanationist culture of practice and the Emanationist world-view are founded on an elaborate conception of life as a ritual sacrifice. Sacrifice is conceived to be the single principle that describes the origin and the structure of the world, the individual, the society, and all the forms of action whereby each part or individual is related to the whole and to every other part or individual. Likewise, in the Emanationist view, sacrifice is the logic of all action on the part of human individuals, gods, and the ultimate God. And sacrifice is the principal means whereby happiness (or "salvation") is attained.

To be sure, all of the separate cultures of the ancient world developed unique cultural features, and as they developed through time, each cult or tradition developed its own language of sophisticated philosophy and theology. But all of the ancient systems were basically founded on the same animistic base. All conceived of Nature and the individual as being inhabited and controlled by invisible being (the "soul" in the individual and, in the case of monotheism, the "Great Soul" or God of Nature) and invisible forces (the individual's life-energy, the spirit-entities that pervaded all space, the "gods" or powers that controlled the natural world, and, in the case of monotheism, the One God-Spirit that pervaded or ultimately controlled all beings and all of Nature). The ancient Emanationist cultures generally conceived of the world as the product of sacrifice (on the part of God or gods). And, likewise, it was presumed that, since individual or creaturely existence was produced by the sacrifice of God or the gods, every creature is under obligation to fulfill the Law of sacrifice if it is to achieve and maintain a happy state in this world and the next. Therefore, the basis of all traditional cultures of the ancient world was the systematic description and performance of all kinds of ritualized sacrifices (whereby the connection was constantly reestablished between individuals and society, and between individuals, or collections of individuals, and the invisible forces or beings that controlled and affected them).

In the cultures of pluralistic animism and polytheism, the system was devoted to establishing magical, religious, moral, and mystical relations with (and, ultimately, control over) all kinds of individuated entities and powers in the realm of Nature. And in monotheistic cultures the system was devoted to establishing magical, religious, moral, and mystical relations with (and, ultimately, control over) the One Ultimate Entity and Power in or above the realm of Nature. In either case, there were complex rituals of personal and social behavior, magical or ceremonial activity, psychological and internal mystical disciplines, and a whole range of associated psycho-physical states or experiences that were the "rewards" or effects of right action (or right sacrifice). And if we understand all of this (which means that we must first be free of the provincial mind of our limited dogma or tradition) it is clear that there is no <u>ultimate</u> or <u>absolute</u> difference between the national traditions of Christianity, Judaism, Islam, Hinduism, and all of the shamanistic tribal religions of the ancient and the modern world. All of the Emanationist systems are variations on the one idea of sacrifice as the means of participatory relationship between individuals, groups, societies, energies, or powers—and between all of these and the Ultimate Energy or Power or Being.

The Vedic tradition was simply the systematic cultural system of ritual action (or sacrifice) in the setting of ancient India. It was devoted to maintaining the orderly process of ritual sacrifices at every level of individual existence, the society as a whole, and in all the hierarchical planes of existence in and beyond the realm of Nature. And that sacrificial system was, like the sacrificial systems in all other animistic, shamanistic, and

Emanationist traditions, founded on one basic exercise. It was the ritual of transforming and "sending up" an offering through submission of the offering to fire.

The essence of ritual sacrifice is, therefore, most concretely summarized and contained in the image of fire. Just as Gautama's (and, in general, the non-Emanationist's) principal and most concrete image of born existence was that of fire or heat, the principal and most concrete Vedic (and, in general, Emanationist) image of born existence was also that of fire or heat. But the two traditions (Emanationist and non-Emanationist) stand, at least in argument, in stark opposition and contrast to one another.

"Gautama's fire" is not the same as the "Vedic fire." Gautama's philosophy was specifically intended to represent an abandonment of the Emanationist views of immortal soul, ultimate God (or Reality as Cause), and life as a ritual bond of necessary sacrifices (all of which were intended to produce one or another result for the pleasure or benefit of the ego). Gautama's fundamental resistance to the Vedic system was not primarily based on a revulsion to priestcraft and ceremonial rituals of sacrifice. What he opposed most fundamentally was the conception of life (or born existence) as a necessary state to be reinforced and continued for the sake of its own continuation and experiential fulfillment. He did not believe there could be any final experiential fulfillment in the conditional realm of Nature, but he did firmly believe that conditional existence in any "born" or manifest form is inherently painful, deluded, self-possessed, fruitless, and unnecessary. Therefore, for Gautama (and for all non-Emanationists or ascetical philosophers) born existence is indeed on "fire" with the causative motion of desire, and that fire should, therefore, be controlled, quenched, and transcended as the means for transcending born existence itself.

By contrast, the Vedic Emanationist philosophers conceived of born existence as the product of Divine Causation, and thus born existence was presumed to be basically necessary, good, and capable of both temporal and ultimate fulfillment. The Vedic Emanationists (along with all other Emanationists) basically conceived of individuated existence as an effect of Divine Causation rather than of merely phenomenal and mechanical causation. They did, however, presume that self-possessed existence (rather than simple created individuation) was the essence of delusion, pain, and negative destiny. Therefore, the Emanationist cultural systems are all based on primary Law—the Law of sacrifice—which is the means whereby individuated existence is to be constantly purified, directed beyond itself, related to beings and powers (or Being and Power) beyond itself, and thus made to cause (or attract to itself) all kinds of pleasurable fulfillment and happy destiny (in this world and in the world or worlds or futures after death).

The non-Emanationist view, exemplified by Gautama's conception of fire, conceives of born existence as a negative or unnecessary and non-ultimate condition. Therefore, that view considers the human being to be on fire (and thus to be in need of cooling, quenching, and the ultimate transcendence of born existence itself). But the Emanationist view, exemplified by the Vedic conception of fire, conceives of born existence as a positive condition, or a condition that can both fulfill and transcend itself (not by bringing itself to an end, but by always releasing and going beyond its present state of limitations, and thus always moving into a higher plane in the scale of manifest existence). Transformation of self (rather than dissolution of self) seems to be the reasonable goal in the Emanationist view, because of the basic presumption that individuated existence is caused by (or inheres in) immortal and omnipotent forces, or even Caused by an ultimate Divine Being or Transcendental Reality. Therefore, that view considers the human being to be a fire-bearer, a kind of priest, who can always go beyond present limitations to future pleasures and fulfillments (either in the human world or in higher worlds) if he or she will conform to the law of sacrifice (and thus use the principle of fire to positively transform his or her existence).

Of course, the Vedic or Emanationist conception of fire does presume that born existence can fail to realize happiness. There is even the idea that human birth is auspicious only because it is capable of changing itself into a higher form via sacrifice (whereas in itself it is merely mortal and low in the scale of Nature). Therefore, the Emanationist idea of life carries with it the implication that one must practice the techniques of sacrifice (ritually, magically, religiously, morally, or mystically) as a great and profound effort of Wisdom if there is to be any hope of positively and ultimately transforming one's state of existence. Just as Gautama's Way requires ascetical success in order to achieve self-dissolution, the Emanationist Way requires magical and mystical success in order to achieve self-transformation. And each Way has its inherent and characteristic or unique double-binds and loopholes that serve as traps for all those who are not yet Awake.

All of the concepts and practices of philosophy, religion, and spirituality in the first five stages of life are expressions of the Emanationist logic (except for the materialistic philosophies that are produced when human beings fail to grow beyond the rudimentary mentality of the first three stages of life). Therefore, all of traditional religion and mysticism in the first five stages of life is based upon the Emanationist idea of sacrifice as the primary means of world-creation and of happiness (or "salvation" from negative destinies). And, for this reason, the primary and most concrete image of all such traditions is that of fire. The Vedic "psychology of fire" is simply one great example of human culture based on these presumptions.

Fire is method (or a means of transformation) in the "idealist" or Emanationist schools, just as fire is the primary characteristic of suffering (or that which is to be released or overcome) in the non-Emanationist or sixth stage "realist" schools (such as that of Gautama). In the Emanationist schools of the first five stages of life (and even in the Emanationist schools of the sixth stage of life—such as those of Upanishadic Advaitism) the basic concrete metaphors for the process of sacrifice come from the ancient ritual use of fire in the making of ceremonial sacrifices. Fire (or heat) originally served as a method for transforming various sacrificed articles (or beings) via the process of cooking. It was through cooking in fire that gross sacrifices were transformed into subtle elements that could rise up and be visibly transported through the air to the subtle powers and beings (and gods or God) that were presumed to reside in the air. And whereas Gautama conceived of practice of the Way as the blowing of a cool breath on the fire of desire (in order finally to quench it), the Vedic tradition conceived of practice as a kind of bellows, or the blowing of air on heated coals to increase the intensity of the flame and its height of ascent, and so make the sacrifice more profound, total, and quick.

The gross ceremonial practices of fire sacrifice were only the lowest or most exoteric form of Emanationist culture. Such practices (and their priesthood) were intended to serve the lower class of humanity (or those not yet grown beyond the first three stages of life). And the same traditions that were devoted to exoteric ceremonialism and incantatory magic were also the bearers of exoteric teachings relative to the moral sacrifice of self. Thus, we can see both ceremonial (or magical) and moral exotericism in all the great ancient traditions (including Judaism and Vedic Hinduism).

The moral exotericism of the Emanationist schools was actually a sophisticated philosophical development of the original fire-culture of animistic shamanism. In that view, the individual self (or soul) was itself conceived to be the subject to be sacrificed (and thus transformed and returned to its original state of purity and subtlety, capable of rising to its natural home in the "air," or the Heaven above the Earth, beyond the daemonic spirits that were presumed to inhabit the lesser airy regions). The method of self-sacrifice was also that of transformation through fire. The "fire" in that case was self-transcending moral activity in relation to all others and to the society as a whole. Such action was conceived to produce "friction" between the self-centered motion of self and the other-directed motion of self, thus producing a kind of useful stress or "heat" that would purify the self-essence or soul of its gross desires and habits of mind, emotion, and body.

And it was this tribal system of moral exotericism (which provided a religious basis for human maturity in the terms of the first three stages of life) that provided the primary basis for the later national religious movements of the Emanationist traditions—such as Christianity and Islam (wherein the ceremonial and magical culture of literal elemental fire sacrifices was no longer to be a central occupation of the practice).

Just so, the Emanationist culture of sacrificial fire also extended into the esoteric domains of the fourth and fifth stages of life. In the fourth and fifth stage cultures, the individual ego or soul continues to be the subject to be sacrificed and transformed and sent upwards. In the fourth stage mode, the focus of practice includes the moral exotericism of self-transcending service or love of others, but it goes beyond the realm of human relations that are embraced for their own sake. The fourth stage "fire" or "heat" of practice is centered on the constant loving Remembrance of God (the One Being above all) or, in pluralistic cultures, constant loving remembrance of invisible creative powers and beings of all kinds (all of which are generally conceived in terms of some kind of ultimate unity). Thus, in the esoteric frame of the fourth stage of life, the desires to fulfill the personal and social possibilities of this world are either made secondary to or entirely abandoned for the purposes of Heaven or the heavens or the Divine in Itself. And in the esotericism of the fifth stage of life this process is extended to the fullest degree, so that the "fire-sacrifice" of self becomes a matter of the application of all kinds of mystical (or technical psycho-physical) means for permanently ascending beyond this world to the heavens or Heaven or Divine Being above the plane of gross Nature. Those mystical means develop the heat (or "tapas") of self-discipline to such a degree that an internal fire (or intensification of energy in the nervous system) develops in the lower or vital region of the body and rises up to the higher brain centers, producing the peculiar physical and psychic effects associated with mystical experience.

The "realist" point of view of Gautama's Buddhism is generally applied to an ascetical Way of practice that seeks to quench (or uncause) desire and bring an end to the causation of conditional selfhood in all its forms and planes. This sixth stage "realistic" method stands in contrast to that of the exoteric and esoteric traditions of the first five stages of life—all of which seek to transform desire (rather that quench it altogether) and to purify and transform and raise up the self or soul (rather than bring it to an end or uncreate it) toward a superior destiny in higher worlds, heavens, Heaven, or in a state of ascended contemplative self-forgetting or absorption in the Divine Being (conceived to be above, at the head of all causes and effects). Therefore, this difference between the traditional ideal of transformation of self rather than the more radical ideal of the cessation of the conditional self is the principal difference between Gautama's "fire" of "realism" and the Vedic "fire" of "idealism."

However, a sixth stage tradition also appeared within the fold of Emanationism. Its primary representatives are the schools of Upanishadic Advaitism and Advaita Vedanta. That tradition based its philosophy and practice on the foundation of the Emanationist design of the cosmos (descending and ascending in hierarchical planes, between relative subtlety and relative grossness). And it also based itself on the idea of self as an inherently undying (and thus immortal) and even unborn (and thus eternal or, ultimately, Transcendental Reality or Being). The sixth stage schools of Emanationist "idealism" simply extended the process of self-sacrifice (or the fiery "tapas" of self-transcendence) beyond the terrestrial and cosmic modes (where results were attained either low or high in the scale of Nature) into the Transcendental sphere of Awakening. Thus, the traditional Advaitist method is not devoted to the purification and transformation of the self-essence into a subtle form that can rise mystically (or in the after-death state) into the regions above. Rather, traditional Advaitism engaged the self (or the "I") in a more radical process of surrender into (or Identification with) the Transcendental Ground of Original and Acausal Consciousness, Being, and Bliss (prior to all categories of mind and conditional form).

The Emanationist view of "fire" is finally epitomized in the sixth stage Advaitist tradition (where self goes beyond transformation to Realize its ultimate Identity by sacrificing itself to the Transcendental Self behind the mechanics of the body-mind). And the non-Emanationist view of "fire" (as pain, or as the very self that is to be transcended) is epitomized in the sixth stage Buddhist tradition. It should be clear once again how Advaitism and Buddhism simply represent two sides of the same coin (or two versions of approach to the same ultimate or seventh stage Transcendental Realization). Both the Advaitist and original Buddhist conceptions of "fire" are associated with the purpose of ultimate and final transcendence of the conditional self (and its apparent states of knowledge and experience). The Buddhist practice, which seeks to cool the "fire" to the point of cessation, does in effect amount to a form of what the Emanationists call "tapas," or the "heat" (or concentrated effort) of self-transforming and self-transcending practice. And the Advaitist practice (which is grown upon the base of all the Emanationist rituals and yogas of transformation of self through application to the method of "fire-sacrifice") actually seeks to bring an end to the illusion or illusory necessity and independence of the conditional self. (Therefore, from the Advaitist point of view, just as much as from the original Buddhist point of view, the "fire" of desires and the conditional self are to be utterly transcended.) But it is in the Awakening of Free Transcendental Realization (or the seventh stage of life) that all the schools and traditions and progressive stages of life transcend their self-based limitations (and their conceptions of Reality or Truth as the Goal of practice rather than the Condition of the present moment).

3. Transcendental Fire

Gautama's "fire" is a concrete conception that epitomizes the final step in the sixth-stage process of progressive self-transcendence in the Way of the "realists." And the

Vedic "fire" is a concrete conception that epitomizes all of the steps (including the final step) in the six-stage process of progressive self-transcendence in the Way of the "idealists." "Transcendental Fire" is a concrete conception that epitomizes That which is finally Realized in the seventh stage of life by all who practice to the point of "Siddhi" or Completeness. And this image of "Transcendental Fire" is, therefore, the most basic concrete representation of the orientation of the Way that I Teach.

The Emanationists (or "idealists") and the non-Emanationists (or "realists") have traditionally considered their Ways in terms of the two basic conventional views of fire: either as cause (or an effective and creative tool of transformation) or as effect (the uncomfortable and apparently destructive heat of burning). In earlier essays I have also indicated how the two conventions (of "idealism" and "realism") also viewed the subjects of consciousness and light (or energy) from two basic but opposite points of view (either as source and cause or as phenomenon and effect). Likewise, the two traditions have considered the subject of "dharmas" (or all the causes of effects) from two basic but opposite points of view.

The Emanationist "idealists" are generally interested in "dharmas" in the sense of <u>causes</u>—or methods or techniques or programs of action that can produce desirable effects. Such "dharmas" include all kinds of ritual action, social action, belief, knowledge, mystical yoga, Transcendental philosophy, and so forth. Therefore, for the "idealist," "fire" (or the "fire-sacrifice") is a "dharma," or a traditionally prescribed technique of self-transformation and self-transcendence.

The non-Emanationist "realists" are generally interested in "dharmas" in the sense of <u>effects</u> (which may function as the causes of subsequent effects, but which have no ultimate status beyond the mechanical cause and effect process of phenomenal existence). Such "dharmas" include all of the elements or basic constituents of composite or phenomenal existence. Therefore, for the "realist," "fire" is a "dharma"—a quality or conditional element of born existence.

Three Fires

For the "idealist," "dharmas" are to be defined, enumerated, and practiced until their results are achieved. And for the "realist," "dharmas" are to be simply observed, understood, and ultimately overcome (in the acausal disposition of Enlightenment).

Even so, both "idealists" and "realists" are ultimately and equally concerned with "Dharma," or the "Dharma," which means the Way and the Truth of the Way—the ultimate Way or Process or Nature—of Transcendental Realization. Therefore, in their sixth stage modes (or in any of the modes of the first six stages of life) the "idealists" and the "realists" (and the Advaitins and the Buddhists) tend to associate their minds with rather opposite views of the same subjects. But both traditions are equally oriented and ultimately concerned with the "Transcendental Dharma," or the ultimate Way and Truth of the Perfected, Completed, or seventh stage of life. And, therefore, the seventh stage Adepts of all traditions Confess, in basically identical terms, the Realization of "Transcendental Fire."

"Transcendental Fire" is the "Dharma." The Ways of progressing toward Its Realization may differ in terms of conventions of mind and effort, but That which is ultimately Realized in the Event of utter self-transcendence is One, Transcendental, Radiant, Free, and beyond or prior to all limitations on Happiness.

The Way by which such Realization is either progressively or directly approached is traditionally considered to be the "Dharma" in all traditions. But in fact all practices that are means of approaching Realization are representations of a consciousness that belongs to the first six stages of life, and, therefore, all such "Dharmas" (or Ways) are actually only "dharmas" (or lesser techniques or "fires," associated with the pain or "fire" of egoity). Even so, such "dharmas" have their utility in the context of the stages of life in the traditional setting. And all the basic traditional "dharmas" or schools of technique can be seen to correspond to the various orientations of the stages of life in a naturally progressive pattern.

The first three stages of life are associated with the gross consciousness and terrestrial fulfillment of human beings. The "dharmas" of the first three stages include "Puja Yoga" (or self-sacrifice and participation in the Divine Sacrifice of world-creation and world-salvation, via ceremonial worship and magical prayer) and "Karma Yoga" (or self-sacrifice via "moral" or social and other-directed action). Both "idealistic" and "realistic" traditions maintain such beginner's "dharmas" (although they may call them by different names), and even such beginner's practices are at least implicitly devoted toward unity with and ultimate Realization of the Transcendental Reality, Condition, or Being.

The fourth stage of life is associated with the "dharma" of self-transcending love, trust (or faith), and surrender in direct relation to the Transcendental or Divine Being (or even to lesser entities or powers that are lower than "Heaven" in the scale of Nature, but which may act as intermediaries between Earth, or Man, and Heaven, or God). The most common name for this method of approach is "Bhakti Yoga," or the practice of <u>continuous</u> and <u>concentrated</u> self-devotion via heartfelt feeling-attention to the Ultimate Reality or Person, generally imaged in the form of God-Ideas, God-Names, and cultic Images, or the spiritually transformed person of an Adept (who is presumed to be transparent to the Divine or Transcendental Being). This "dharma" is grounded in the terrestrial ego, but it matures and gradually ascends into the cosmic scale.

The fifth stage of life is the basic stage of ascent into the cosmic domain above and beyond the material or lower elemental planes of Nature. It is the stage of life that represents the limit of fulfillment by conventional mystical means. The "dharmas" of this stage include all of the technical yogas of mystical ascent via progressively subtler techniques of psycho-physical self-sacrifice. And the results include the various conditional "samadhis" attainable during human embodiment (such as the visionary "savikalpa samadhi" and the ascended or conventional and conditional form of "nirvikalpa samadhi," which is associated with the transcendence of all mental forms or images). The "dharmas" of this stage include all kinds of yogic techniques, such as "Hatha Yoga" (in its complete classical form), "Kundalini Yoga," the mystical form of "Kriya Yoga," "Mantra Yoga," "Nada Yoga" (or "Shabd Yoga"), "Tantra Yoga" in all its forms, and the "Six Yogas of Naropa."

The sixth stage of life is the last of the progressive stages previous to Transcendental Awakening. It is the basic stage in which the transition is made from terrestrial and cosmic conceptions of the Divine or Real Being to conceptions of the Ultimate as the Transcendental Reality and Condition and Identity of all apparent beings and conditions. And the process of self-sacrifice is thus transformed from an effort that serves the development of knowledge and experience in the planes of the psycho-physical personality to a direct effort of utter self-transcendence. The principal traditional "dharmas" of this stage of life are the "Jnana Yoga" of the Emanationist or "idealist" tradition of Advaitism and what I call the "Buddhi Yoga" of the non-Emanationist or "realist" tradition of Buddhism.

All of the "dharmas" or methods or yogas of the first six stages of life are basically techniques of self-transcendence. As the stages progress toward the sixth, the functional level of the human being that provides the base for the exercise moves progressively from the grossest (physical or elemental) to subtler (emotional, then psychic) and finally to the most essential (or egoic essence). And the plane of awareness in which the goal or effect of the exercise is sought moves in a like manner, from the terrestrial (or gross) to the cosmic (or subtle) and finally to the Transcendental. But all of these efforts of self-sacrifice are basically involved in one process and effect: the transcendence of conditional attention (or of self, mind, body, and the relations of these) in the Condition that is their Ultimate Source. In other words, all of the "dharmas" are essentially forms of mind-control.

There is an old traditional text that summarizes all the stages of progression of the "dharmas" or practices that lead toward Transcendental Awakening. It is the *Yoga Aphorisms* of Patanjali. His system, which reflects the ancient system of techniques that progressively move toward the Realization that characterizes the seventh stage of life, is called "Ashtanga Yoga," or the "dharma" of eight stages. Those eight practicing stages can be seen as the progressive phases of the first six stages of life (although all of the phases are to one or another degree incorporated into the yoga of each stage of life). The "yamas" and the "niyamas" include all the basic things to do and not to do that constitute the original practical, moral, and ethical base of the first three stages of life as well as the religious and devotional base of the fourth stage of life. The practices of "asana" (or body-control), "pranayama" (or control of nerve-force and emotion via discipline of the breath), "pratyahara" (or control of sensory desires and outer-directed or sensory awareness), and "dharana" (or concentration of attention in a selected object) are the basics of self-control and mind-control in the fourth stage of life and the ground of the subtler techniques of the fifth stage of life. "Dhyana" (or meditative absorption in one or another object, high or low in the scale of possibilities) is the essence of maturity in the fourth stage of life and the basic practice in the fifth stage of life. And "samadhi" (or self-forgetting trance-absorption of attention in an object or condition) is the goal of the fifth stage of life. Just so, "samadhi," as a direct process or exercise that transcends the absorptive mystical techniques of the earlier steps in the "Ashtanga Yoga," is the essence of practice in the sixth stage of life. Beyond that, "Samadhi," or Awakening to the Transcendental Condition beyond the conditional context of the psycho-physical exercise of self (or attention), is the final goal of the sixth stage of life. And such "Samadhi" is the prior or already Realized basis of the seventh stage of life, so that "Samyama" (which is a capability associated with the mastery of all of the eight limbs of the yoga, and which ultimately involves tacit "recognition" or inherent transcendence of all phenomenal conditions) is the natural or inherent and spontaneous process in the seventh stage of life. (Whereas "samyama," in the conventional yogic sense of the demonstration of uncommon psycho-physical powers, is either an ordinary expression of success in the fifth stage of life or, at best, a secondary expression of Free Radiance in the seventh stage of life.)*

The six progressive stages of life are finally fulfilled in the seventh stage of life. All of the "dharmas" or yogas of progressive practice are forms of self-transcending mind-control that are finally fulfilled in the transcendence of conditional attention (or self-based awareness) in the Realization of Perfect Identification with the Love-Bliss of Radiant Transcendental or Divine Being. And that Realization, that Love-Bliss, that Radiant Transcendental (or Nirvanic) Identity or Being or Condition is the "Transcendental Fire."

4. Transcendental Fire and the Way That I Teach

The Way that I Teach is the radical or seventh stage process of understanding, or <u>prior</u> transcendence of the self-contraction in the Radiant Transcendental or Divine Being. But I address my Argument to all kinds of individuals, most of whom are suffering the most benighted predicaments of egoic failure in the first three stages of life. Therefore, those who consider my Argument are invited toward the ultimate practice via a progressive process of preparation, purification, and growth, wherein energy and attention are at least gradually released for the ultimate practice. That progressive process (or "yoga of consideration of the Way") is related to the various stages and forms of experiential attention that characterize the first six stages of life—<u>but</u> those forms of attention or experience that characterize the first six stages of life are constantly considered in a manner that gradually weakens and finally overcomes the compulsive tendency to associate with them.

Those who are just beginning this "yoga of consideration" generally take on the practices and disciplines of the "Way of

---

* In the *Yoga Sūtra* (III. 4) of Patañjali the term *saṃyama* or "constraint" refers to the practice of concentration, meditation, and *samādhi* upon one and the same object.

Divine Communion," which is a yoga of devotion to the Transcendental Divine that overcomes the neurotic complications of the first three stages of life and establishes equanimity via the ecstatic disposition of the fourth stage of life.

Those who become more mature through the "Way of Divine Communion" then begin to practice the "Way of Relational Enquiry," which represents the beginning of a more direct exercise of the point of view of understanding.

The "Way of Relational Enquiry" eventually develops into non-verbal re-cognition (or knowing again) and transcendence of the forms of self-contraction, and so the "Way of Re-cognition" begins. The "Way of Re-cognition" initially develops as self-transcending consideration of all of the features of the first five stages of life. And when that consideration achieves maturity, a form of instruction is given that considers or re-cognizes and directly transcends the mechanics of the sixth stage of life.

Finally, the disposition of the seventh stage of life Awakens, and the ultimate practice, or the "Way of Radical Intuition" begins.

The practice founded in the radically intuitive Awakened disposition of the seventh stage of life is the "Yoga of Transcendental Fire." In the seventh stage of life, there is no strategic effort to make attention ascend in the scale of Nature, but neither is there any strategic effort to separate attention from objects. There is no strategic effort to suppress or to exploit the self or the not-self. There is no strategic effort to fulfill the self or to achieve any particular plane of the not-self. Rather, self and not-self are simply understood and inherently transcended in the Blissful Reality. The practice is to Abide naturally in the Condition of prior Identification with the Radiant Love-Bliss of Transcendental or Divine Being and, on that basis, to recognize whatever arises to be only a transparent, unnecessary, and non-binding modification of the Transcendental Condition. In this manner, attention is naturally transcended in Transcendental Consciousness (Self, or Being), and the body-mind and its objects (high or low in the scale of Nature) are naturally Transfigured, Transformed, and ultimately Outshined through the recognition of their perfect inherence in a state of unqualified Identification with the Self-Radiance or Love-Bliss of the Transcendental Being. Therefore, both self (or attention) and not-self (or the objects of attention) are tacitly recognized and inherently transcended in the seventh stage disposition.

In every moment of recognition of self and not-self in the seventh stage of life, the body-mind is spontaneously released into a state of Identification with the "Transcendental Fire," Self-Radiance, or Love-Bliss of Divine Being. This process Transfigures and Transforms the body-mind, and it may, therefore, be associated with the movement of living energy in the body, toward (or to and from) the crown of the head (as in the fifth stage yogas). As long as there are objects arising to attention, the living energy is stationed at one or another functional level of the body-mind, or in one or another plane of the hierarchical scheme of Nature. But the process in the seventh stage of life is one in which attention (or self) and living energy (or objects and states) are recognized and transcended in the Transcendental Condition (which is eternally prior to all of the structures of the Realm of Nature). Therefore, energies may move, but the movement of attention is transcended via Identification with its Transcendental Source, and all moving energies are themselves finally Outshined in that same Source-Identity or Transcendental Condition.

In the seventh stage of life, all conditions of self and not-self are merely effective Reminders of the Transcendental Condition, and so they are transcended in the instant of their arising. Even so, they may continue to arise (although in an utterly "recognizable" form), and, in that case, the seventh stage of life is expressed in the form of "Sahaj Samadhi" (or Realization in the midst of conditions). But recognition of all events in the "Transcendental Fire" of Divine Being at least gradually (but inevitably) becomes the Outshining of self and Nature (or the radical transcendence of all conditional "noticing," all motions of conditional attention, or all appearances of self and/or not-self). Such is Bhava Samadhi, Nirvana Samadhi, or the ultimate (nondependent or unconditional) form of Nirvikalpa Samadhi (which is utterly beyond all mental modifications as well as all association with the ascending-descending mechanics of the nervous system, or embodied attention in the planes of Nature).

XIII
Worldliness, Selfishness, and Transcendence

The primary practical concerns of the Emanationist tradition are associated with the not-self (or the relations and conditions of the self). Because of its original or base orientation toward the Source of all emanations, the Emanationist tradition is primarily concerned either with (1) the acquiring of desirable conditions from the Divine Source or (2) the abandonment and transcendence of all relations and conditions for or in the Divine Source. The Emanationist schools of the first three stages of life are associated with the first of these two orientations—the magical and moral improvement of the relations and conditions of the self, or all that comes to the self from the Divine Source. The Emanationist schools of the fourth and fifth stages of life are concerned with the progressive abandonment of grosser relations and conditions of self for (or in order to attain) the Divine Source. In that case, the Divine Source is conceived to be eternally located above all non-eternal conditions and relations, but the Realization of the Divine Source does not require the dissolution or transcendence of either the eternal part of the self or any of the possible eternal relations and conditions of the eternal self. In contrast to the "idealism" of the Emanationist schools of the first five stages of life, the Emanationist (or Advaitist) schools of the sixth stage of life are concerned with the direct transcendence of all relations and conditions (and thus, ultimately, the conditional self itself) in_ the Divine Source (conceived to be the Transcendental Self behind the self and the not-self).

In contrast to the basic practical orientation of the Emanationist tradition, the non-Emanationist tradition (epitomized in the schools of Buddhism) is associated with concerns relative to the self. The non-Emanationist tradition is not based on the "idealism" of communion with the Source of self and not-self, but it is based on a "realistic" criticism of the self as the cause of association with the not-self. Therefore, its primary practical concerns are not associated either with improving the not-self (or the conditions and relations of the self) or with returning the self to a state of absorption in the Source of self and not-self. Rather, its primary practical concerns are associated with the transcendence of the conditional self.

Because of these basic differences in the original orientations toward life and the possibility of ultimate or Transcendental Realization, the practical concerns of the Advaitist and the Buddhist schools can be characterized in terms of two distinct and separate attitudes. The Advaitist schools are, as a practical matter, concerned to avoid worldliness, or attachment to all the forms or mechanics of not-self (and so the ultimate Emanationist discipline is the Advaitist discipline of inversion upon the essence of self). And the Buddhist schools are, as a practical matter, concerned to avoid selfishness, or attachment to all the forms or mechanics of self (and so the primary Buddhist discipline involves renunciation of self-centeredness).

The Way that I Teach is not founded on the worldly or other-worldly "idealism of Source" that characterizes the Emanationist tradition. Therefore, it is free of the overt and obsessive concerns for self-improvement (or improvement of the conditions and relations of self) that characterize conventional religious desire and effort in the first three stages of life. Likewise, it is free of the fourth to sixth stage taboos against worldliness (or full participation in the total functional life that characterizes the human psycho-physical personality).

The Way that I Teach is, like the traditional schools of

Buddhism, founded on a criticism of the self (although not in the terms of conventional "realism"). Therefore, it is associated with direct self-transcendence (rather than with self-fulfillment, self-transformation, or self-inherence). Even so, since it is founded on moment to moment understanding and transcendence of self as contraction, rather than on the "realistic" Buddhist method of strategic self-dissolution and strategic dissolution of self-centeredness, it is free of the conventional and often fetishistic taboos against selfishness and "selfness," or existence as the phenomenal self.

The Way that I Teach is the direct Way of the inherent transcendence of self and not-self. It is associated with both self-transcendence and Realization of the Transcendental (and thus Acausal) Source, Self, Reality, or Condition of all forms of conditional existence. And its primary practical discipline is the free (or non-problematic) observation, understanding, and transcendence of the act of self-contraction and all of its limiting power and effect.

XIV
Realization and Belief

1.

The Emanationist tradition has developed many forms of practice, according to the stage of life represented by the concerns of each particular school. One major common element that can be found in all of the Emanationist schools (or the Emanationist cultures of the first six stages of life) is the idea that faith (or the affirmation of belief) is the necessary basis for practice and the precondition for the attainment of the ultimate Revelation or Realization.

This basic notion is to be found in all the religions and all the magical and mystical systems of the first five stages of life. It is even the basis for the materialistic and social idealism of the first three stages of life (as can be seen in the fact that all atheistic political movements focus their first and primary efforts on the propagandization of a belief system and an idealistic orientation of self toward social altruism). Even Buddhism has historically accepted cultural modes and practices that reflect the "idealistic" motives of the first five stages of life (rather than the "realistic" disposition that characterizes the original Buddhism of the sixth stage of life), and in doing so, the affirmation of belief (or faith) in the Eternal Buddha and/or the "ideal" of Enlightenment was made an important part of Buddhist culture. And the tradition of Advaitism (which is, in its basic form, a sixth stage epitome of the Emanationist or "idealist" tradition) is also an epitome of the Way of faith (or affirmed belief), and, in its case, faith involves the affirmation of belief in the existence of the Transcendental Reality and Its unique identity with the inner self-essence or consciousness.

A practice cannot be based on the affirmation of belief (as a <u>precondition</u> for attaining the Revelation or Realization of Truth) unless it is presumed that there has already been an historical or universally applicable Revelation that justifies and calls for belief. Indeed, previous <u>general</u> Revelation is the basic means generated in the Emanationist cults for justifying and propagandizing the <u>method</u> of belief, or belief as <u>means</u>, for attaining the <u>personal</u> Revelation.

People in the West are profoundly familiar with this tactic in the domain of religion, politics, and science. The lives, incidents, and words or Revelations of such individuals as Moses, Jesus, Mohammed, Copernicus, Galileo, Newton, Jefferson, Darwin, Marx, Lincoln, Freud, and Einstein are the standard basis for propagandizing and motivating the mass culture of the Western world, and more and more of the total world. Indeed, the popular or exoteric mass culture of mankind has always depended on belief systems (or the motive and method represented by prior belief). And, therefore, there are so many historical Revelations of the "ultimate and final Truth" that the Truth Itself has become all but impossible to discern.

What I call the "Great Tradition" is that entire mass of traditions, reflecting all of the seven stages of human existence, that is the common inheritance of all of mankind in this time of universal communication, interrelatedness, and interdependence. It is no longer appropriate or even possible for individuals, cultures, or nations to justify absolute independence from other individuals, cultures, or nations—and it is no longer appropriate or possible to grant absolute or ultimately superior status to any historical Revelation, belief system, or conception of how things work. The entire Great Tradition must be accepted as our common inheritance. We need not (as a method for achieving Realization or Enlightenment) base our lives on the affirmation of belief in the Great Tradition (in part or as a whole) as Revelation, but we must overcome the provincialism of our minds (and, ultimately, the provincialism that is mind itself).

In most of its features or movements, the Great Tradition (whether materialistic or religious, secular or spiritual) bases itself on (1) the propagandization of a particular historical Revelation as a unique and sufficient, if not final, presentation of the Truth Itself (and not merely the Way to Truth), and (2) the propagandization of a Way of achieving personal Realization of that Truth via disciplines that express the affirmation of belief in the previous historical Revelation.

The sixth stage Way of Advaitism is simply an epitome of the Way of belief in the original Revelation that characterizes the Hindu approach to Truth in the first five stages of life. All the Hindu schools of the Emanationist tradition found their particular conceptions of the Way on the basis of what they conceive to be a faithful and orthodox appeal to the ancient "Holy Books" of the Vedic and Upanishadic eras. The Vedas and the Upanishads are granted the same status in Hinduism that is granted to the Bible in Christianity or the Koran in the religion of Islam. The traditional "Holy Books" are all considered to be the "Word of

God," given through prophets and seers, and eternally applicable to all human beings (if not binding on them). The trouble is that those ancient books were produced in times in which cultures could develop in relative isolation and independence from one another, and as a more and more intimate world civilization has developed during the course of the last one or two thousand years, the self-contained cultures of the ancient times (and their books) have entered into more and more open contact (and conflict) with one another. The result has been a seemingly interminable sequence of absurd wars, all based on the efforts of one or another anciently (or modernly) independent system of mind and culture to achieve a state of power and dominance over all other systems. (Historically, Christianity and Islam are, among religions, the most conspicuous in their consistent pursuit of world-wide political power and universal cultural dominance, whereas the capitalistic and communist political systems, each in league with the amoral and transcultural technical idealism of scientific materialism, are, in the modern era, the most conspicuous secular enterprises engaged in usual pursuit of power and dominance.)

By allowing the process of world culture to develop through the conflict of self-contained systems we have, in effect and in actuality, placed the world in the hands of self-centered lunatics (as if all of the madmen and madwomen who imagine themselves to be Cleopatra, Jesus, or Napoleon were given principal offices in each government and institution in the world). Therefore, I call for the universal acceptance of the total tradition (or Great Tradition) of mankind as the common inheritance of mankind. And, rather than merely put all these eggs in a basket to be sampled at random (or in one soup, to be tasted all in one bite), I have communicated a critical approach to understanding and transcending the limitations of the Great Tradition of human existence.

Therefore, all the "Holy Books" are _our_ books, and all of us must go to school and be transformed in our minds by the Great Tradition. Only a critical approach to our inherited and traditional cultural and philosophical limitations of mind and action can purify us of the habit of brute conflict and self-delusion.

If we go to school with the Great Tradition, we must go through a trial of self-transformation. My Teaching provides the critical basis for that school of self-transformation. In the beginning, I call you to consider and overcome the provincialism of your mind, and, therefore, I Argue the Way in relation to the traditions and stages of life. (And this is the justification for my consideration of my own Teaching in terms of the Great Tradition as a whole and the ultimate traditions of Buddhism and Advaitism.) But my Argument finally goes beyond this schooling of the provincial or conventional mind. The radical Argument of my Teaching is a consideration that transcends the mind itself, even the entire body-mind, the apparent world, and attention itself. Therefore, my Argument considers the Great Tradition positively and critically, but it ultimately transcends all the conventions of the Great Tradition and all of the systems of approach to Truth based on either beliefs (as in the Emanationist or "idealist" schools) or problems (as in the non-Emanationist or "realist" schools).

2.

I have already considered the limitations inherent in the "realism" and the problem-based conceptions of sixth stage Buddhism. In this essay I want to consider an aspect of limitation that pertains more specifically to the tradition of Advaitism. To be sure, the sixth stage considerations of original Buddhism have commonly been used as, in effect, a belief system for the followers of Gautama. The "realist" propositions of Gautama are a conceptual framework for progressive practice, and they are commonly affirmed simply because they are overtly propagandized. And the "problem" that motivates the usual seeker for Nirvana is a belief (or mental state) that he simply has not yet understood. But Gautama's fundamental approach was not one that appealed to belief in the conventional propaganda of Revelations and means that were the common basis of the culture of his day. He called simply for a direct exercise of present insight and intuition (rather than the exercise of belief) as the means for Realization. And Gautama's orientation is thus, at least in principle, remarkably free of the limitations of the first five stages of life. However, the efforts toward Realization via sixth stage means are also founded in the conventional or yet un-Enlightened mind, and Gautama's Way (as practiced by yet un-Enlightened individuals and schools) is, therefore, reflective of the problems and beliefs of ordinary mind. In any case, we should understand that Gautama's Way at least calls for the direct exercise of insight and intuition, rather than the method of belief in Transcendental Being, God, gods, immortal self, or the efficacy of magical and mystical techniques for transforming the self or its conditions. (But we should also understand that Gautama did not otherwise deny the ordinary factuality of cosmic and subtle powers, the continuation of existence after death, or the conventional reality of psychic, magical, and mystical abilities, processes, and states.) Gautama's call for the exercise of insight and intuition rather than conventional belief represents a unique orientation that also characterizes the Way that I Teach. (And this likeness is one of the reasons for considering the Way that I Teach to be a form of Buddhism.)

The Advaitist tradition, like the Emanationist tradition as a whole, calls for the exercise of belief based on an appeal to the Revelation of Truth represented by the Vedic and Upanishadic "Holy Books" and traditions. The technique of practice in the schools of Advaitism is apparently a very subtle and direct exercise of insight and intuition, but that subtle and direct exercise is founded on the prior affirmation of two primary philosophical beliefs: (1) Reality is Transcendental Being, Consciousness, and Bliss, and (2) that Reality is identical to the immortal or eternal essential self (or "atman") of every living being.

These two beliefs are presumed to be the core of Revealed Truth that was first made Evident to the seers of the Vedic and

Upanishadic epochs. And the Way that is proposed is not merely a direct Way to Realize what may also have been Realized by others in the past. The Way the Advaitists typically propose is based upon prior and continuous affirmation of the Revealed Truth in the form of <u>propositions</u> believed by the yet un-Enlightened mind.

I have Argued that the Obvious Truth, or the Transcendental Truth that is Realized in the seventh stage of life, is not merely a factual Truth that can rightly be believed by those who have not yet <u>Realized</u> It. Until the Truth is Realized, It cannot, as an alternative, be wholly believed (or believed to the degree of being Realized). One of the basic limiting errors of traditional Advaitism is that it proposes a Way <u>based on belief</u> in the Transcendental Reality and the concrete and exclusive <u>identification</u> of that Reality with the essential or most internal self. As a result, the Way in practice (previous to ultimate Awakening) becomes one of conventional (and inherently Narcissistic or contracted) <u>self-inherence</u> rather than <u>self-transcendence</u>.

The Transcendental Reality is not, in any unique or exclusive sense, the essential self-nature of the individual being. That essential self-nature is only one among all of the conventional and conditional forms of contraction that comprise the "samsaric" or yet un-Enlightened awareness of existence. The Transcendental Reality is Realized to be the <u>Condition</u> of the individual being (or the total self) and the entire realm of Nature (or the not-self). The Transcendental Reality cannot be <u>conceived</u> in the mind. Therefore, It cannot, previous to Realization, be wholly believed in, or affirmed as It is, to the degree of Realization. The Transcendental Reality is not a proposition in the mind, to be believed or confronted in or by the mind. The Transcendental Reality is not to be believed, but It is to be Realized. It cannot be <u>concentrated</u> upon, as if It were one among the possible objects of attention. It is not an object (or Object) of attention. It is not factual, or <u>a</u> fact, but Transcendental. And It cannot, therefore, be directly concentrated or meditated on in the form of the self-essence (which is only one possible and factual object or direction of attention), or in any other form of self, not-self, or contraction. It is Realized only in the case of <u>utter</u> self-transcendence, not self-inherence or inherence in any form of self or not-self.

The Transcendental Reality or Condition is Obvious <u>only</u> in Enlightenment (or self-transcending Awakening). Apart from such Awakening to the Obvious, there is no wholly real or most profound presumption that there is, as such, a Transcendental or Ultimate Divine Condition. Such cannot be wholly believed by the ego (which is utterly contracted from the Transcendental Condition) and is not completely believed by anyone (or any mind). It is only doubted and otherwise wondered about, until it is Realized. Therefore, all propagandized beliefs in the Ultimate or Transcendental Divine Being and Condition are nothing more than hopeful and apparent beliefs, or conditional, easily mutable, and chronically doubted structures of mind. Apart from Enlightenment, those apparent belief structures are merely bits of mimicry, or inherited mind-forms, prattled in the midst of an endless conflict between themselves and other inherited mind-forms that propose, even with equal force, totally other and even antagonistic beliefs or presumptions.

Those who propose ultimate beliefs as a means for attaining or assigning the Truth are merely trying to make the Truth seem to be compatible with the ego and with the world as it seems to the conventional view. And those who claim utter belief in the Condition of Transcendental Being without yet Realizing It are merely glorifying the face (or lie) of Narcissus in the pond. The Way of the Realization of the Transcendental Condition cannot be based upon propositions of belief, but only and directly upon the understanding and transcendence of the conventionally presumed self, mind, body, world, and God. All other approaches are merely consolations for the ego in the un-Enlightened stages of life.

3.

I do not speak of the Transcendental Reality as the essential nature of Man. This is a conventional sixth stage point of view, a reflection of traditional Advaitism, which is oriented to self-inherence rather than self-transcendence. The Transcendental Reality cannot be directly Realized by inverting upon the essential being. The Transcendental Reality can only be Realized when the essential being (and the motive to invert upon the essential being), as well as all the other psycho-physical extensions of the being, is understood and transcended. Ego-transcendence, and not ego-inherence, is the radical Way of the Realization of the Transcendental Reality.

In the literature of the Way that I Teach I constantly criticize the sixth stage method of inversion. If we are to Realize the Transcendental Reality, we cannot continue to make any feature of the world or any of the "sheaths" of the being into an object of ultimate belief or absorptive meditation. Therefore, I constantly criticize this tendency. The essential being of Man can, in the actual case of Awakening or Realized Enlightenment, be recognized in the Transcendental Reality. In that case, and in that sense, we may say that the Transcendental Reality is the "Nature" of Man, but such a proposition is true only in the case of Realization. And, in that same and only case, all of the parts of the world and all of the parts or "sheaths" of individual being are equally recognizable in the Transcendental Condition—but apart from Realization, or the self-transcending recognition of the essential being in the Obvious Transcendental Reality, the Transcendental Reality is no more to be equated with the essential nature of Man than with any other "sheath."

I do not propose a Way of practice that is based on <u>belief</u> in the Transcendental Reality. The fundamental Argument of the radical Way that I Teach is not a description of the Divine or Transcendental Reality, nor a prescription for practice based on the affirmation of belief in that described Reality (or its equation with the whole or any part of the self or the not-self). My fundamental Argument is simply a criticism of the self-contraction in all its forms. I call for the practice of self-observation and insight into the self-contraction, until "Whatever" or "Whoever" or "Itever" It is that transcends it stands out as the Obvious. When my Argument has been thoroughly considered, when the self is discovered to be Narcissus or the activity of self-contraction, and when all the forms of self-contraction, appearing as self and not-self, have been re-cognized and transcended, then the Transcendental Reality is Realized as the Obvious. But only then.

The principal limiting error of the Advaitic point of view is the claim that the Transcendental Reality is identical to the essential nature (or "atman") of Man. This error transforms the Transcendental Reality into a proposition to be believed and a conventional object to be meditated upon rather than a Condition that is Obvious only in Enlightenment. This conventional Advaitist error is equivalent to the conventional Buddhist error of believing that "Nirvana and samsara are the same" as a matter of conventional fact rather than of ultimate Realization. And it is clear to me that Gautama's refusal to base his Way upon the idea of an eternal soul or "atman" was an expression of his unwillingness to found the Way on the basis of this "Advaitist error." (His refusal should not be interpreted to mean that he did not believe or know that there is actual survival of death, and so forth.) And he refused to support un-Enlightened <u>belief</u> in (or conventional description and affirmation of) the Transcendental Reality or Condition Itself for the same reason—not because there is no Transcendental Condition, but because it is errorsome and useless relative to actual Realization to believe or affirm It via the necessarily un-Enlightened structures of mere mind.

A certain conventional level of belief in the Transcendental Divine and a sense of self-inherence in the Transcendental Divine are perhaps inevitable and also natural to the human condition as it matures in the first six stages of life. These propositions of mind and the feeling psyche may, therefore, appear at the beginning of the practice of approach to the Way that I Teach, in the form of the Way of Divine Communion, which is a beginner's practice offered to those who have not yet become fully mature in relation to the functions and conditions of the first three stages of life, and who, therefore, are not yet free to understand and directly transcend the mind of the self-contraction in the context of the fourth stage of life. In any case, such propositions or conventional beliefs are only reflections of the egoic mind of the earlier stages of life. They are not fundamental to the Way itself. Therefore, the approach to the Way that I Teach will eventually proceed (in the form of the Way of Relational Enquiry) on the basis of direct understanding, or insight and intuition, alone. In its ultimate or most direct and radical form, the Way that I Teach is simply to see that there is self-contraction and to re-cognize it utterly. When the self-contraction is utterly re-cognized, the Transcendental Reality stands out as the Obvious.

One cannot perfectly believe in the Transcendental Reality, but one can Realize It. It cannot be Realized by concentrating upon and identifying It with any conditional form at all. It is only Realized when It Reveals Itself as the Obvious. Therefore, the Way is to understand and re-cognize conditional existence. When the play of conditionality is thoroughly understood and re-cognized, then the Transcendental Reality is Revealed as the Obvious.

In the Way that I Teach, there is Help for those who once "hear," or understand, and then continually practice that same understanding. The life and Teaching of the Spiritual Master are not offered as conventionally objective Revelations of Truth, merely to be believed and imitated. They are offered as Argument, or the means of consideration. And relationship to the person of the Spiritual Master is likewise offered as a living means of Transmission or Help (and not merely as an objective symbol or surrogate for belief in the Divine Being). Those who understand and practice in the Company of the Spiritual Master also naturally experience the Transmission of Helping Power and the Grace of Awakening, and so they cultivate that relationship in a naturally responsive manner. But the Way that is served by all of that Help is not a conventional and self-based believer's path. It is the Way of practice of self-transcendence, founded on direct understanding (or insight and intuition) only.

The Radiant Transcendental or Divine Being is not Obvious to the un-Enlightened mind or being. Therefore, It is not merely to be affirmed or believed. Such affirmation or belief is always superficial, a consolation to the ego, a supporter of egoity (rather than a means for transcending ego-centeredness), and an illusion of mind. Belief may console the ego, but it also deludes it and supports it. Therefore, the struggle with the ego (or the discipline in which it is understood and transcended rather than consoled) is useful for Realization, whereas belief is more of a vacation or relief from the struggle itself. The Radiant Transcendental or Divine Being is only Revealed as the Obvious after one has considered the Argument of the Teaching, discovered self to be Narcissus, and seen or re-cognized and transcended all of the forms of self-contraction (or all of the conventions and illusions of the first six stages of life). It is only in the case of actual Awakening (or insight that goes beyond the self-contraction) and Enlightenment (or free, direct, and radical intuition of the Condition of self and not-self) that the Radiant Transcendental or Divine Being is Obvious. Only then are all conditions recognizable in the Transcendental Condition. Only then are the conditional self and the "samsaric" or mechanical round of Nature discovered to inhere in Radiant Free Divine Love-Bliss.

Only Realization is true faith. It is not necessary first to believe ultimate propositions in order to Realize the Transcendental Condition. Such affirmations of belief tend to appear as psychological and psychic phenomena in the stages of life, but they are nothing more than the poetry of philosophical mind. The fundamental process of the Way is simply a matter of "hearing" (or understanding) and "seeing" (or quickening via Transmission) in the Company of the Adept. That hearing and seeing are expressed via self-observation and insight into the mechanism of self-contraction. The practice progresses as re-cognition and transcendence of all the forms of self-contraction, until energy and attention are free of the conventional bondage of the first six stages of life. Then energy and attention are themselves recognized in the Radiant Transcendental Being, the Divine Self, the Transcendental Condition, the Love-Bliss or Happiness of the Real.

Therefore, do not settle for belief or mere ego-consoling faith. Do not vacate the struggle for long with the dope of pleasures and mind. Such a life is merely a cycle of motivation and frustration, with occasional moments of imaginary attainment and mock-release—a calendar of wants, incarnate memory, no ease. Not even doubt, but the struggle with doubt is the sensation of real practice. And that very doubt is transcended in every moment of real understanding.

XV
The Practices of Insight and Devotional Idealism in the Way of Divine Ignorance

The basic form of Buddhist reasoning: "All 'dharmas' (including all phenomenal conditions as well as every kind of action and result of action) are temporary and limited expressions of the play of causes and effects. At the level of human awareness, all conditions are nothing but temporary forms or modifications of mind. If I react to them by attachment, I am limited to them. If I react to them by seeking an alternative to them (or an escape from them) I am still limited to them by virtue of my struggle against them." On the basis of such logic, the Buddhist schools have developed a basic and consistent orientation to the understanding of this apparent double-bind as a fundamental but conventional and emotional struggle of mind, or an unnecessary double-bind of conscious being.

This is the ultimate logic of Buddhism: Neither "samsara" (conditions) nor "Nirvana" (the absence of conditions) can be happily and finally embraced or attained. Relative to conditions there is only struggle. But the struggle is <u>added</u> to conditions. It is the result of attachment to conditions and the convention of independent self. Mind and self are added to or hallucinated upon conditions. The "Nature" of mind and self is not <u>other</u> than mind and self. It is the prior Condition of mind and self. It is not other than the world of phenomenal conditions itself, in its "natural" or spontaneous mode or moment of arising, prior to any addition or reactive qualification in the form of thought, desire, aversion, or psychic differentiation of self. The "natural" state of mind is one that does not react to conditions but is at ease, uncreated, tacitly aware of events without clinging or aversion.

From the point of view of conventional mind (or thought, which reflects, reacts to, and is superimposed upon the world as well as upon the simple awareness that witnesses the world) the world of phenomena is a double-bind of alternately pleasurable and painful limits. Thus, the mind proposes either fulfillment of pleasurable possibilities or else escape from all conditions. The proposition of pleasurable fulfillment (even at the risk of painful frustration) is the proposition of "samsara." The proposition of dissociation and escape from conditional states is the proposition of "Nirvana." Therefore, both samsara and Nirvana are conventional propositions of the mind. The two propositions are, as such, mutually exclusive or contradictory. Thus, they represent the internal contradictions, or the inherent problem-structure of the mind.

The trend of Buddhist philosophy is to criticize mind and all propositions of mind as artificial and binding artifices. Indeed, it is the convention of mind as such that is, from the Buddhist point of view, the source and essence of non-Enlightenment, or ego-bondage. And Enlightenment is, therefore, a matter of the transcendence of mind (and thus the conventional self-idea as well as all other limiting and binding conceptions).

The Awakening associated with Enlightenment in the traditions of Buddhism is an Awakening to the native and natural state of awareness prior to identification with mind. It is a matter of being aware of mental states as a simple flow (prior to any act of choice or evaluation or reaction)—and it is a matter of being thus aware of even physical states or conditions (rather than relating to such states or conditions via identification with the structures of mind). Once the position of simple awareness is established as the native state (rather than the conventions of the body-mind-self), then the ultimate "Nature" of mind and body and world events suddenly becomes obvious in the form of a tacit or "mindless" intuition.

To put it in the terms of my own Teaching, the psycho-physical contraction-reaction to phenomena produces the self-convention and the emotional struggle of mind, high and low. If this contraction-reaction is transcended, the manifest being continues to arise spontaneously in the plane of phenomenal Nature, but the being abides in its native or natural state (prior to contraction-reaction and all clinging and seeking). In that native or natural state, which is unqualified or, as a Buddhist would say, void or empty (since it adds nothing to what is spontaneously arising), there is blissful clarity in which the "Nature" of Nature is obvious.

In the conventions of our limited born state, we react and contract as the body-mind. Thus, we become possessed by the idea (or presumption) of limited independent self and by the flow of ideas (or presumptions) about phenomena. But both the ego-idea and the flow of phenomenal ideas are superimposed on the actual situation by the reactive contraction. If this can be rightly understood, the reactive contraction can be transcended in the equanimity of right practice. And in that self-transcending and mind-transcending equanimity, there is inherent freedom from the self-idea. Instead, there is natural abiding in the "Nature" or original state of mind. And in that native state of consciousness or being, prior to mind and the conception of self, there is neither attachment to phenomena nor the revulsion from phenomena that gets expressed in the search for a state that excludes phenomena.

The Practices of Insight and Devotional Idealism in the Way of Divine Ignorance

In other words, "samsara" is not a problem, and, therefore, "Nirvana" is not needed as a solution. In place of conventional attachment to phenomena ("samsara") or to the absence of phenomena ("Nirvana") there is the native state of no-contraction, no-reaction, no-mind, no-ego, no-clinging, no-aversion. And the "mood" of such Enlightenment is that naturally associated with the native state of being. It is the blissful mood of innate freedom, in which phenomenal conditions are naturally or spontaneously permitted (neither sought nor suppressed) as a pure or mere event, without binding implications. On the basis of this pre-mental and pre-egoic equanimity, the intuition ultimately arises that all phenomena are a display or spontaneous modification of inherently Radiant Transcendental Being.

This is the ultimate sense of Buddhist philosophy. In *Nirvanasara* and in *The Lion Sutra** (as well as in previous works) I have made it clear how this fundamental process of insight, developed in somewhat different terms as a process in practice, is also the essence of the Way that I Teach.

In the course of my own practice there arose a spontaneous understanding of the source of the "problem" that was motivating my own search. It was a matter of direct insight into the reactive contraction of the body-mind. As this insight became more and more profound, the sense of "problem" weakened. The presumed goals of religious, mystical, yogic, and philosophical effort were understood to be nothing more than attempts to solve the "problem"—but it was clear that no such solution was more than a temporary, conditional, or non-ultimate convention of the self and its problem. What was ultimately necessary was understanding and transcendence of the problem at its root (which was present psycho-physical self-contraction) and thus transcendence of the entire search for solutions built upon the problem. Thus, in the Event at the Vedanta Temple, native Enlightenment or Awakening to Truth was restored.†

---

* *The Lion Sutra* is Da Free John's forthcoming comprehensive revelation of the wisdom of the seventh stage of life, the transcendence of attention or the practice of Enlightenment.

† Master Da Free John's own spiritual transformation was spontaneously perfected

Paradoxically, the Vedanta Temple Event was followed by the spontaneous development of various "siddhis" or higher powers of manifest being. Instead of my own self-problem, the focus of consciousness was expanded, so that the mind began spontaneously to reflect the states of others—even countless others. And soon I was drawn into the Work of struggling with others in a Teaching Ordeal. In that Ordeal, a remarkable history of instructive play developed, full of extraordinary wonders and all the theatre that attends the undermining of egoic conventions in a group of ordinary people. As a result, a complete and newly considered Teaching of Enlightenment was developed, and a full culture of practice was elaborated. And it was only when all of that had stably appeared, thus fulfilling the purpose of my original submission to those who are alive in this time and place, that I was able to retire again into a relatively secluded and private circumstance—to bless all beings unobserved and to serve mature practitioners of the Way.

In summary, relative to the historical precedents for the Way that I Teach, I would say that the process of insight into the problem-consciousness is the most fundamental practice, and, therefore, there is a clear line of sympathetic affinity between the Way that I Teach and the philosophical features of traditional Buddhism. But the Realization of Transcendental Wisdom and the Transfiguring Radiance of Reality is not different from the Realization of the Transcendental Divine proposed in the schools of high Hinduism (as expressed in the *Bhagavata Purana,* the *Bhagavad Gita,* and in the spiritual demonstrations of many great "Siddhas" or Free Adepts in the high Hindu tradition, and finally epitomized in the sixth to seventh stage Teachings of the Sages of Advaitism). Therefore, the Way that I Teach enjoys sympathetic affinity with the spiritual idealism of high Hinduism and Advaitism, just as it does with the insight schools of Buddhism.

The ideal of rigorous application to Realization via devotion

---

while sitting in meditation in a small temple on the grounds of the Vedanta Society in Hollywood, California, in September, 1970. For a full discussion of these events, see pp. 131-139 in *The Knee of Listening.*

(or self-sacrifice) to the Radiant Transcendental Being is, ultimately, fruitful in the same sense as rigorous application to the process of insight into the conventions of the self. In the Way that I Teach, the practice of devotional idealism, or self-sacrifice into the Divine Being, is basic to the foundation level of the discipline (or the Way of Divine Communion)—although, clearly, even the foundation level of practice requires discriminating intelligence, insight into the conventions of self, conversion or release of feeling-attention from the self-contraction, and continuous maintenance of the self-sacrifice into Divine Communion via all functional and conditional structures. But rigorous application to the process of self-transcending insight is, in the Way that I Teach, most fully developed in the "esoteric" and the "radical" stages of practice (or in the progression to the Way of Relational Enquiry, then the Way of Re-cognition, and, finally, the Way of Radical Intuition). In the form in which I Teach it, the Way of Divine Communion is founded on the disposition that characterizes the ultimate or seventh stage of life. Thus, if it is rightly and rigorously engaged, it will naturally and inevitably lead to the esoteric and radical stages of practice.

The conventional philosophy of Hinduism does tend to posit a Divine Reality over against phenomena, so that the method of practice often tends to become one either of exclusive inversion toward the essential self or exclusive ascent and expansion toward the Divine and away from the grossly concentrated phenomena of body and mind. This is understood from the Buddhist point of view to be a beginner's approach to Reality, the results of which are fruitless asceticism, false views, the neophyte's "stink of Enlightenment," and an attachment to "Nirvana" (to the exclusion of "samsara") that makes native Enlightenment impossible to Realize. Likewise, in the Way that I Teach, the false effort that comes from the tendency to <u>objectify</u> the Divine as a concept over against and separate from phenomena must be understood as a convention produced by the ordinary self-based mind. Thus, I have communicated a Way of practice that enters into Divine Communion on the basis of

Ignorance (or awareness free of mind, conventionally objectified ideas of God, problem conceptions, strategies of problem solution, and so forth). Therefore, the idealism of Divine Communion is, in my view, a viable form of the Way, once it is established on a base of right understanding and expressed as an ordeal of moment to moment self-sacrifice or self-transcendence in Divine Communion rather than a problematic effort to escape the world or the self. If the Way is engaged as self-sacrificial (or ecstatic) Communion with the Radiant Transcendental Being, then every kind of necessary insight into the self and mind will arise naturally as practice matures. But if the Divine is pursued merely by attempts to dissociate from states of mind and body, the sufferings and illusions of self are only magnified in the form of religious and philosophical conceits.

The dissociative method and its illusions have also been a part of the Buddhist tradition. The convention of dissociative effort to escape conditions has traditionally been criticized as "nihilism." And the false or illusory concretization or objectification of the Ultimate Reality or Truth has been criticized as "eternalism." The *Lankavatara Sutra,* one of the greatest of all Buddhist scriptures, dwells on the criticism of all such false views that come from the conventional mind in its struggle with phenomenal limitations. And what is called for is insight into mind, or the process of conceptual and experiental consciousness in relation to phenomena, so that mind (or consciousness) may Awaken from thoughts and mentally based propositions to the native state of phenomena (including the body-mind). It is natural identification with the native state of awareness (rather than conventional identification with any particular or conditional state of attention, or the suppression of awareness, or the attainment of any higher object or state of mind) that is the disposition called Enlightenment in the high tradition of Buddhism.

Ultimately, the traditions of Buddhism and of high Hinduism demonstrate the same Enlightenment in the case of actual and complete Realizers. Both traditions have provided the cultural framework for the appearance of Free Adepts. The Way that I Teach is a new tradition that refreshes the Way as an opportunity for humanity in this epoch. I have communicated this Way as I have Realized it. Likewise, I have criticized and appreciated the historical traditions of Hinduism, Buddhism, the Semitic religions of Judaism, Christianity, and Islam, the animistic and magical traditions of shamanism, and all the mystical cults of terrestrial and cosmic Emanationism. I have done this in order to clarify the minds of those who consider the sacred ordeal in this time and place, when the historical traditions have lost their clarity, face, and power due to the accretions of centuries of conventional influences.

Enlightenment <u>remains</u> the ultimate Realization of Man. It is the Truth of Nature Realized by Man, and, once Realized, it is the Truth or Radiant Reality that Outshines Man and the world. The Realization of Truth liberates, but the Truth Realized is also the Reality to be Realized for Its own sake. To Realize the Truth is to be entered into a new Destiny, gone beyond even the conventional transmissions and limitations of light in space.

XVI
Insight, Intuition, and the Heresy of Progressive Enlightenment

Much of the original literature of Buddhism (usually referred to as the "Pali canon") reflects a culture of response to Gautama's considerations at a lesser level than that of Enlightenment. That is, the original literature embodies responses to Gautama and not merely the ultimate Teaching of Gautama, and those responses are largely characteristic of the beginner's mind.

The culture of practice described in the Pali literature of Buddhism is primarily monastic and associated with a rudimentary form of practice. It is the practice of programmatic strategies of self-purifying activity that are intended to bring an end to desire and the subsequent generation of negative effects or states of phenomenal being. That practice was to be carried out in great detail in every level and moment of functional, personal, and relational existence. And it was presumed that only after a long period of such discipline (even after many lifetimes of self-purifying discipline) would Nirvanic Enlightenment be attained.

The problem created by the dominance of this beginner's conception of the Way is that it suggests a conception of Enlightenment that is conditional and indirect. It suggests that Enlightenment (or Realization of the Nirvanic Condition) is a conditional effect of phenomenal activity (or a state that can somehow be <u>caused</u> by action).

Gautama Awakened in a moment of perfect intuition that was indeed <u>preceded</u> by self-purifying activity, but it was <u>founded</u> on insight (or radical understanding) alone. Those who considered his Dharma or Teaching were mostly beginners. Attention and energy were not sufficiently free in them to represent a capability for direct Realization of the Nirvanic or Transcendental Truth. Therefore, they were offered a progressive Argument and a progressive practice of the Way, in the form of the "Noble Eightfold Path," a complex system of behavioral rules, and so forth. And that culture of progressive Argument and practice later became the basis for a complex systematic analysis of the "dharmas" (or constituents of phenomenal existence) and a Way of practice that included routines of analytical meditation.

Gautama's own <u>ultimate</u> consideration or insight was most simple and direct: Conditional existence (apparent as the phenomenal self and the phenomenal not-self) is inherently painful (or disturbed) and unnecesasry. This insight permitted Gautama to Awaken suddenly and spontaneously into the Transcendental Samadhi or most profound Realization of the most prior, "unborn," or unconditional Reality. And it is this insight and intuitive Realization that is the core of Gautama's Teaching.

The Hinayana (or Theravada) tradition of Buddhism has continued to maintain the progresive culture of self-purifying activity as the necessary means of Nirvanic Enlightenment. But the Mahayana tradition began as a philosophical reaction to the conceptions associated with the progressive method. The original Mahayana philosophy was based upon the granting of dominance to Gautama's core Teaching—the Teaching of radical insight leading directly to Awakening. And the meditative schools of the Mahayana (such as Ch'an and Zen) are all devoted to this most direct form of the Way.

The great Mahayana philosophers saw that the conception of a progressive Way was founded on un-Enlightenment, or the tendency to be serious about concepts and conditions that should simply be understood and directly transcended. They were well aware that people must generally grow (or gradually release energy and attention for the ultimate Realization) through a difficult and even prolonged regimen of disciplines and learning situations, but the Mahayana philosophers were not willing to allow the practical necessity of progressive discipline to transform the philosophical conception of Enlightenment into that of a conditional Realization. Therefore, they proposed Enlightenment as a matter of direct knowledge, radical insight, on intuitive Wisdom—rather than as the effect or result of self-purifying action.

The Advaitic (or non-dualist) tradition is also associated with a radical consideration of Enlightenment as a matter of direct insight and intuition rather than as the result or effect of action. Indeed, this insistence upon the Way as "knowledge" rather than as action is one of the most fundamental Arguments of Advaita Vedanta. The Vedantic Emanationist schools of the first five stages of life are all basically dualistic, and they always advocate progressive forms of the Way, founded on action and the results of action, that will eventually produce "Realization" in the form of terrestrial contemplations, phenomenal rewards, and cosmically mystical states of one kind or another. But the sixth stage schools of Advaitism advocate only direct "knowledge" (or insight and intuition) rather than progressive action. Therefore, the <u>ultimate</u> consideration or insight of the Emanationist tradition is, like that of Gautama, simple and direct: Conditional existence (apparent as the phenomenal self and the phenomenal not-self) is only an unnecessary or merely apparent disturbance in, to, and of Transcendental Consciousness.

The sixth stage Advaitists, like the philosophers of the Mahayana, certainly offer a culture of progressive disciplines that generally correspond to the first five stages of life, but that culture of discipline is not directly associated with Enlightenment or Self-Knowledge. Rather, as in the Mahayana schools, that beginner's culture is regarded to be simply an ordinary means of preparation (or the preliminary effort devoted to the release of energy and attention from the stream of phenomenal limitations), after which the primary and direct exercise of intuitive insight becomes the basis of practice. And it is only that ultimate practice that qualifies philosophically to be the true Way in the Advaitist tradition.

Therefore, both the Buddhist and the Advaitist traditions are historically associated with a radical or ultimate philosophy of practice. It is the Way of (1) direct insight into the status of conditional existence, and (2) direct intuition of the Transcendental or Unconditional Reality. Gautama's form of the Way is based primarily on moment to moment inspection of the event of self and not-self, until the merely conditional and unnecessary status of all of that becomes obvious and, on that basis, Transcendental Awakening appears spontaneously. The Advaitist form of the Way is based primarily on two exercises. First is the exercise of insight, done by locating the actual self, or the consciousness, which has no form, but merely witnesses the body-mind and its relations. And the second exercise is that of intuition, done by constantly remembering that consciousness until its Transcendental Status and the illusory or unnecessary status of self and not-self become spontaneously obvious. In either case, the Way is conceived in terms that transcend the cause/effect, subject/object, or self/not-self dichotomies of conventional and dualistic consciousness. Both traditions are basically opposed to any conception of Enlightenment as an effect or result of conditional causes (or actions). Therefore, in both traditions, all forms of practice that take the form of action (or the efforts of the first five stages of life) must be understood to be conventionally useful and even inevitable disciplines that belong only to the preliminary, preparatory, or beginner's domain of the Way. In all of the Buddhist and Advaitist schools, actions are regarded to be phenomenal, karmic, or effect-producing, but the Way is intended to transcend karmas, effects, births, deaths, and thus all actions. Therefore, the ultimate form of the Way involves a natural or free relaxation of attention from the plane of actions (or self-transcending efforts) and a direct resort to insight and intuition (which are inherently self-transcending).

The Way that I Teach is, likewise, a radical Way of observation, understanding, insight, and intuition. Its simple, direct, and ultimate consideration or insight is this: Conditional existence (or the play of the phenomenal self and not-self as a mortal machine, independent of perfect Happiness) is an unnecessary apparition created by the self-contraction (or contraction within and recoil from the Real Condition). The Way is to observe the self as contraction (rather than as entity or merely factual being), and re-cognize all the forms of the self-contraction, until the Transcendental or Divine Condition stands out as the Obvious. Thereafter (or in the seventh stage of life), it is simply a matter of Abiding in and as that Condition, tacitly and continually recognizing self and not-self in That. The practice may necessarily be associated at the beginning (and for a long time) with disciplines of the active and functional body-mind-self—but all of that is a "yoga of consideration" that gradually releases energy and attention from the binding concerns of the first five stages of life (and even the sixth stage of life). When energy and attention are profoundly free, understanding of the self-contraction and radical intuition of the Transcendental Condition appear in the form of a most profound and direct process in which Radiant Transcendental Being is Self-Revealed as the Obvious. And once there is the Awakening of the seventh stage of life, neither action nor the abandonment of action helps, supports, maintains, threatens, or dissolves the Awakened Realization—but the Power of Self-Abiding in the Transcendental Condition, recognizing all conditions (and all actions) as transparent, or merely apparent, unnecessary, and non-binding modifications of unconditional Happiness (or Radiant Love-Bliss), at least gradually reduces the activities of the body-mind to a state of motiveless simplicity (or apparent renunciation), and, finally, all conditions and all actions are Outshined in Radiant Transcendental or Divine Being.

XVII
The Way of Radical Understanding and the Traditional Formulae of Enlightenment

The principal traditional summation of the "point of view" of Enlightenment is expressed in the language of Upanishadic Advaitism: (1) The world (or any and all objects, conditional existence, suffering, etc.) is un-Real. (2) Only Brahman (or Transcendental Being) is Real. (3) Brahman is the world. The Mahayana Buddhist tradition restates the same point of view in the formula: Nirvana (Transcendental Being or Existence) and samsara (or conditional existence) are the same. And the Advaitic schools also maintain other versions of the same point of view, expressed in such Upanishadic formulae as "Thou art That" and "The atman (or the essence of the individual self) and Paramatman (or the Transcendental Self) are identical."

Each of these conceptual summations is based upon Transcendental Realization. Therefore, in the form in which they are stated, none of these formulae represents a means for attaining Realization or Enlightenment. That is, from the un-Enlightened or conventional point of view, the world is not un-Real, Brahman is not Real, Nirvana and samsara are the opposites of one

---

Reprinted from Da Free John, *The Bodily Sacrifice of Attention* (Clearlake, Calif.: The Dawn Horse Press, 1981).

The Way of Radical Understanding and the Traditional Formulae of Enlightenment

another, and the individual self is not the Transcendental Self or Source of the world. However, traditionally, these formulae have been used as guides to belief, philosophical presumption, meditation, and even the presumption of a logic wherein Enlightenment is regarded to be the case merely on the basis of acceptance of the ideas contained in these formulae.

Truly, these formulae may be affirmed to represent the point of view in Enlightenment—but only those who have Realized Enlightenment can affirm them. Otherwise, the process of Awakening must somehow be entered into—since the Truth of the traditional formulae cannot be affirmed by the un-Awakened.

Of course, the traditional guides also generally propose practice for the sake of Realization, but the schools of practice tend to base themselves on fundamental errors, problems, and the search for release or ultimate solutions. Thus, depending on the stage of life to which any school most basically belongs, certain objects of belief, meditation, contemplation, or experience are recommended—and such objects or states are regarded to be the Truth or Ultimate Reality and Condition.

The fourth stage schools generally regard one or another Divine Name, presumed Incarnation, or God-Idea to be the Ultimate Object. The fifth stage schools regard certain subtle internal objects (such as sound or light), or the various yogic states of trance-absorption in such objects, to be the Way and the Truth. And the sixth stage schools generally regard the self-essence (or the atman, exclusive of objects) to be the Ultimate Identity. But all such schools and their methods are based upon the search for Realization—that is, the search itself is founded upon un-Enlightenment or the conventional mind.

Truly, none of the "ultimate" objects proposed by the traditions is the Truth. Absorption in those objects is not Enlightenment. Even the traditional formulae tacitly condemn such enterprises as false views. Each of the traditional formulae specifically regards the world, or all objects, to be un-Real or non-Truth or "samsara"—except from the point of view of <u>prior</u> Enlightenment.

The principal traditional summary could be applied directly to the enterprises that are commonly built upon it. (1) The "x" (where x is any object) is un-Real. (2) Only Transcendental Being (not even any Ultimate Object) is Real. In this manner, not only any object or state of conventional daily awareness and experience but any conventional or conditional meditation object or experience is denied Reality.

This denial of Reality to merely conditional or conventional objects and states is in fact the essential first step in the process wherein Reality or Truth is actually Realized. Realization or Enlightenment cannot be attained either by denying the un-Reality (or merely conditional and conventional status) of any or all objects and states or by asserting the Ultimate Reality of any particular object or state. The traditional viewpoint is generally based upon the search to solve or attain release from existence proposed as a problem. Therefore, many objective and subjective conceptions or experiences are proposed to be Reality, Truth, the Goal, and the Way. But the Way that is Truth is based, first of all, on discriminative insight or understanding, wherein it is clear that all of the conventions, objects, conditions, experiences, and presumed knowledge of the six stages of life (apart from Enlightenment, or the seventh stage of life) are not the Truth or the Way to Truth.

Such insight is itself a profound Awakening, wherein the Ultimate Truth simply stands forth as the Obvious. Therefore, on the basis of such insight (traditionally expressed in the form "The world is un-Real; Only Brahman is Real") the ultimate expression of Enlightenment is made (as a spontaneous Confession of Enlightenment, not merely as a convention of conditional belief or logic).

It is only when "Brahman" (or the Transcendental Condition of Being) is Realized that <u>any</u> object or condition is seen in Reality. Otherwise, any object or condition is seen in its un-Real aspect (that is, in its apparent form rather than in its equation with Reality or Transcendental Being). And if Brahman is Realized, <u>all</u> objects or conditions are seen in Reality. (Therefore, in the case of Enlightenment, no particular object or state is regarded to be Reality in an exclusive or special sense. Neither the atman—or self-essence—nor any mystical or physical or gross or subtle or presumed Divine object is, from the "point of view" of Enlightenment, regarded to be the Reality. Rather, the unique characteristic of Enlightenment is utter freedom from the conventional or exclusively samsaric mind, and thus freedom from both the vision of un-Reality itself and the vision of Reality as an exclusive attribute of any particular object or state.)

It is only as Brahman (or in Reality) that any object or state is Real. And as long as Reality seems to pertain only to certain particular objects or states, Brahman has not yet been Realized.

Therefore, none of the gross or subtle objects of attention to which human beings become oriented in the first five stages of life is Reality, Truth, or Brahman. Transcendental Freedom or Bliss is not Realized via the attainment of any of the objects of knowledge or experience, high or low.

Likewise, the essence of subjectivity, the atman or internal witness, is not Reality, Truth, or Brahman. It is proposed as Reality, Truth, or Brahman in the sixth stage schools (particularly of Advaita Vedanta), based on the ancient scriptural pronouncements of the traditional formulae of Realization. But it is only as Brahman that the atman or basic consciousness is identical to Reality or Truth. Until the Realization of Brahman, the atman is merely the atman, and it is, therefore, un-Real, merely conditions, or not-Brahman.

The sixth stage schools favor the atman as the only appropriate object of meditation, even as the usual man or woman prefers the gross objects of sensation and thought, or the fourth stage schools prefer the Words and Names and Ideas and Incarnations of God, and the fifth stage schools prefer the subtle objects and states of mind and self-absorption. But the internal witness or self-essence is only one of the possible "objects" or orientations of attention. Absorption in the atman is merely another conventional state. All of the objective and subjective orientations of mankind are "sinful"—that is, they "miss the mark," or merely express and affirm the presumption of un-Happiness or separation from the Real Divine Condition.

It would seem, therefore, that the only proper object of attention is Brahman (since It is the only Reality) rather than any of the possible gross or subtle objects or experiential states, or the witnessing subject of objects and experiential states. Such would seem to be an appropriate conclusion based on a right understanding of the traditional formulae. But Brahman, or Transcendental Being, is not an object. It is not associated with any particular experiential state. And it is not a particular being. Therefore, it is impossible to "think" Brahman, meditate on Brahman as an object, or invert upon Brahman as if It were by definition identical to the self-essence. Even so, it is only if Brahman can be Realized that any and all conditions, experiences, objects, and beings can be seen in Reality.

It is not by means of any formula for objective or subjective meditation that Brahman can be Realized. Brahman is not by definition identical to any object or subject. Therefore, no conventional meditation is of any Ultimate consequence. It is necessary to exercise discriminative intelligence or profound understanding for Reality to be Realized. It is only in such understanding that the conventions of object and subject are inherently transcended. It is the tacit transcendence of the conventions of object and subject that is Enlightenment. What is un-Real is the "world" (objects or subject-modes seen in themselves, as their conventional apparency). "Brahman" is not any object or any particular subject. It is, therefore, unfortunate that the term "Brahman" has the appearance of a name or a conventional reference pointing to particularity in the form of an object or a subject. The term "Nirvana" is equivalent to the term "Brahman," but it has the limitation of appearing to point to the mere negation of any and all objects or subjects. The best "term" of reference to Reality is perhaps silence, no-thought, no-indication, or no-action. Or, perhaps even better, all possible references, forms of speech, thoughts, indications, and actions are the best term of reference. Therefore, any term will do. (I commonly use the term "Radiant Transcendental Being.")

The Way of Radical Understanding and the Traditional Formulae of Enlightenment

The necessary point is not contained in the substantial meaning of any form of reference to the Real or Transcendental Condition. Rather, the point to be made is a process of intelligent understanding and tacit transcendence of conditional and conventional limitations. Whatever the term of reference applied to the Real and its Realization, what is signified or called for is that profound understanding that inherently transcends the conventions of un-Reality (or objective and subjective conditionality).

To turn upon any object, or condition, or experience, or the subjective being itself, <u>as</u> Reality or Truth, before the Truth is Realized, is <u>the</u> primal error of un-Enlightened being. And that very error is not only fundamental to everyday life (or the first three stages of life). It is fundamental to all of the sacred, magical, mystical, religious, spiritual, and high philosophical schools of the fourth, fifth, and sixth stages of life.

How can Brahman, or Reality, or Truth, or Radiant Transcendental Being be made the "object" or the "subject" of meditation? Reality cannot be <u>reduced</u> to any convention of the subject-object realm of being. At best, <u>when</u> Transcendental Being is Realized, <u>then</u> any and all objects, states, and subjects are inherently recognizable <u>as</u> Really the Transcendental Being.

Then what is the Way of Realization of That which inherently Transcends objective and subjective references? It is the radical Way of understanding, or present and direct transcendence of the objective and subjective conventions of the moment. The radical Way of understanding is the moment to moment process of presently transcending the limiting power or implications of any and all objects that are arising to the notice. It is not a matter of intentionally meditating on any object or attaining any state of manifest knowledge or experience, high or low. Rather, it is a matter of direct transcendence of any object or state that is presently arising.

Likewise, it is not a matter of intentionally turning attention away from psycho-physical objects or states and toward the subjective consciousness that witnesses all objects and states. That subjective consciousness is not by definition identical to Brahman (but only by virtue of Realization). By definition, and by virtue of experience, the subjective consciousness is the independent self-essence, exclusive of objects, different in kind from objects, and apparently different from other essential individual selves. The traditional Buddhist view of the self is that it is not at all founded upon an immortal conscious or subjective entity (or atman) but is merely a phenomenal appearance implied by or based upon the temporary arising of the constituents of the body-mind. Thus, the Buddhist tradition tends to recommend a practice based on rigorous denial of the existence of an internal being or atman separate from the body-mind. But the ultimate Goal of Buddhist meditation is not negation but Transcendental Awakening. And such Awakening indeed transcends the conditional categories of object and subject wherein the existence of an "atman" is either affirmed or denied. Therefore, the Buddhist point of view is not epitomized in the denial of the Reality of the atman.

The denial of the atman as Ultimate Reality is, however, a basic proposition of the original understanding in which the Truth becomes obvious. It corresponds to the formula "x (or the object in question) is un-Real." And, as an argumentative proposition, it is traditionally placed in opposition to the apparently conventional Vedantic or Upanishadic proposition that the atman exists. Actually, the original Buddhist denial of the existence of the atman is based on the same logic that appears in the traditional Upanishadic assertion that the world, or samsara, is un-Real and only Brahman is Real. And the traditional Vedantic proposition that the atman exists is based on the "common sense" observation of experience, the facts of life after death, reincarnation, and so forth, and it is justified by the later part of the traditional Upanishadic formula, which affirms the Reality of conditional states of being on the basis of Ultimate Realization. Therefore, the proposed conflict between Buddhism and Advaitism is merely a consequence of certain conventions or styles of logical analysis, although certain differences in the technique of meditation and so forth also follow from the independent propositions of the two great traditions.

The Way of Radical Understanding and the Traditional Formulae of Enlightenment

In my view, the "atman" exists in the conventional sense. That is, the manifest self is an apparent or phenomenal process that continues to change even beyond bodily death. The Buddhist criticism of the concept of atman tends to be used to justify a materialistic or mortal and ultimately nihilistic view of human birth, but such was not the original view of Gautama (who was psychically aware of the continuum before and after bodily death). But the Buddhist criticism can be a useful interpretation of the facts insofar as it helps us to maintain the view that the manifest self is merely or wholly a phenomenal process, rather than a phenomenal appearance superimposed on an immortal soul that should be systematically separated out from the world (as commonly proposed in the fourth and fifth stage schools). Likewise, the Buddhist criticism of the traditional concept of the atman is rightly disposed to abandon all meditative exercises based on the idea of the separable atman (or salvation via gnostic separation of the soul from the body and the lower worlds). The Buddhist view is thus also rightly disposed to abandon meditation on the atman or self-essence (as proposed in the sixth stage schools of Advaita Vedanta).

However, I regard the ultimate Realization of Upanishadic Advaitism (expressed in the formula epitomized by the Confession "Brahman is the world" and other formulae, such as "Thou art That" and "Atman and Paramatman are identical") to be the same as that proclaimed in the Buddhist schools as the correct view of Nirvana and expressed in such formulae as "Nirvana and samsara are the same."

The radical Way of understanding is the ultimate Way of Truth. It is implicit and often, to one or another degree, explicit in the traditional schools (particularly in the great traditional formulae of the Upanishads and ultimate Buddhism and such seventh stage texts as the *Ashtavakra Gita* and the *Lankavatara Sutra*). The Way of Radical Understanding is a matter of presently transcending the conventional objective and subjective modes of phenomenal being. It is a matter of directly and presently transcending the meditative techniques of object-meditation and subject-meditation—or the error of ascribing necessity, independence, or Reality to any of the possible objects or subject-modes that condition phenomenal existence according to the various preferences that characterize the first six stages of life.

What Transcends or stands beyond any present object—What is Obvious when the self-contraction that defines self and objects independent of the Radiant Transcendental Being, Brahman, or the Nirvanic Reality is itself presently and directly transcended—is the Condition or Identity in which all objects, the self, all beings, or the fundamental contraction that differentiates the un-Real from the Real are arising as apparent modifications of Itself.

Real meditation (or that meditation in which Reality is directly, tacitly, or already Obvious) is not a matter of meditation on any object (high or low in the chain of phenomenal appearances). Nor is it a matter of meditation on the self-essence, the witness of objects, or the atman. Real meditation is a matter of unmediated transcendence of the conventional limitations, implications, or consequences of attention. It is a matter of direct, present understanding or recognition of attention itself. It is a matter of present understanding and transcendence of the self-contraction that is the basic or primal element of every form or object of knowledge or experience.

When the habit of attention is presently understood, or when the idea of the self-essence as being or a being separate from objects and even from other beings is transcended, or when the conception of self, not-self, and the separation between self and not-self is gone beyond, then the Real is Obvious. And when the Real is Obvious, then any and all objects or subject-modes that presently arise are recognizable in That, without any dependence on strategic fixation on any object or strategic and exclusive inversion upon the essence of being.

XVIII
Atman, Brahman, Shunyata, and Nirvana

The Radiant Transcendental Being is not the "atman," the soul or presumed eternal individual self-essence. There is no such <u>eternal</u> individual. What is presumed to be the individual self is a temporary configuration that is the present result of a continuous play (without apparent beginning or end) upon the Only Eternal, which is the Radiant Transcendental Being. Therefore, the "atman" is <u>Really</u> Brahman, or Transcendental Being, in which all beings and conditions appear to arise, but which is characterized as Void ("Shunyata"), the Nirvanically or Transcendentally Real. All conditions arise in the Radiant Transcendental Being or Void like thoughts arise in the mind. There is no ultimate substantiality, eternality, or necessity to any of it.

If conceived relative to the conditions of manifest being, the Transcendental Reality or Being may seem to be an ultimate negative. But if the Radiant Transcendental Being is actually Realized, It is found to be the Radiant Fullness of Love-Bliss.

The Radiant Transcendental Being or Reality is the Identity (or Self) of all beings and the Condition (or Source-Substance) of all conditions. Therefore, this Realization does not require a self-negative, body-negative, or world-negative presumption. Realization is not associated with rejection or non-awareness of the world, but it is a matter of tacit, unmediated, or non-problematic recognition of the world. Therefore, all conditions may simply be recognized in the Radiant Transcendental Being and thus permitted their spontaneous arising, changing, and passing away. But this same recognition of conditions and self in the Radiant Transcendental Being also ultimately Outshines conditions and self in the Nirvanic Love-Bliss or Void-Fullness of the Truth.

The radical or seventh stage Realization is not a matter of the separation of the ultimate Self from the body-mind (or

"Purusha" from "Prakriti"). They are One, ultimately Identical to one another (or equally and simultaneously recognizable in the Radiant Transcendental Being). Thus, radical Realization is a matter of the recognition of all such separate categories (or states of cognition) in the One Reality. All that is cognized or experienced as existing (such as self, mind, thoughts, body, others, the world, God, and all objects, relations, or "others" than the self) is to be recognized in the Radiant Transcendental Being. Thus, in the case of such recognition, there is inherent transcendence of conditions (and even of self) without strategic or problematic separation from them. And, therefore, the evidence of Transfiguration and Transformation may appear in the process of the seventh stage of life, before the Outshining (or Translation in Bhava Samadhi) becomes complete.

XIX
Transcending the Hierarchy of Errors

The tradition of ascetical or Nirvanic Transcendentalism is a path of seeking based on a problem. This tradition is epitomized by Theravada or Hinayana Buddhism. By means of ascetical effort (founded on an intelligent appreciation of the negative and non-necessary status of conditional existence) the Transcendental Condition is pursued as a future attainment necessarily associated with the non-arising of all conditional states of self or its objects. Thus, such Nirvana comes to be the basis for the definition of Enlightenment (or the Realization of Reality), and this is an error.

The tradition of Advaitic (non-dual) or subjective Transcendentalism, epitomized by the Upanishadic or Vedantic non-dualism of Sri Shankara, is free of the problem-basis of the conventionally ascetical path. It is not fundamentally a path based on a negative evaluation of conditional existence (and a methodical attempt to destroy the mechanism of its arising). Rather, it is a path based primarily on most positive evaluation of the unconditional Reality, which is, as a matter of practice, located directly as the essential awareness behind the various functional mechanics of the subject-self. Thus, the method of the path is one of constant resort to identification with that essential awareness. If this is done, conditional states are simply and naturally dropped from attention. Whereas in the ascetical path there must be a completely successful dropping of all such conditions before Nirvanic Enlightenment can be attained, in the Advaitic path Enlightenment is equivalent to simple identification with the fundamental awareness (and the dropping of conditional motives or states is a secondary expression of that very Enlightenment). However, exclusive subjectivism (or the identification of Enlightenment with awareness in the specific locus of the conditional self and qualified by the specific exclusion of objects) is a fundamental error of this path.

The Way that I Teach can certainly be felt to bear an affinity with the great traditions of Buddhism and Advaitism (although my life and Teaching developed spontaneously, without any significant or guiding influence from those traditions). However, I have, in my own Teaching consideration, found those traditions to contain certain limiting errors, and those errors are fundamental tendencies that belong to the sixth stage of life.

Those who live on the basis of the limits represented by the first three stages of life tend to suffer from the error of reductionism, or the tendency to conceive of existence in exclusively materialistic and terrestrial (or elemental and lower functional) terms. And those who live on the higher basis of the limits represented by the fourth and fifth stages of life tend to suffer from the error of misplaced ultimacy, or the tendency to regard the phenomenal attainments of the higher functional or cosmic scale as Reality or Truth. In turn, those who live on the basis of the limits represented by the sixth stage of life tend to suffer either from the error of nihilistic or radically ascetical realism (the problem-based effort to bring an end to conditional experience and functional subjectivity as a pre-condition for and a definition of Enlightenment or Reality) or subjective idealism (the exclusive identification of Reality with the eternal subject-awareness independent of objects).

The Way that I Teach is considered in terms that transcend the traditional errors, which are simply expressions of the errors inherent in the structures of the various stages of life previous to the seventh. Therefore, the ultimate (or seventh stage) consideration of the Way is specifically free of the limits or errors of the sixth stage of life. It is for this reason that I have entered into a thorough consideration of Buddhism and Advaitism.

In the seventh stage of life, Sahaj Samadhi ultimately becomes Bhava Samadhi. Bhava Samadhi, in my usage of the term, is equivalent to Nirvana. But Enlightenment, or Transcendental Realization of Truth or Reality, is prior to Bhava Samadhi (or Nirvana). If there is true Enlightenment (or Sahaj Samadhi) then Bhava Samadhi (or Nirvana Samadhi) will eventually and inevitably be the case. Considered in this manner, the Way is free of the problem-basis of all negative or "realistic" reactions to phenomenal existence, and the Way is inherently free of association with conventionally ascetical programs.

The Way that I Teach is developed on the basis of understanding the whole process and context of the phenomenal or conditional self. Therefore, the Way of Radical Understanding bears an affinity to the "realist" traditions (such as are epitomized by the various schools of Buddhism). However, the Way of Radical Understanding is not an ascetical path, focused on a strategic program of functional self-negation. Rather, it is a Way focused on the self-transcendence inherent in real understanding, and that self-transcendence is the moment or Context in which the Transcendental Reality is priorly Realized (even in the apparent context of conditional existence). This does not mean that discipline, renunciation, and Nirvanic Transcendence are not also characteristic of this Way. Rather, they appear on the basis of prior understanding and Awakening rather than as means for achieving such Enlightenment or Awakening.

The Way of Radical Understanding is thus free of the nihilistic error of ascetical realism, even though it is aligned to a realistic disposition (expressed via constant understanding and transcendence of the self-contraction).

The Way of Radical Understanding can also be said to bear an affinity with the "idealist" traditions (epitomized by the schools of Advaita Vedanta and such Sages as Ramana Maharshi). This is clear, since the Way is founded on self-transcending understanding, or re-cognition of self in the Transcendental Reality. However, the Way of Radical Understanding is not bound to the strategically subjectivist orientation of traditional Advaitism. The essential self-consciousness (or "atman") must be re-cognized or transcended as a focus of attention just as much as any other objects, high or low in the scale of perception or conception. The mechanism of attention itself must be re-cognized, and this ultimately requires the transcendence of attention not only to objects but also to the subject-consciousness (or the locus of awareness internal to the conditional or functional self, or the body-mind-self).

In the course of the development of spiritual maturity in the Way that I Teach, individuals may encounter, pass through, and only then fully transcend the mechanics and motives of the various stages of life previous to the seventh. But ultimately there is steady establishment in the Enlightened disposition of the seventh stage of life. In that disposition, the errors of elemental reductionism, misplaced ultimacy, ascetical realism, and idealistic subjectivism are inherently transcended. Therefore, in the seventh stage of life the Way that I Teach is practiced in its fullest or ultimate and most radical sense. In that case, all conditions of self and its objects are tacitly or directly recognized in the Transcendental Condition, Identity, Consciousness, or Radiant Being in which they are apparently and mechanically or spontaneously arising. That Transcendental Reality or Consciousness is not merely inside the subject self. It is not Realized via interiorization in the self but in direct recognition of the self.

Therefore, the Realization is inherently free of the sixth stage error of subjective idealism. Likewise, all conditions or objects of the functional self are recognized in that same Reality or Consciousness. That Reality or Consciousness is neither inside nor outside the functional self. It is not located via any "point of view," or on the basis of any reference to the conditional self. It is Realized Itself, directly, as and by Itself. It is the Transcendental Self or Real Consciousness. Even the Substantial Energy or Objective Matrix of all objects is recognized in the Transcendental Self. The world, the body, the mind, the Light above the head, and the self-knot in the right side of the heart are all recognized in the Boundless and Centerless Heart, the Radiant Self, the Transcendental Reality or Divine Consciousness. Therefore, in the seventh stage of life, the Transcendental Self is Radiant in the form and actions of the conditional self and world, but all conditions are recognized in the Self (which is the same Transcendental Reality or Consciousness Realized in Bhava Samadhi, or the Nirvanic Realization associated with the non-noticing or non-arising of conditional or subject-object phenomena). Thus, the conditional self and world are without necessity or binding power, and at last they become utterly transparent in that Radiant Consciousness, the Infinite Domain of Love-Bliss.

XX
Transcendentalism

From the "realist" point of view, I am a temporary and unnecessary form, the result of moving thoughts, passing from birth to death. But conventional "realism" is finally transcended in the point of view of Transcendental Realism, wherein form and thought are transparent in the Unborn.

From the point of view of exoteric "idealism," I am the

creaturely servant of God and mankind. From the point of view of esoteric "idealism," I am an eternal being, a fraction of total light, cycling back through the planes of Nature to the Eternal Being Who is the God and Cause and Sun and Unity of all the rays. But conventional (or exoteric and esoteric) "idealism" is finally transcended in the point of view of Transcendental Idealism, wherein the separately individuated self is transparent in the Only Self.

From the point of view of Radical Transcendentalism, or the Way that I Teach, there is, simply and only, Radiant Transcendental Being—and self, mind, body, world, and God are not other than This, but all are inherently transparent when recognized as This Only.

XXI
Advaita Vedanta, Classical Buddhism, and the Way of Radical Understanding

Advaitism: Meditate on (or invert attention upon) the essence of self (or witnessing consciousness) until all objects are excluded and the Transcendental is Revealed.

Buddhism: Meditate on (or clearly observe) all presently arising objects until the self (or the conventional sense of consciousness as individual and independent of objects) is overcome and the Transcendental is Revealed.

Advaitayana Buddhism: Understand and directly transcend the contraction that generates the sense of self and of objects as conventions of limitation (independent of one another and of the Transcendental), and so in every moment recognize self and objects (and the binding power of self and objects) in the Transcendental (or That which is always already Revealed).

XXII
The Three Teachings of the One Way

There are three principal Transcendentalist (or sixth to seventh stage) Teachings: Realist Buddhism (or Realist Transcendentalism), Idealist Advaitism (or Idealist Transcendentalism), and Advaitayana Buddhism (or Radical Transcendentalism).

The Buddhist Teaching of Realism is epitomized in the considerations of Gautama, and the Realization based on that Teaching is epitomized in texts such as the *Lankavatara Sutra* and the Sixth Patriarch's *Altar Sutra*. In this view, manifest existence, seen in itself, is regarded to be unnecessary suffering. The Way is to inspect every aspect of self, mind, body, and the world and see that every part is conditional, temporary, limited, and merely the result or effect of other conditional, temporary, and limited motions or events. When this inspection has become most profound, then it is obvious that no part of self, mind, body, or the world is anything but a form of conditional motion—an effect of previous motions and a cause of motions that will follow it. Therefore, it becomes obvious that Happiness is not in the form of any part of self, mind, body, or the world—or any form of effect or cause. The Truth is Transcendental (prior to effect and cause), and the Realization of Truth is a matter of Awakening to the acausal (or Nirvanic) Condition on the basis of first inspecting and transcending attachment (and conceptual confinement) to all forms of cause (or desire, or motivation, or motion) and all forms of effect (or self, mind, body, or world).

The Advaitist Teaching of Idealism is epitomized in the considerations of the *Yoga Vasishtha* and the philosophers Gaudapada and Shankara, and the Realization based on that Teaching is epitomized in the Confessions of Adepts such as

The Three Teachings of the One Way

Ashtavakra and Ramana Maharshi. In this view, manifest existence, seen in itself, is regarded to be an unnecessary illusion. The Way is not merely to turn attention away from the world, the body, the mind, and the self, but to turn or invert it toward the Transcendental Self or Consciousness in which the thought of self (or "I"), all other thoughts, and the experiential conception of the body and the world are arising. If this is done most profoundly, then the illusory independence of the phenomenal self, mind, body, and world will vanish in the Bliss of Unconditional Being. Therefore, it becomes finally obvious that self, mind, body, and world are not in any sense or to any degree independent from the Transcendental Self-Source, and it also becomes obvious that self, mind, body, and world have no necessity or binding power when viewed in the context of the Transcendental Self. The Truth is the Transcendental Self-Reality, and the Realization of Truth is a matter of Awakening to the Original or Natural and Native State of Identification with that Self-Reality on the basis of the inversion (or conversion) of attention into its noumenous Ground.

The Teaching of Advaitayana Buddhism (or Radical Transcendentalism) and the demonstration of its Way of Realization have their origin and epitome in my own Teaching Work. In this view, manifest existence is not a problem to be solved or escaped, but it is simply to be always already understood (and thus natively and naturally transcended, but not strategically avoided or egoically embraced). The Way is to observe that all problems and all seeking for solutions arise on the basis of self-contraction (or the Narcissistic effort that is the ego). Therefore, it is a matter of constantly observing, re-cognizing (or knowing again), and transcending this self-contraction (which is chronically manifested as the avoidance of relationship in the midst of all the kinds of psycho-physical relations).

When this process of understanding has become most profound, the relations, activities, and states of body and mind will have all been observed and felt beyond, so that only the most primary evidence of the self-contraction remains in view. That primary evidence is the rudimentary sense of relatedness. Therefore, the ultimate exercise, by which a natural transition is made to the seventh stage of life, is to re-cognize the sense of relatedness itself (which is the primal cognition or root-event of conditional existence, on the basis of which both the separate self and its apparently independent objects of all kinds are subsequently and simultaneously conceived and differentiated). The sense of relatedness is itself to be re-cognized as contraction, directly, free of any strategic resort to introversion upon the self or to extroversion, beyond direct cognition of the sense of relatedness itself, into the wandering of attention in the differentiated field of objects. When this ultimate form of re-cognition is most profound, the Consciousness in which self, mind, body, world, or all forms of contraction are arising stands forth as the Obvious Reality, and Its Status as the Divine or Transcendental Identity and Condition of self and not-self is also inherently Obvious. Since Reality, or the Real Condition, is necessarily That which is always already the case, prior to all subsequent acts that cause It to appear other than It is, the re-cognition of all such acts, or of the primary action that is the root-constant of all such acts, necessarily and naturally or inevitably Reveals That as the Obvious. That which is ultimately Obvious is the ultimately Real. And the Obvious, prior to all forms of contraction, and prior to the cognition of separate self, its objects, or the primary sense of relatedness, is unqualified consciousness, or Radiant Transcendental Being.

In the view of Advaitayana Buddhism, the Truth is Radiant Transcendental Being, Consciousness, Love-Bliss, or Happiness, and all arising conditions are transparent, or merely apparent, unnecessary, and non-binding modifications of That. Realization of That is a matter of the inspection, re-cognition, and inherent transcendence of the self-contraction, which is conventionally perceived via the dual sense of separate self and the otherness of all conditions that confront the self, but which is singly or most basically evident in the sense of relatedness itself (prior to the conventional distinctions and elaborations of the play between self and not-self).

The Three Teachings of the One Way

All three of these most basic and unique Transcendentalist Teachings ultimately involve a practice and a Realization that goes beyond or transcends the world, the body, the mind, and the separate or egoic self. But there is no such transcendence until there is in fact such transcendence. Therefore, until the Way becomes most profound, practice is inevitably associated with various disciplines of the body-mind and attention. But the purpose of such disciplines is always secondary or supportive to the ultimate consideration, or the practice and process in consciousness. Therefore, the basic purpose of the supportive disciplines is to release energy and attention from the bind of egoic habituation, so that the conscious process may become most profound.

The traditions of Buddhist Realism and Advaitist Idealism are the two Great Schools coming out of the two primary ancient streams of consideration—or the "realistic" and "idealistic" traditions of philosophy. Buddhist Realism is a Transcendentalist philosophy that founds its Argument on the language of "realism," and that language is specifically intended as a criticism of the speculative metaphysical and "eternalistic" views of the tradition of subjective "idealism." Even so, the Way of Buddhist Realism eventually leads to a Realization that transcends all of the conventions and structures (or "dharmas") of "realism" (all of which are, from the beginning, regarded as unnecessary suffering). In contrast to the tradition of Buddhist Realism, Advaitist Idealism is a Transcendentalist philosophy that founds its Argument on the language of subjective "idealism," and that language is specifically intended as a criticism of the "nihilistic" tendencies of the "realist" position. Even so, the Way of Advaitist Idealism eventually leads to a Realization that transcends the Narcissistic or world-excluding subjectivism of conventional "idealism." Advaitayana Buddhism, which is only now appearing, epitomizes the Transcendental tradition as a whole, but the language of its Argument transcends the conventional limitations of both "realism" and "idealism," so that, from the beginning, its Way transcends the orientations of the two ancient attitudes of consideration.

Realist Buddhism is the Way that Realizes the Transcendental Truth beyond the not-self (or all phenomenal conditions—all of which, including the ego, bear the characteristic of not-self or no-self).

Idealist Advaitism is the Way that Realizes the Transcendental Truth beyond the self (and thus also beyond all that is not-self, or all the insentient phenomenal relations of the conscious phenomenal self—all of which relations bear the illusory appearance of independence from the conscious self).

Advaitayana Buddhism is the Way that Realizes the Transcendental Truth beyond (or prior to) the primary sense or cognition of relatedness, which is the single basis or prior and original sign of the subsequent and simultaneously arising pair of opposites—the self and the not-self. Both the self and the not-self are simply apparent (and apparently different or opposite) aspects of the same unnecessary contraction from the Condition of Radiant Transcendental Being, and neither of them is directly and finally transcended unless the conventionally unconscious or uninspected contraction is directly inspected in the form of the primary sense of relatedness.

The Transcendental Truth realized via each of these three principal Ways is the same. The Way that is chosen depends, apart from the karma or accident of mere cultural proximity, on the quality or kind of intelligence that moves the individual. And the Way of Advaitayana Buddhism (or Radical Transcendentalism) is the epitome or ultimate fulfillment and single form of the two separate Ways conceived according to the logical opposites of Buddhist Realism and Advaitist Idealism.

XXIII
Nirvanasara

"I" is the body (or the total body-mind). There is no "I" inside, other than, or separate from the body-mind (or conditional self).

"I" is contraction—a separative (self-defining and other-defining) effort added to That which is always already the case. As an ordinary or foundation discipline (to maintain psycho-physical equanimity and release energy and attention from entrapment by the conditions of the body-mind), the "I" (or psycho-physical self) should be relaxed, surrendered, and expanded beyond its own knot or gesture of contraction. But mature practice develops only in the event of the stability of true equanimity—that state in which energy and attention are relatively free of the tendency to be distracted or bound by the psycho-physical symptoms of the self-contraction. That mature practice begins when self-observation has developed to the point of certainty that the "I" (or body-mind-self) is contraction, inherently, and in every form of its appearance. Therefore, the mature practice is one that transcends the motives of self-expansion (and the obsessive search to achieve pleasurably distracted psycho-physical states). Such mature practice is simply the re-cognition (or direct transcendence through always present understanding, or knowing again) of "I" (or all forms of the body-mind-self) as contraction.

When the self-contraction is utterly re-cognized, it becomes clear that it is only a transparent, or merely apparent, unnecessary, and non-binding modification of Nirvanic, Transcendental, or Divine Being, Consciousness, or Love-Bliss. Such is radical intuition, or the ultimate basis of the Way that I Teach.

The Way of Radical Understanding, or Divine Ignorance, or Advaitayana Buddhism is not a conventional path of self-seeking or God-seeking based on being the "I" rather than transcending the "I." The Way truly begins only when it is observed and understood that the "I" is only contraction. All the forms or developments of the "I" that are observed in the first six stages of life are only contraction. All that is body, all that is mind, and all that is self is only contraction. And the conventional cognition of all the objects of the body-mind-self—the world, all beings, thoughts, subtle forms and states, and all apparitions or conceptions of God—is rooted in and determined by that same contraction. When this understanding is most profound, only That in which "I" (and its states and relations) is arising stands out as the Obvious. Therefore, the essence of the Way is to understand and thus tacitly transcend the self-contraction (rather than make all kinds of conditional and self-based efforts to expand beyond the knot of self-contraction). And the radical fulfillment of the Way is in the native, direct, or spontaneous Realization of That which is No-contraction, prior to all contraction, prior to Its own modification in the form of contraction and all subsequent appearances. It is to Realize That in which contraction or modification is apparently (but not by virtue of ultimate necessity) arising. Such Realization is Sahaj Samadhi, or Divine Ignorance.

In Sahaj Samadhi, the self-contraction is inherently transcended through its prior re-cognition and ultimate or radical Identification with Radiant Transcendental Being. And all of the parts of the total Realm of Nature (including all of the phenomenal structures of the body-mind) are only then tacitly and inherently and spontaneously recognized to be transparent, or merely apparent, unnecessary, non-ultimate, or non-binding modifications of that same Radiant Transcendental Being. Therefore, in the seventh stage of life, self and not-self are no longer merely defined and separated (on the basis of the self-contraction) but equally recognized and transcended in Radiant Transcendental Being—the Ultimate Divine, prior to separation, otherness, and limitation. In the Awakening of the seventh stage of life, the self-contraction (or "I") is already and inherently or priorly transcended, and the not-self (or Nature) is thus also inherently or tacitly recognized.

The Way in the seventh stage of life is to Abide in Divine Ignorance, or tacit and prior Identification with Radiant Transcendental or Divine Being, spontaneously recognizing whatever arises (as mind, or phenomenon, or action) in That, until all is forgotten or Outshined in That.

When there is no self-contraction, the Realm of Nature is Obvious as it is. The self-contraction and the entire Realm of Nature are arising as transparent, or merely apparent, unnecessary, and non-binding modifications of the same One Radiant Transcendental Divine Being or Reality! Therefore, transcend the self-contraction via radical understanding until the Awakening of the seventh stage of life, wherein self and not-self are equally and simultaneously transcended and ultimately Outshined in the One that is Love and Happiness and the Peace of Bliss.

This is "Nirvanasara," the Essence of the Teaching of Nirvana, or Radical Transcendentalism.

About Master Da Free John

Worldly genius is rare enough, but only once every so often humanity is graced by the appearance of a spiritual giant. Master Da Free John was born fully enlightened, on the third of November 1939, into an unsuspecting middle-class family of Jamaica, Long Island (New York), and a starkly materialistic environment. Master Da's birth was a free, spontaneous incarnation with the specific and compassionate purpose of instructing spiritually sensitive people of the twentieth century in the "Way of Life." His enlightened Condition remained stable throughout the gradual maturation of the personality of "Franklin Jones," as he was formerly known.

From earliest childhood on he underwent spontaneous purificatory experiences caused by his awakened *kuṇḍalinī*. At first these would manifest in the form of sudden attacks of intense fever and skin rashes, traditionally recognized as one of the symptoms of an active *kuṇḍalinī*. But he also experienced the whole range of physical and psychic phenomena associated with this extraordinary process. In his eighth year all these *kuṇḍalinī* symptoms subsided, and he entered a period of "relative latency" during which, as he puts it, he "took on a social personality." This period of social adaptation lasted until he was about seventeen years old when the spontaneous yogic process resumed its manifest activity.

After several years of exposing himself to all manner of experiences, situations, and trials, he experienced a "crisis of despair" about the world around him. This led to a profound reawakening in 1960 while he was doing undergraduate studies at Columbia College. In his widely-read spiritual autobiography *The Knee of Listening*, Master Da Free John recollects:

> I experienced a total revolution of energy and awareness in myself. An absolute sense of understanding opened and arose at the extreme end of all this consciousness. And all of

the energy of thought that moved down into that depth appeared to reverse its direction at some unfathomable point. The rising impulse caused me to stand, and I felt a surge of force draw up out of my depths and expand, filling my whole body and every level of my consciousness with wave on wave of the most beautiful and joyous energy.

I felt absolutely mad, but the madness was not of a desperate kind. There was no seeking and no dilemma within it, no question, no unfulfilled motive, not a single object or presence outside myself. (p. 13)

This experience left him with two important insights: Firstly, where there is no seeking, no consciousness of being caught in dilemmas and contradictions, there is only and simply Reality. Secondly, man is essentially enlightened and the nescient mind is merely a superimposition upon that prior illumination. From that point on, the individual Franklin Jones began a conscious spiritual discipline (*sādhana*) based on "an internal process of a kind of listening." From 1962 to 1964, while living in secluded retreats, he engaged in an exhaustive and constant observation of the "myth of Narcissus," the separative self-sense which his college experience had disclosed to him forcefully. He writes about this period:

I would simply perceive every form of memory or internal imagery, every form of thought or perception, every indication or pattern in my daily experience, every intention, every imposition from without, in fact every possible kind of experience. (Ibid., pp. 16–17)

In order to facilitate this comprehensive self-inspection, he continued to pursue "every kind of means, every method of interiorization and exteriorization of awareness that could possibly dredge up the lost content, the controlling myth." (Ibid., p. 17)

Then, in 1964, the process of psychic transformation reached a new peak, corresponding to Franklin Jones's move toward the outside world. The same accelerated process of inner change led to his witnessing of the psycho-physical, synchronous nature of reality. (This principle of synchronicity, rather than that of conventional causality, is fundamental to a proper understanding of the maturation of Franklin Jones into the Enlightened Being that he always was. The external events in the Master's life are never merely causes or effects of something else, but correspond to the psychic process of unfoldment within him.) During this phase he had countless psychic experiences, including recurrent visions of an Oriental art store in New York where he would, in the same year, meet Swami Rudrananda ("Rudi"). Under the guidance of this American-born teacher, he dedicated himself to the practice of a form of *kuṇḍalinī-yoga*.

He submitted himself wholeheartedly and completely to the disciplinary demands of this teacher, and at Swami Rudrananda's behest even entered a Lutheran seminary.

In the spring of 1967, while studying at the seminary, Franklin Jones passed through a "death" experience analogous to the one reported by Sri Ramana Maharshi.

> When all of the fear and dying had become a matter of course, when the body, the mind and the person with which I identified myself had died, and my attention was no longer fixed in those things, I perceived or enjoyed reality, fully and directly. There was an infinite bliss of being, an untouched, unborn sublimity, without separation, without individuation, without a thing from which to be separated. (Ibid., p. 63)

At that point he saw that all his life's search had been founded on the "avoidance of relationship in all its forms." He realized that conventional human life was in fact determined by this chronic avoidance of relationship, of the unqualified love which is Reality. From then on, he simply tried to live in the light of this recognition by "maintaining this true understanding under all conditions."

The momentum of this critical insight and consequent change in his spiritual practice led Franklin Jones, in 1968, to approach Swami Rudrananda's own teacher, Swami Muktananda. After only four days in the company of this renowned Indian adept, Franklin Jones experienced, for the first time in his adult life, the "formless ecstasy" (*nirvikalpa-samādhi*) prized so highly in the yogic tradition. Several auspicious factors converged to bring about this breakthrough, including spiritual encounters with Swami Nityananda and Rang Avadhoot as well as the whole intense yogic environment of Swami Muktananda's Ashram in India. And a year later, Swami Muktananda confirmed in a rare written document that Master Da Free John had indeed attained "the highest human condition" (*mūla-manāvāta*), "yogic liberation" (*yoga-mokṣa*).

Master Da knew, however, that the perfect Enlightenment which he had enjoyed on the transcendental level from his birth was still only imperfectly expressed in the body-mind he happened to be associated with. These last limitations on the psychophysical level were finally removed in the "Vedanta Society Temple" event of September 1970. At that point Franklin Jones truly died as a separate personality and entered the permanent disposition of *sahaja-samādhi,* the ecstasy with "open eyes" as Master Da calls it. In his spiritual autobiography, he describes this momentous event thus:

> In an instant, I became profoundly and directly aware of what I am. It was a tacit realization, a direct knowledge in consciousness itself without the addition of a communication from any other source. I simply sat there and knew what I am. I was being what I am. I am Reality, the Self, and Nature and Support of all things and all beings. I am the One Being, known as God, Brahman, Atman, the One Mind, the Self.
>
> There was no thought involved in this. I am that Consciousness. There was no reaction either of joy or surprise. I am the One I recognized. I am that One. I am not merely experiencing Him.
>
> Then truly there was no more to realize. Every experience in my life had led to this. The dramatic revelations in

childhood and college, my time of writing, my years with Rudi, the revelation in seminary, the long history of pilgrimage to the Ashram, all of these moments were the intuitions of this same Reality. My entire life had been the communication of that Reality to me, until I am That. (Ibid., p. 134–35)

Master Da's whole early life had been a paradoxical struggle to bring his body-mind to a point of receptivity where it would fully incarnate his prior Enlightenment. With the realization in the Vedanta Society Temple, this process came to its unsurpassable culmination. There was now no more need for him to meditate or to enter any of the mystical or yogic states of ecstasy. His God-Realization remained constant throughout all the experiences of daily life.

He was (and is) from that time in a perpetual state of *sahaja-samādhi*, with both "natural" awareness and uncommon psychic awareness. In this *samādhi*, he would spontaneously see the contents of other minds arising in him, which he would then meditate. He humorously compared his role to "an old lady cleaning a bird cage." This confirmed to him his obligation to teach others. Soon people began to seek out his illumined company who had had "inexplicable" meditation experiences which changed their whole outlook on life.

At first, Master Da granted frequent access to spiritual aspirants or devotees, but gradually, as they matured more, he would insist on an increasingly formal relationship and stricter discipline all round. In order to help those who had found their way to him, and those who were still to come, he developed a whole new way of life which facilitates spiritual growth in a truly human community.

That way of life is founded on the principle of *satsaṅga* or "true relationship," which Master Da has been teaching from the very beginning. *Satsaṅga* is traditionally understood to refer to the practice of spending time in the company of a saintly person, but one can also enjoy *satsaṅga* with a sacred locality or object, or indeed with the Divine itself. Master Da Free John uses the term to denote the transcendental relationship between a God-Realized Adept and his devotees. In this relationship Reality itself is communicated directly on all levels of consciousness and life.

In August 1973, Franklin Jones went on a pilgrimage to India where he visited many traditional sites and a number of spiritual teachers as a kind of *yajña* or ceremony of sacrifice to his own spiritual sources. When he returned, he returned as "Bubba Free John," which is a spiritual rendering of his birthname "Franklin Jones" prefixed with "Bubba," meaning "brother" (a name by which he had been called since childhood). Subsequently he served his devotees through "teaching demonstrations" during which he would graciously allow them to participate temporarily in higher states of consciousness and thus to witness the truth of his teaching. In particular, he wanted everyone to understand the futility of all experiences, high or low, and that the only worthwhile concern should be the transcendence of all experience, including the traditionally valued "formless ecstasy."

In November 1976, he was spontaneously moved to discontinue his frequent personal contact with hundreds of devotees and spent the following years producing much of the new community's "source literature." In mid-September 1979, the Master abandoned his name "Bubba" for the spiritual title of "Da," meaning "Giver." Having created a spiritual culture for a growing community of devotees, he now lives in seclusion and only occasionally sits with devotees in formal meditation. But his presence makes itself felt throughout The Johannine Daist Communion, and his persistent demands for more and more rigorous spiritual practice are a constant inspiration for all the practitioners: they understand that access to the Adept must be earned through mature practice. That Master Da Free John's retirement from active teaching does not signal the end of his compassionate activity in the world is evident from the essays in this new book. And he is still calling for real practitioners who are prepared to devote themselves to the highest ideal of God-Realization in his company.

I am interested in finding men and women who are free of every kind of seeking, who are attendant only to understanding, and who will devote themselves to the intentional creation of human life in the form and logic of Reality, rather than the form and logic of Narcissus.

Thus, I would find a new order of men and women, who will create a new age of sanity and joy. It will not be the age of the occult, the religious, the scientific, or the technological domination of humanity. It will be the fundamental age of Real Existence, wherein Life will be radically realized, entirely apart from the whole history of our adventure and great search.

(Scientific Proof of the Existence of God Will Soon Be Announced by the White House!, pp. 110–11)

About The Johannine Daist Communion

The spiritual fellowship of devotees of the Adept Da Free John, who practice the Way of Radical Understanding or Divine Ignorance that Master Da Teaches, is called THE JOHANNINE DAIST COMMUNION. Its name derives from the name and title of Master Da Free John. "Johannine" means "having the character of John," which means "one through whom God is Gracious." "Da" is a name of the living, eternal, infinite Divine Being or Reality. When used to refer to the Spiritual Master, it is a title of respect and an indication of spiritual stature, much as the traditional titles of "Rabbi," "Swami," or "Holiness."

The Communion has four divisions:

THE LAUGHING MAN INSTITUTE is the public education division of the Communion offering programs about the Way to the public, to friends and supporters of the Teaching, to beginning practitioners, and to those preparing for practicing membership in the Communion.

THE CRAZY WISDOM FELLOWSHIP is the educational and cultural organization of maturing practitioners of the Way of Radical Understanding.

Those who have completed their preparation for the Way and who are maturing in the higher or esoteric stages of practice are members of THE ADVAITAYANA BUDDHIST ORDER. The term "Buddhism" refers to the ancient teachings of the great Adepts (including but not limited to Gautama) who Realized and Taught the transcendence of conditioned reality (samsara). "Advaita" refers to the tradition of Upanishadic non-dualism, or the Way of the Adepts who Taught the Realization of That which transcends conditioned reality. The Way that Master Da Free John Teaches brings together these two highest expressions of spiritual Realization and, at the same time, is their culmination, transcending the limitations peculiar to each of the two.

The term "yana," meaning "vehicle" or "way," has traditionally been used to distinguish the three great branches of Buddhism (the Hinayana, or "narrow" way of original Buddhism; the Mahayana, or "wide" way of lay practice; and the Vajrayana, the "diamond" or "essential" way of tantric practice). Master Da characterizes the Way that he Teaches as the fourth vehicle: Advaitayana Buddhism, or the Way of Radical Transcendentalism.

THE FREE RENUNCIATE ORDER consists of devotees who have Realized the ultimate stage of practice of the Way. These Enlightened individuals are served by members of THE HERMITAGE SERVICE ORDER, who, while practicing in the lower stages of the Way, live the disposition of spiritual renunciation. The Hermitage Service Order is thus the operational limb of the Free Renunciate Order, and its members manage the fulfillment of the responsibilities of the Free Renunciate Order, which are to preserve, protect, and provide access to the spiritual Treasures of the fellowship—the Spiritual Master, his Teaching, and the Holy Sites he has empowered.

AN INVITATION

If you would like to learn more about the study and practice of the Spiritual Teaching of Master Da Free John or about how to begin to practice the Way, please write:

THE LAUGHING MAN INSTITUTE
P.O. Box 3680
Clearlake, California 95422

INDEX

Absolute, the, 19
absolutism, 121
adepts, 8, 51, 89f., 96, 122, 133, 150, 159, 162ff., 214
Advaita Vedanta (Advaitism), 10, 27, 34f., 65, 67, 70, 89f., 102ff., 129, 184f., 217, 235
  and Buddhism, 71, 148ff., 218ff.
  limitation of, 167
Advaitayana Buddhism (The Way that I Teach), 45, 72, 98ff., 112, 142f., 148, 168, 235ff.
  and Advaitism, 73
ahimsa, 39
Ajivikas, 39
Ajnana school, 39
Akbar, 45
alaya-vijnana, 42
Altar Sutra, 236
alcoholism, 25
anandamaya-kosha, 126n, 166
Ananda Mayi Ma, 51
anatman, 27. *See also* non-self
Angeles, P. A., 29n
anima, 29
animism, 29, 176 et passim
  and Advaitism, 109
  magical, 60, 158
  pluralistic, 31, 59, 60, 66, 177
  singularistic, 31
  and Vedic tradition, 64
Arhat (arahant), 41, 139
asana, 190
Asanga, 42
asceticism, 90, 96, 183, 213, 230
ascent
  shamanistic, 79
  yogic, 60, 140
Ashtanga Yoga, 190
Ashtavakra, 72, 120, 133, 237
Ashtavakra-Gita, 120n, 227
atheism, 19f., 37, 80ff., 123
atman, 27, 110, 128, 148, 170, 205, 223, 226, 229. *See also* self, Self
attention, 26, 88, 91, 115, 191, 208, 219, 228
  free, 174
  inversion of, 92, 131, 166, 235
  transcendence of, 27, 192f., 233
Avadhoot, 160
avatara, 53f.
awareness, transcendence of, 93
  native state of, 214

Baha'i, 46
behavior, unconventional, 96
being, manifest, 87
belief, 154, 197f., 204f.
  method of, 201
Benjamin Minor, 13
Bhagavad-Gita, 12, 19, 38, 65, 130, 212
Bhagavata-Purana, 53, 130, 212
Bhakti Yoga, 188
Bhava Samadhi, 97, 116, 139, 147, 157, 160, 193, 230, 232
Bible, 198
Bliss, 93, 147 et passim
bodhisattva, 42, 139f., 156
Bodhisiddha, 162
body-mind. *See also* self

and ego, 9, 241
Transfigured, 193
brahma-bhuta, 19
brahman, 43, 96, 110, 138, 148, 220ff.
Brahmajala-Sutta, 39
Brahma Samaj, 46
brainwashing, 151
Buddha-Mind, 101, 103, 145
buddhi, 167
Buddhism, 32f., 39, 42, 89f. et passim
  and Advaitism, 71, 98ff., 107ff.
  Madhyamika, 42, 144
  Mahayana, 42, 67, 100, 102, 105, 139ff., 144ff., 217
  not nihilistic, 103, 124
  "pop", 148f.
  Tantrayana, 67
  Theravada (Hinayana), 64f., 99, 103, 139ff., 208f., 216, 230, 235
  Vajrayana, 67, 100, 102, 139ff., 158ff.
  and Vedic tradition, 184
  Vijnanavada, 42, 106, 144f.
  Yogacara, 42, 144f.
Bu-ston, 54

causation
  Buddhist chain of, 40, 67, 92
  Divine, 180
Ch'an, 133, 146
Christianity, 49, 57, 74ff., 83, 178, 183, 198f., 216
cognition, suprasensuous, 18
Columbus, 11
compassion, 14, 42
consciousness, 41, 65, 91, 117ff., 210, 214
  mythical, 11
Consciousness, transcendental, 115, 117ff., 129, 135ff., 169, 233f., 238
conversion, to the Way, 58
Copernicus, 11
cosmology
  and atheism, 80
  and Divine Emanation, 65
cosmos, dimensions of, 58. *See also* Nature
Crazy Wisdom, 96, 133, 153, 160
Cues, Nikolaus of, 45

Da Free John, as adept, 8ff.
darshana, six classical, 37ff.
Darwin, 197
Dattatreya school, 160
da Vinci, 11
death
  and consciousness, 127
  existence after, 68, 226f
desire, 24, 184
Devi school, 160
Digha-Nikaya, 53n
dharana, 190
dharma, 41, 92, 113, 123, 126f., 132, 145, 186f., 208, 239
  as Truth, 135, 187
dhyana, 190
discipline, 174, 239
Divine Communion, 213f.
Divine Emanation, 32, 61f., 69, 176
  and consciousness, 127
  and seventh stage, 66
Divine Ignorance, 19n, 115, 241

Index

doubt, 16, 57, 93, 208
drug addiction, 25
dynamism, 30

education, 15
ego, 20, 34, 99 et passim
  and atheism, 80
  development, 89
  as error, 51, 84
  and God, 77
  as Master, 149
  salvation, 89
  and seventh stage, 79
  as unnecessary, 174
Einstein, 197
Eliade, M., 176
emanationism, 32, 44, 104, 128, 159, 194f. *See also* Divine Emanation
energy, 137
  and animism, 31, 59
enlightenment, 113, 209, 215, 224 et passim
  deferred, 156
  definition of, 87f., 91, 95f.
  positively regarded, 180
equanimity, 85f., 114f., 136, 211
essentialism, 33
eternalism, 40, 43, 125, 214
esoteric, and exoteric, 61 et passim
esotericism, 31, 61
evil, 78f. *See also* good
evolution, psycho-spiritual, 23
existence
  after death, 58, 68
  nature of, 116
  positively regarded, 180
  as a problem, 66, 98 et passim
  and suffering, 40, 68, 99
  as unnecessary, 101
eye, third, 26

faith, 18, 26, 96f.
  Realization as true, 207
feeling-attention, 23, 213
fire
  image of, 172ff.
  as method, 181
  Transcendental, 51, 186f.
  Vedic, 176
Fire Sermon, the Buddha's, 173
freedom, religious, 64
Freud, 197

Galileo, 11, 197
Gaudapada, 43, 102, 236
Gautama, the Buddha, 32, 74 et passim
  his reluctance to teach, 165
  silence of, 103
God
  as Creator, 34, 77ff.
  mystical knowledge of, 60
  as Reality, 84, 86 et passim
God-Realization, 87
good, and evil, 34, 78f., 84f.
Gospel of John, 75
Great Tradition, 17ff., 47, 121, 198f.
  and Advaitayana Buddhism, 73, 107f., 154f.
  definition of, 57n, 71

Happiness, 86, 93, 136, 138, 187, 220, 236, 238, 243
Hatha Yoga, 189
"hearing," 174, 206f.
"heart," 26, 28

heaven, 183, 188 et passim
Hebrews, the early, 59f.
Hinduism, 37 et passim
   and Buddhism, 66
   and Christianity, 178
Holy Books, 189
Hugh of St. Victor, 13

idealism
   in Buddhism, 27, 70, 146
   and consciousness, 120
   materialistic, 63
   of Source, 195
   subjective, 65, 110, 232, 239
   and theism, 80
ideocentrism, 36
imitatio Dei, 50
inexpressibles, the fourteen, 33
insight, 67, 73, 91f., 101, 201, 207, 213, 219, 222
inspection, 236, 238
institutions, 162f.
inversion, 111f., 115, 131, 166f., 204. *See also* attention
invisible, the, 17ff., 58f.
Islam, 43, 83, 178, 183, 198f., 215

Jainism, 38f., 64f., 130, 176
Jefferson, 197
Jesus, 49f., 74ff., 150, 197
Jnana Yoga, 166f., 189
Judaism, 49, 83, 178, 215

kali-yuga, 43
Kalkin, 53f.
karma, 240
karma, laws of, 58

Karma Yoga, 188
Kepler, 11
Khan, Hazrat Inayat, 46
King, J., 30
knowledge
   embedded in theory, 33
   mystical, 84
   and power, 81ff.
Koran, 198
Krishna, 150
Kriya Yoga, 189
Kundalini Yoga, 189
kutastha, 12ff., 19

language
   emanationist, 67 et passim
   limitations of, 44, 68
   radical, 67, 122, 134
   realist, 69, 103
   religious, 66, 126
   Vedic and Buddhist, 71
Lankavatara-Sutra, 144f., 214, 227, 236
liberation, 27, 38
life
   emanationist idea of, 181
   as frustration, 208
Life-Current, 26, 28
life-force, 30, 79
light, 118ff.
Lincoln, 197
Lokayata school, 39
love, 24, 26, et passim

magic, elemental, 59
   taboos against, 62
Mahamudra, 161f.
maha-siddha, 7, 21, 55, 139f. *See also* adepts
Mahavira, 39
Maitreya, 53f.

Index

Majjhima-Nikaya, 33
man
  as fire bearer, 180
  less than human, 151
mana, 30
manomaya-kosha, 126n
Mantra Yoga, 18
Mark, 20, 197
Marx, 20, 197
mass culture, 82, 197
materialism
  and Buddhism, 66, 68
  definition of, 63
  political, 63, 82
  scientific, 17, 57, 63, 120, 199
Matthew, 48, 53
maya, 88, 94
megbe, 30
meditation, 175, 228, 235
method
  vs. methodos, 18
  scientific, 61
Miceli, V. P., 20
middle path, of the Buddha, 32
Mimamsa, 37
mind. *See also* ego, self
  higher, 36, 151
  insufficiency of, 154
  natural state of, 209
  primitive, 29
  scientific, 57
  total, 58
Mohammed, 197
monotheism, 60f., 64, 66
Moses, 197
mountain, metaphor of, 12ff.
mystery, 75
mystical experience, taboos against, 62

mysticism, cosmic, 79

Nada Yoga, 189
Naropa, Six Yogas of, 189
Nagarjuna, 115, 133, 144
Narcissus, 154, 205, 207. *See also* ego, self
Nature
  as energy, 117
  play of, 84ff.
nervous system, 79
Newton, 15, 197
Nicodemus, 75f.
nihilism, 16, 33, 40, 126, 149, 214, 239
nirvana, 27, 68, 89, 100, 116, 144f., 148ff., 205, 208ff.
Nirvana Samadhi, 193, 232
Nirvanasara, meaning of, 243
nirvikalpa-samadhi, 129, 138, 161, 188, 194
niyama, 190
Noble Eightfold Path, 216
no-mind, 211
no-self, 194 et passim
Nyaya, 38

objectivity, ideal of, 15
observation, 196, 219, 237. *See also* self-observation
ontology, 38
origination, dependent, 114

Padmasambhava, 54
pain, 87. *See also* suffering
Pali literature, 215
Patanjali, 38, 189, 191n
Petrarca, 11ff.
phenomena, 210f.
  nature of, 145
phenomenalism, 126

phenomenon, noumenal, 130
philosophy, transcendental, 118
play, spiritual, 97
polytheism, 59, 61, 66, 176
pop culture, 36, 149ff.
popularization, 151, 155
power, 81ff. *See also* siddhi
practice, spiritual, 87
prajna, 12, 14
prakriti, 38, 129, 135, 138
pranayama, 190
pranamaya-kosha, 126n
pratyahara, 190
problem consciousness
  in Buddhism, 66, 69, 163ff.
  transcendence of, 87, 92, 98, 131, 134, 211ff., 237
process, conscious, 92
projection, 29
prophecies, about Dharma Bearer, 54f., 72
prophets, false, 50
pudgala, 42
Puja Yoga, 188
purification, of humanity, 58
purusha, 27, 38, 129, 135, 138
purushottama, 129, 135, 138
psychism, taboos against, 62

Radical Transcendentalism, 45, 73, 170, 236f.
Ramana Maharshi, 51, 72, 120, 133, 233, 237
rationalization, 20
realism
  of Advaitayana Buddhism, 73, 168
  atheistic, 80
  and Buddhism 65, 69, 110, 125, 164, 239
  and consciousness, 120
  vs. idealism, 44, 126ff. et passim
  materialistic, 63
  phenomenal, 74, 145
Reality
  and Buddhism, 68, 103, 146
  and faith, 197
  transcendental, 65, 112, 202
  as unborn, 103, 108f.
re-cognition, 28, 92, 115, 238, 241
reincarnation, 226
relatedness, sense of, 238
religion
  esoteric, 79, 81
  popular, 150ff.
  and stages of life, 77
  study of, 29
  transcendental unity of, 46, 48
Renaissance, 11
Rgveda, 48
Richard of St. Victor, 13
Roy, Ram Mohan, 46
Russia, 64

sacrifice, idea of, 177f.
sadhana, Master Da's own, 143
sahaja-samadhi, 28, 96, 111, 113, 116, 139, 147, 157, 160, 175, 193, 232, 242
Sahajayana, 43
Sai Baba, 51f.
shakti, 138

salvation, 152, 177
samadhi, 26, 68, 74, 129, 190
  ultimate, 73, 114, 133, 164, 175, 190
Samkhya, 38, 64f., 130, 135n, 176
samyama, 190, 191n
samsara, 88f., 94
  and nirvana, 146ff., 155ff., 205, 208ff., 220
Satsang, 172
savikalpa-samadhi, 138, 188
scholars, and traditional sources, 58
science
  nature of, 16
  and paradoxes, 118
  and prejudices, 61
scientism, 16f., 82, 123
scientists, conformism of, 15
"seeing," 18, 207
seeking, strategy of, 93 et passim
self, 96, 115, 237 et passim
  as hallucinated, 209
  and not-self, 91, 100, 106
  as noumenal, 104
  to be sacrificed, 182
  as unnecessary, 70
Sen, Keshab Chandra, 46
self-contraction, 86, 92, 115, 171, 175, 191f., 196, 206, 210, 219, 228, 237, 241ff.
self-convention, 210
self-devotion, 188
self-enquiry, 91
self-essence. *See* atman
self-forgetting, 184
selfishness, 195
self-root, 92

self-transcendence, 10, 25, 185, 189, 196
shamanism, 176, 182, 215
  of sky magic, 60, 161
Shankara, 38, 43, 45, 72, 102, 133, 230, 236
sheaths, of body-mind, 126, 166, 204
siddha, 39, 158f. *See also* maha-siddha, adepts
siddhi, or higher power, 161, 212
  as Completeness, 186
silence, on metaphysics, 27, 38, 42, 103, 133
society, modern, 62
soul, Buddhist denial of, 68f.
spirit, 75, 118
Spiritual Master, as means of Transmission, 55, 206
spirituality, and ego, 77
stages of life, 22ff. et passim
  fifth, 188
  seventh, 79, 86, 95, 147, 193, 188
  sixth, 79, 86, 108, 131, 189
suffering, 40, 68, 80, 87, 99f., 104f., 131, 170
Sutrakrtanga, 39

Tantrayana, 43
Tantra Yoga, 189
Tantrism, 67, 159
Taoism, 158f.
tapas, 183f.
Teaching, Master Da's method of, 153, 172, 175, 212
technology, 17
theism, 80ff.
theology, conventional, 35, 78

theosis, 35
Third World, 17
Tillich, P., 35
transcendence
  in Buddhism, 69f.
  of egoity, 35, 84, 101, 110, 125, 146, 192, 204
  inherent, 196
  of mind, 161
  and popular movements, 154
  of seeking, 93
Transcendentalism, 103f., 125. *See also* Radical Transcendentalism
tulku, 162
Tylor, G. B., 29

underground, of asceticism, 38, 64, 176
understanding, radical, 30, 88, 98, 154, 168, 171, 175, 191, 196, 206f., 219, 225, 237
United States, 60, 64
Upanishads, 198 et passim
Upasani Baba, 54

Vaisesika, 38
Vasubandhu, 42
Vedanta, 37f. et passim
Vedanta Temple Event, 211f.
Vedas, 32, 198
Vedic tradition, 64, 102, 176, 178
Vesalius, 11
vijnanamaya-kosha, 126n, 166f.
Vishnu, 53

Visuddhi-Magga, 10
Void, 106f., 229

Way of Divine Communion, 192, 206, 213
Way of Divine Ignorance, 22
Way of Radical Intuition, 192, 213
Way of Radical Understanding, 232f., 241
Way of Re-cognition, 192, 213
Way of Relational Enquiry, 192, 206, 213
waken, 31
will, free, 34
witness, transcendental, 27
Wisdom. *See also* Crazy Wisdom
  in Buddhism, 101, 146
world
  as a double-bind, 209
  as unnecessary, 69f.
worldliness, 195
World Teacher, 50f.

yama, 190
yin and yang, 160
Yoga, 38, 135n, 161, 185, 188f.
  of consideration, 95, 114, 191, 219
  of Transcendental Fire, 192
Yoga-Bhashya, 12
Yoga-Vasishtha, 129, 236

Zaehner, R. C., 13
Zen, 133, 146

The Books of Master Da Free John

". . . a Spiritual Master and religious genius of the ultimate degree."

—Ken Wilber
editor, *Re-Vision*
author, *The Spectrum of Consciousness*

What Others Have Said about Master Da Free John . . .

"It is obvious, from all sorts of subtle details, that he knows what IT's all about . . . a rare being.

"What he *says*, and says very well, is something that I have been trying to express for thirty-five years, but which most people seem quite reluctant to understand. He has simply realized that he himself as he is . . . is a perfect and authentic manifestation of eternal energy of the universe, and thus is no longer disposed to be in conflict with himself."

—Alan Watts

"If there is a man in this country today who is God-illumined, that man is Da Free John. The proof is in his books. Here is the most ancient tradition of mankind expressed in a way that is startlingly modern. Da Free John is a force to be reckoned with. Speaking the language of the Hindu-Buddhist tradition, the language that is 'drunk with infinity,' he is completely of the Now, one hundred percent on the side of life."

—Henry LeRoy Finch
author, *Wittgenstein, the Early Philosophy*

THE KNEE OF LISTENING
*The Early Life and Radical Spiritual Teachings of
Da Free John*

Master Da Free John's own account of the Awakening, testing, and fulfillment of the whole Way that he Teaches. This is the life story and original Teaching of one who was born in a literally illumined state. Master Da Free John describes the Condition of Enlightenment as he enjoyed it at birth. He chronicles his years of struggling and miraculous transformation as he experienced the disciplines and transcendental fulfillments of traditional Western and Eastern spirituality. And he relates the event of his ultimate resumption, in September 1970, of Perfect Illumination, the indestructible and highest esoteric Realization of God or Truth, which transcends all ordinary possibilities. His essays in Part Two interpret this Revelation with respect to all the spiritual and worldly traditions of the great search of Man. Written in the weeks and months immediately after his Re-Awakening, these essays demonstrate the eternal wisdom and perfect insight of the Enlightened Man.

Foreword by Alan Watts, with a new, updated introduction. Now in its third printing—over 38,000 copies sold.

$10.95 cloth
$5.95 paper

SCIENTIFIC PROOF OF THE EXISTENCE OF GOD WILL SOON BE ANNOUNCED BY THE WHITE HOUSE!
Prophetic Wisdom about the Myths and Idols of mass culture and popular religious cultism, the new priesthood of scientific and political materialism, and the secrets of Enlightenment hidden in the body of Man

"This book does two things absolutely critical for the survival of Man. First, it exposes the fundamental flaws of organized religion, science, and politics. Second, it gives clear indications for establishing a culture based on wisdom and love. Anyone who is the least bit concerned about his or her own well-being—physical, mental, spiritual—and that of the world should consider the words of Da Free John. He teaches and is a living demonstration of the present Divine Condition and evolutionary future of the human race."

John White, author, *Pole Shift*

$12.95 paper

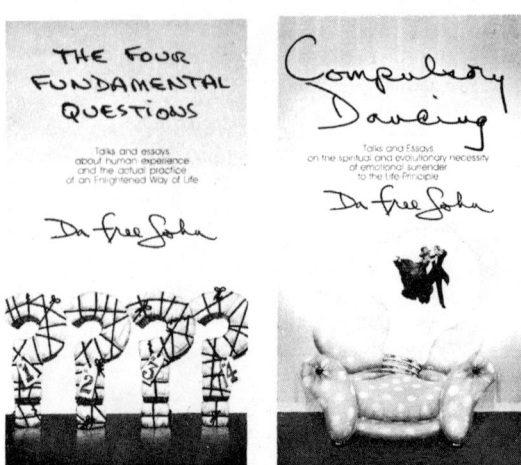

THE FOUR FUNDAMENTAL QUESTIONS
Talks and essays about human experience and the actual practice of an Enlightened Way of Life

Beginning with the question "Are you the one who is living you now?" this classic of disarming simplicity has the power to evoke in us the authentic intuition of Enlightenment. An easy to read, inexpensive introduction to the Teaching Work of Master Da Free John.

$1.95 paper

COMPULSORY DANCING
Talks and Essays on the spiritual and evolutionary necessity of emotional surrender to the Life-Principle

"If you want to be Happy, you have to change your way of life!"

Da Free John

There is no ultimate psychiatric enlightenment weekend. There is no pop salvation, no plastic nirvana, no Oz in the world or the mind. Human un-Happiness in our time is real. In this book, Da Free John considers the only true alternative—the compulsory dance—the emotional and spiritual conversion of human existence from self-possession to God-love in every moment, every occasion, every relationship.

$2.95 paper

THE ENLIGHTENMENT OF THE WHOLE BODY
A Rational and New Prophetic Revelation of the Truth of Religion, Esoteric Spirituality, and the Divine Destiny of Man

This book is Da Free John's ecstatic confession of God-Realization, and the principal source text for all students of the Way that he Teaches. Awesome and brilliant in its depth and scope, it contains the prophetic fire and philosophical majesty of the ancient classic spiritual literature and goes beyond it to present the most illumined testimony of Divine Life ever to appear. With brilliance and clarity, Da Free John discusses his own life and Teaching Work, the moral necessity of conversion to love, and the actual process wherein the body-mind of Man is transfigured in God.

$10.95 paper

LOVE OF THE TWO-ARMED FORM
The Free and Regenerative Function of Sexuality in Ordinary Life, and the Transcendence of Sexuality in True Religious or Spiritual Practice

More than any other current title on sex, LOVE OF THE TWO-ARMED FORM reveals an evolutionary understanding of human sexuality and its profound significance for ordinary happiness and true spiritual realization.

Part One helps the reader to understand and release all emotional obstructions to love, relationship, and sexual pleasure. Part Two describes the process of *sexual communion*, the enlightened approach to sexual embrace.

$10.95 paper

CONSCIOUS EXERCISE AND THE TRANSCENDENTAL SUN
The principle of love applied to exercise and the method of common physical action. A science of whole body wisdom, or true emotion, intended most especially for those engaged in religious or spiritual life

This is a classic manual for Enlightened equanimity, the way to look and feel and be and act completely Happy in every moment and in all relationships. Simple instructions on sitting, standing, walking, and brief daily routines of calisthenics, hatha yoga, and pranayama, or control of life in breath—a whole-body dance of constant Communion with Life, the "Transcendental Sun." Beautifully illustrated.

$10.95 cloth

THE EATING GORILLA COMES IN PEACE
The Transcendental Principle of Life Applied to Diet and the Regenerative Discipline of True Health

God, or Transcendental Life, is our true Food. We are also the food of God, for the universe is a meal in which all are devoured. This text is a practical manual for applying that radical understanding of "food" to life from birth to death: "the wholly regenerative vegetarian diet"; the seven stages of life; whether or not to fast, and how; pregnancy and childbirth; how to treat illness, lay on hands, balance and rejuvenate the body—always releasing your life into God, and receiving Life in return.

"In my own experience as a practitioner, Da Free John's suggestions for life and health management have dramatically demonstrated their validity amongst my patients, which to my mind is the ultimate test of truth. For anyone interested in maintaining and raising their health, I recommend this book as the fundamental cornerstone."

Bill Gray, M.D., N.D.
coauthor of *The Science of Homeopathy—A Modern Textbook*
$10.95 paper

THE PARADOX OF INSTRUCTION
An Introduction to the Esoteric Spiritual Teaching of Da Free John

This book comprehensively states the fundamental Spiritual philosophy of Da Free John's Teaching. It offers a thorough comparison of traditional approaches to religion and spirituality with the radical illumination he proposes. The insights into the nature of ego, the condition of human suffering, and true Awakening in God will challenge many readers, particularly those with a philosophical bent.

$10.95 cloth
$5.95 paper

THE WAY THAT I TEACH
Talks on the Intuition of Eternal Life

A book that uniquely documents examples of Da Free John's direct way of Teaching to students, recorded during the earlier Teaching years. Includes: "God Is Not an Alternative Reality," "The Grace of Suffering," "Renouncing the Search for the Edible Deity," "Love Is the Sacrifice of Man," and many others.

$10.95 cloth
$5.95 paper

THE METHOD OF THE SIDDHAS
Talks with Da Free John on the Spiritual Technique of the Saviors of Mankind

In the first months and years of his Teaching Work, Da Free John invited ordinary people to sit with him and discuss true spiritual life. This book records the dialogues that took place. Often using both humorous stories and profound parables, he answers questions and urges his listeners to participate in "Satsang," or Enlightened association with the Adept. First published in 1973, it remains one of the most useful and enjoyable volumes of his radical Spiritual Teaching.

$5.95 paper

Back in Print

WHAT TO REMEMBER TO BE HAPPY
A Spiritual Way of Life for Your First Fourteen Years or So

A delightful and easily understood message on how to feel and breathe the Mystery of Life and be always happy every day. When read aloud, both children and adults are delighted by its capacity to reawaken the sense of being alive and full of feeling in a wondrous World. 44 pages, fully illustrated.

$3.95 paper

What Teachers Say About This Book...

"WHAT TO REMEMBER TO BE HAPPY is a clear and simple presentation of the most relevant spiritual matters for children. As the Teaching of Master Da Free John in its most basic form, the words and simple practices instill a fundamental understanding of life, death, love, and happiness. And most importantly, children do respond to the essence of spiritual life contained in this book. Master Da Free John artfully and ingeniously describes that which cannot be known, that which we all recognize as Truth, Reality, or God, as 'the Mystery.' He calls the book 'A Spiritual Way of Life' and it is actually an in-depth study of the primary principles of the 'Life of Ignorance,' as it always brings the children back to the liberating fact that they 'do not know what a single thing is.' This book is a shining example that the essence of spiritual life can be brought to children in a way that will enliven and enrich their personal understanding."

—Jennifer Lynn, B.A. Ed.
Big Wisdom Free School

What Readers Say About This Book...

"When I read WHAT TO REMEMBER TO BE HAPPY it makes me feel the Mystery. It helps me to be happy. I feel that I am in God. It tells me the Truth."
Kirstin Kantner, age 7

"This book is full of ways that help you to feel God. It has changed my life elaborately. I've read this book a lot. It might help you too for your first fourteen years or so."
Dylan J. Morris, age 11

"WHAT TO REMEMBER TO BE HAPPY helps me to feel good. Master Da Free John is happy in his heart. I've seen him. He helps me to be happy too."
Pan Esterle, age 6

"WHAT TO REMEMBER TO BE HAPPY gave me a clear and straightforward feeling and understanding of how we are more than what we look like. Reading this book itself helps me to feel the Mystery very strongly. This book is wonderful."
Brett Harper, age 13

Understanding and the Beginnings of True Practice

THE BODILY SACRIFICE OF ATTENTION
Introductory Talks on Radical Understanding and the Life of Divine Ignorance

"All of the [traditional] sects and schools and all of humanity in general are calling us to devote attention to one or another conditional state or objects. All of that is sin! All of that is un-Enlightenment.

"Enlightenment is a totally other process than all of this desiring, all of this using of attention for a worldly purpose, a religious purpose, a mystical purpose, or an apparently transcendental, intuitive purpose that moves via the process of inversion upon the inner self. All of these activities are conventional exercises that appear within the traditions, and yet from the point of view of Truth they are utterly unnecessary, fruitless, and false. They are built upon an error.

"The Way that I Teach is founded upon the transcendence of this error. It is founded upon fundamental understanding. This understanding is the summation of my life and spiritual practice and Teaching."

—Da Free John
The Bodily Sacrifice of Attention

These recent talks are a product of the longest teaching lesson in the history of The Johannine Daist Communion. Master Da Free John spent most of 1981 in hermitage retreat, granting esoteric instruction to a small group of devotees. But they, and his "beginning" students, all tended to confuse his radical Way with conventional, self-based religious and spiritual approaches. In October 1981 the Master returned to The Mountain of Attention Sanctuary to "reclaim" the Teaching and the culture of practice for the radical Way and to transmit the Power of understanding to prepared devotees.

These talks bring perspective to the entire ten years of the Master's instructions on Satsang, Narcissus, understanding, Divine Ignorance, and the Way of Divine Communion. A demanding text, and absolutely necessary study for anyone who wishes to consider this Way and its practice.

$9.95 paper

The Art and Science of
Conducting the Life Force Bodily
So That Spiritual Practice May Begin

"I" IS THE BODY OF LIFE
Talks and Essays on the Art and Science of Equanimity and the Self-Transcending Process of Radical Understanding

"Make the practical basics of the Way your life-practice, and thereby develop more and more free energy and attention—free of obsessive, unbalanced, and overstimulated involvement with the conventional, superficial, and apparently problematic conditions of existence. Thus, by cultivation over time, you will Awaken more and more into the Radiant Life-Power of Transcendental Being. And that Power of Being is the Circumstance in which we move into and through the higher stages of life to the Realization that characterizes the seventh stage of life."

—Da Free John
"I" Is the Body of Life

Throughout human history conductivity or "the capacity of the body-mind to conduct or be surrendered into the All-Pervading Life Current" has fascinated yogis, saints, and magicians. As Master Da Free John says, "When the body-mind is opened to the Life-Current and coordinated with it through feeling-attention, breathing, relaxation, disciplines that purify and balance the body, then extraordinary experiences begin to arise." If a person becomes enamored of these experiences, then he will obstruct himself from true spiritual Happiness and practice. But if a person rightly practices conductivity, it will free attention for the senior spiritual practice: the "conscious process," or the present exercise of fundamental intuitive consciousness.

In November 1980, Master Da Free John entered into a one-year consideration with a small group of devotees. In a secluded retreat setting, all forms of conductivity were tried and their effect on true spiritual practice was considered. *"I" Is the Body of Life* shares the wisdom relative to conductivity coming from this period.

$10.95 paper

PARTIAL CONTENTS
- The Golden Great Bright-Foreheaded Warrior
- The Most Difficult Stage
- Does God Exist?
- The Divine Self Is the Only Reality
- Narcissus, Ignorance, and the Way of Life
- Hearing, Seeing, and Practicing
- The Subtle Error
- The Natural Vision
- The Simple Technical Practice of Conductivity
- The Bodily Secrets of Conductivity
- Let the Body Achieve True Equanimity
- Transcend All Illusions
- How to Live
- Basic Practical Advice
- Surrender Is Universal Worship
- The Two Crises of Student Practice
- Exercise and Equanimity
- The Three Stages of Sexual Practice
- Service Is Self-Transcendence
- Equanimity
- Spiritual Neurosis
- The Crisis of Meditation
- Spiritual Maturity
- The Essence of Meditation

What to Understand to Be Happy

THE BODILY LOCATION OF HAPPINESS
On the Incarnation of the Divine Person and the Transmission of Love-Bliss

"We tend to wander in excursions of attention into the dualisms of self and not-self, and thus attention tends to be located in un-Happiness. Observe and understand this, and so Remember to locate Happiness in every moment. Happiness is not an object of the self and not-self. Find 'Where' you are Happy—completely Happy, already, now. Contemplate and feel into that Happiness. It is not affected by bodily, emotional, mental, psychic, egoic, or cosmic limitations. It is always already Free. It is always already the case. It is always already There."

—Da Free John
The Bodily Location of Happiness

$12.95 paper

The practice of true or Spiritual Happiness is brought to life in this book through stories of those who have entered into Spiritual relationship with Master Da Free John. The profound, apparently miraculous, and often humorous events and revelations that are a part of the play in relationship to the Divine Adept demonstrate the Truth and Wisdom of his Teaching.

An extremely useful book, *The Bodily Location of Happiness* can be called the world's first handbook of true Happiness. And, although this book is an indispensable tool for students practicing the spiritual discipline of Happiness, it will also be helpful to anyone who is interested in Happiness.

THE BODILY LOCATION OF HAPPINESS EXPLAINS:

- Your native ability to look, feel, act, and be completely Happy
- Why the ultimate form of spiritual life is devotion to Happiness
- How students of Da Free John practice relationship to a Spiritual Teacher
- The lesson of life—that Happiness cannot be attained or achieved
- The understanding of un-Happiness and the conversion to the Way of Happiness
- The transforming yogic processes spontaneously activated in the life of Master Da Free John
- The miracles of Master Da Free John
- The two sides of un-Happiness
- The esoteric mysteries of the *New Testament* and the *Bhagavad Gita*

Find Out the Great Secret

THE YOGA OF CONSIDERATION AND THE WAY THAT I TEACH

"There is a secret, something hidden, something uninspected, that must be Realized. It is not really things as they are that we must engage and improve. We must understand. We must discover the secret of our existence, not merely fulfill its mechanical destiny. Find out the great secret."
—Da Free John
The Yoga of Consideration and the Way That I Teach

Contained within the Argument of Master Da Free John is a secret. The Argument criticizes all conventional human endeavor, both high and low. But constant consideration of this criticism does not leave you in mere despair and negativity. Instead it leads to Awakening, and to the free life of understanding.

In *The Yoga of Consideration and the Way That I Teach*, Master Da Free John distills the Argument to a potent, succinct statement. Reading and rereading this book keeps the consideration of the Argument alive. And if you base your life on this consideration, the "great secret" will be revealed.

$7.95 paper

CONTENTS —

Death and Joy
The Way of the Lion
  Transcending What You Seem to Be
  The Way of the Lion
  The Yoga of Consideration and the Way That I Teach
  The Disappearance of the Separate Self and Its Objects
  The Progress of Practice and the Great Principle
  The Free Renunciate Order

The Argument
  A Summary of the Argument of This Way
  Understanding
  Real Meditation
  Sahaj Samadhi
  The Fundamental Error
  If You Are Serious
  Choose What You Will Do

Unique Book Unveils the Results of a Decade-Long Experiment
The Optimum Diet for Spiritual Practice

RAW GORILLA
The Principles of Regenerative Raw Diet Applied in True Spiritual Practice

Prepared by The Radiant Life Clinic and Research Center based on the Wisdom Teaching of Da Free John

"RAW GORILLA makes a valuable contribution to the understanding of the diet. With its focus on 'radical understanding' and human maturity as prerequisites for spiritual transformation, and with its safe, accurate, flexible guidelines for dietary transitions and for purification, healing, and maintenance of bodily health. I read it with great pleasure.

"With RAW GORILLA you will not get lost in the jungle of dietary sensationalism and physical imbalances. Instead, the spiritual aspirant can anticipate an inspirational and life-supportive approach to diet that enhances true spiritual worship."

—Viktoras Kulvinskas
author, *Survival into the 21st Century*

The optimum diet for enlightened living featured in *Raw Gorilla* emerged from a practical experiment by Master Da Free John and his students. The experiment took the form of a decade of unparalleled investigation, research, and personal experience that yielded the insight for diet optimization.

$4.25 paper

RAW GORILLA OFFERS GUIDANCE ON:
- The effects of a purifying diet
- The relationship between diet and radical healing
- The relationship between diet and spiritual maturity
- Ideal weights for men and women, age 25 and over
- How raw diet balances the body-mind
- How we must become sensitive to the Life-Current to practice diet
- How to make an easy transition to the raw diet
- How to manage the "symptoms" of purification
- What to do when you are enervated
- The unique properties of foods and food groups
- Sample diets

The Laughing Man Magazine

On the Principles and Secrets of Religion, Spirituality, and Human Culture

"Particularly in the time in which we now live, when the ideas of all the provinces of Earth are now gathering together for the first time in human history, and all the absolute dogmas find themselves casually associated, to be judged like a crowd of silly Napoleons or mad Christs in an asylum, the complex mind of Everyman is remembering itself all at once.

"What is the Truth? What stands out in the wilderness of doctrine as singly as the 'I' of the body-mind?"

—Da Free John

THE LAUGHING MAN magazine considers the Truth of our existence, and the Truth of the entire "Great Tradition" of religious, spiritual, and philosophical persuasions that we have inherited in this era.

• The life and wisdom of the American-born Adept, Da Free John, whose Teaching and miraculous Spiritual Work epitomize the Great Tradition and stand as a radical alternative to it
• "The Seven Stages of Eternal Life." How all religious and secular communications express the disposition of one or more of the inevitable stages of human growth and awakening, as described by Da Free John
• The heresies of both religious provincialism and scientific and political materialism

"I am here to demonstrate that the universe is a laughing matter, so that you will transcend it. I am here to tell the ultimate jokes. There are seven eternal jokes, which are not revealed in words—they are not one-liners, but whole pieces of existence. The seven stages of life are the seven original jokes. When you transcend them by fulfilling them, then you are able to see the wonderment of God."

—Da Free John

Annual subscription, four issues $18.00

Please make check or money order payable to The Dawn Horse Press and mail to:
        The Laughing Man Magazine
        P.O. Box 3680
        Clearlake, CA 95422

Forthcoming

THE LION SUTRA
On the Transcendence of Attention

This is a major new book by Da Free John—an ultimate expression of a living Adept. It carries the full majesty and poetic elegance of Realization. In these essays and talks, Da Free John Teaches the highest expression of true spiritual practice, the transcendence of attention, which is the practice of Enlightenment. THE LION SUTRA contains a comprehensive and critical consideration of the traditional schools of religion and spirituality, especially the highest philosophical expressions of Truth found in the traditions.

EASY DEATH

Here is the definitive book on death and dying—Da Free John's radical, enlightening wisdom on:

- Why "there is no self that dies," and what that means for you
- How to prepare for death by surrendering to God while alive
- How to serve a dying person
- How to aid the surviving personality's "three-day transition" after death
- What can happen at death and afterwards
- Wills, mutual forgiveness, pain and medication for the dying, why to avoid autopsies and embalming, cremation vs. burial
- The truth about ghosts, heaven worlds, reincarnation, "near-death experiences"
- The heresies of scientific materialism, religious belief, and esoteric spirituality

The heart of this illumined manual is the marvelous story and actual transcripts of Da Free John's Teaching Work in relation to death during the last ten years. His liberated humor, his constant efforts to help others understand the paradoxes of this life and the beyond, the profusion of miraculous phenomena in his own life and the lives of his students—the whole story is told here with many dramatic incidents, accounts, and testimonials.

The Dawn Horse Press

We are dedicated to the publication of classic spiritual literature, the work of authentic spiritual genius, from all traditions and times, through the present day. We are committed to the preparation of well-designed and yet reasonably priced editions and we are determined to see that these books stay in print from generation to generation. We consider publishing to be a form of spiritual practice and service that promotes the great tradition of true knowledge and implements the growth of a genuine human intelligence in the world.

Classic Spiritual Literature

THE SPIRITUAL INSTRUCTIONS OF SAINT SERAPHIM OF SAROV
edited by Da Free John
Saint Seraphim of Sarov is the most famous saint of the Eastern Orthodox Christian Church. He lived in the late eighteenth and early nineteenth centuries in the forests and monastery of Sarov, Russia. His life combined great periods of solitary hermitage with years as the *staretz*, or spiritual overseer, of the monastery. THE SPIRITUAL INSTRUCTIONS contains the famous "Conversation" of Saint Seraphim with Nicholas Motovilov in which Seraphim reveals the vision and power of God, much like the *shaktipat*, or mystical initiation, of the oriental traditions.
$2.95 paper

THE YOGA OF LIGHT: THE CLASSIC ESOTERIC HANDBOOK OF KUNDALINI YOGA
by Hans-Ulrich Rieker
Translated by a modern Western yogi, this text is the most lively, accessible, and useful version of the great ancient classic *Hatha Yoga Pradipika*. To Mr. Rieker, yoga is a means of bringing happiness into one's life, not merely a dry science. Thus his translations and commentary reflect a sense of relaxed joy.
$4.95 paper

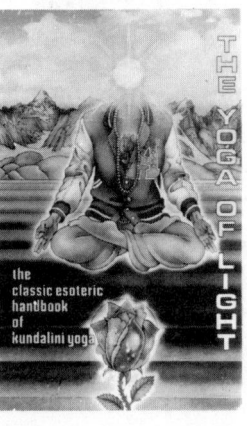

Only a Few Select Texts Communicate Without Limitation the Ultimate Spiritual Realization

THE SONG OF THE SELF SUPREME
Astavakra Gita
Preface by Da Free John
Translation by Radhakamal Mukerjee

"Neither any good nor any evil is associated with my stability, movement, or repose. Hence I live in true happiness whether I am at rest, move about, or sleep."
      THE SONG OF THE SELF SUPREME
            Astavakra Gita (13:5)

"The Adept simply confesses the Realization of the Divine Reality. From the point of view of God-Realization all that is inevitable as a human exercise becomes clearly unnecessary. It has fulfilled its purpose and is transcended."
      From the Preface by Da Free John

$8.95 paper

The Story of Ashtavakra and King Janaka

The great Hindu epic the Mahabharata tells the legend of Ashtavakra and King Janaka. While still in his mother's womb, the learned Ashtavakra expostulated with his father, Kahoda. His father became so enraged that he cursed the embryo Ashtavakra. As a result, the boy was born crippled.

Later Kahoda, Ashtavakra's father, went to the court of King Janaka where he was defeated in an intellectual duel with Vandin. Because he lost the debate, Kahoda was immersed in the ocean.

At the age of twelve, Ashtavakra learned of his father's fate and journeyed to the court of Janaka. There he confronted and defeated Vandin in a philosophical debate. As Vandin was being immersed into the ocean, Ashtavakra's father promptly reappeared and Ashtavakra's limbs were miraculously healed.

The Ashtavakra Gita is the account of Ashtavakra's esoteric instruction to King Janaka.

ABOUT THE ASHTAVAKRA GITA

The Song of the Self Supreme or Ashtavakra Gita represents the culminating expression of the great Vedic and Upanishadic tradition. The author of this soaring poem or "song" belongs to that class of rare beings who have realized the living truth of Enlightenment. This Gita, then, is not a mere speculative treatise but a Teaching given from the vantage point of Enlightenment to prepare an advanced practitioner for the transition to full realization. It is one of a few select texts that communicate the ultimate realization, unmediated by the limitations characteristic of practices and points of view of less mature spiritual adaptations. This grand classic does more than titillate the intellect; it inspires the heart and stimulates one's desire for spiritual practice.

It is not surprising that this extraordinary Sanskrit scripture was a favorite of Sri Ramakrishna, one of modern India's greatest spiritual heroes, as well as of his equally famous disciple Swami Vivekananda.

Master Da Free John's illuminating Preface is a unique commentary on the Ashtavakra Gita and similar rare texts that ecstatically speak without limitation of the ultimate spiritual Realization. Master Da incisively shows how these texts not only culminate the traditions from which they arose but move beyond their inherent philosophical limitations. His penetrating consideration of popular misinterpretations and misapplications of such texts allows the serious spiritual practitioner to make effective use of works like the Astavakra Gita in authentic spiritual practice.

VEDANTA AND CHRISTIAN FAITH
by Bede Griffiths
A beautiful capsulization which compares the spiritual and mystical traditions of India with those of the Christian West. Of interest to scholars and discriminating readers alike.
$2.95 paper

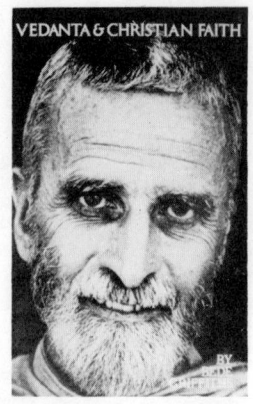

GOPIS' LOVE FOR SRI KRISHNA
by Hanumanprasad Poddar
GOPIS' LOVE FOR SRI KRISHNA contains the very essence of the devotional way of Love-Communion with God. Highly recommended for everyone interested in a devotional way of life. This book reveals the Divine Play of Krishna and the cowherd maidens who loved him. Printed on fine paper, illustrated with original hand-cut Indian wood blocks, and with an exquisite cover.
$9.95 paper

BREATH, SLEEP, THE HEART, AND LIFE
by Pundit Acharya
Born a Brahmin in India, Pundit Acharya lectured for forty years in America on his system of retraining the body for increased health and longevity. "In earlier times it is recorded that men lived to the age of three hundred years. In those days there was also a science of agelessness known to the sages of India. This was the mission of Acharya when he came to America: to rediscover the meaning of this science and reinterpret it to the world in the light of modern practical sciences." (from the Introduction)
$4.95 paper

A NEW APPROACH TO BUDDHISM
by Dhiravamsa
Seven lectures by the modern meditation master Dhiravamsa. In his description of the "new approach" to Buddhism, he says, "We are enquiring into the possibility of having a new dimension in our attitude to life as a living reality, in which everything is integrated because it is understood. This requires freedom from attachment to the dogmas of organized religion, and the renunciation of the self...."
$1.95 paper

These books are available by mail order from The Dawn Horse Book Depot. Add $1.25 for the first book and $.35 for each additional book. California residents add 6% sales tax. Ask for our free catalog.

**THE DAWN HORSE BOOK DEPOT
DEPT. N, P.O. BOX 3680
CLEARLAKE, CA 95422**